NEW GENDER MAINSTREAMING SERIES ON GENDER ISSUES

Gender and Human Rights in the Commonwealth

Some Critical Issues for Action in the Decade 2005–2015

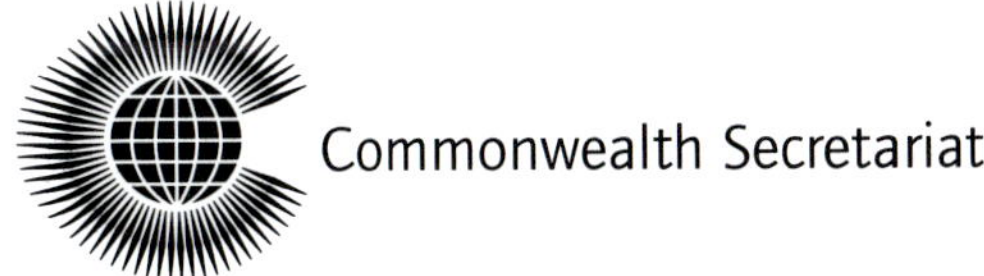

Gender Section,
Social Transformation
Programmes Division,
Commonwealth Secretariat,
Marlborough House, Pall Mall,
London SW1Y 5HX
Tel: +44 (0)20 7747 6284
Fax: +44 (0)20 7930 1647
E-mail: gad@commonwealth.int
www.thecommonwealth.org/gender

Layout design: Wayzgoose
Cover design: Pen and Ink
Cover photo: Hamish Wilson/
Panos Pictures
Printed by The Charlesworth Group, Huddersfield, UK
Published by the Commonwealth Secretariat

Wherever possible, the Commonwealth Secretariat uses paper sourced from sustainable forests or from sources that minimise a destructive impact on the environment.

Copies of this publication can be ordered direct from:
The Publications Manager,
Communication and Public Affairs Division,
Commonwealth Secretariat,
Marlborough House,
Pall Mall, London SW1Y 5HX
United Kingdom
Tel: +44 (0)20 7747 6342
Fax: +44 (0)20 7839 9081
E-mail:
r.jones-parry@commonwealth.int

Price: £10.99

ISBN: 0-85092-808-7

Gender Management System Series

Gender Management System Handbook
Using Gender Sensitive Indicators: A Reference Manual for Governments and Other Stakeholders
Gender Mainstreaming in Agriculture and Rural Development: A Reference Manual for Governments and Other Stakeholders
Gender Mainstreaming in Development Planning: A Reference Manual for Governments and Other Stakeholders
Gender Mainstreaming in Education: A Reference Manual for Governments and Other Stakeholders
Gender Mainstreaming in Finance: A Reference Manual for Governments and Other Stakeholders
Gender Mainstreaming in Information and Communications: A Reference Manual for Governments and Other Stakeholders
Gender Mainstreaming in Legal and Constitutional Affairs: A Reference Manual for Governments and Other Stakeholders
Gender Mainstreaming in the Public Service: A Reference Manual for Governments and Other Stakeholders
Gender Mainstreaming in Science and Technology: A Reference Manual for Governments and Other Stakeholders
Gender Mainstreaming in Trade and Industry: A Reference Manual for Governments and Other Stakeholders
A Quick Guide to the Gender Management System
A Quick Guide to Using Gender Sensitive Indicators
A Quick Guide to Gender Mainstreaming in Development Planning
A Quick Guide to Gender Mainstreaming in Education
A Quick Guide to Gender Mainstreaming in Finance
A Quick Guide to Gender Mainstreaming in the Public Service
A Quick Guide to Gender Mainstreaming in Trade and Industry
A Quick Guide to Gender Mainstreaming in Information and Communications

New Gender Mainstreaming Series on Development Issues

Gender Mainstreaming in HIV/AIDS: Taking a Multisectoral Approach
Gender Mainstreaming in the Health Sector: Experiences in Commonwealth Countries
Promoting an Integrated Approach to Combating Gender-Based Violence
Gender Mainstreaming in Poverty Eradication and the Millennium Development Goals
Gender Mainstreaming in the Multilateral Trading System
Engendering Budgets: A Practitioner's Guide to Understanding and Implementing Gender-Responsive Budgets
Integrated Approaches to Eliminating Gender-Based Violence
Mainstreaming Informal Employment and Gender in Poverty Reduction
The GMS Toolkit: An Integrated Resource for Implementing the Gender Management System Series

Publication Team

Project Co-ordinator: Cindy Berman
GMS *Series Co-ordinator:* Rawwida Baksh
Editor: Tina Johnson
Production: Rupert Jones-Parry

Contents

Foreword

At their 7th Ministerial meeting in Fiji on 2 June 2004, Commonwealth Women's Affairs Ministers adopted a new ten-year Plan of Action for Gender Equality 2005–2015. The Plan reflects a strong rights-based approach in all four critical areas of concern – Democracy, Peace and Conflict; Human Rights and Law; Poverty Eradication and Economic Empowerment; and HIV/AIDS. The Plan places emphasis on *implementation* and the critical partnerships that are needed to achieve its goals over the next decade.

The Human Rights section of the Plan of Action has been developed through wide consultation and the involvement of experts, policy-makers and civil society organisations to reflect the key Commonwealth priorities for action in the next ten years. The gender and human rights issues addressed in the Plan are wide-ranging – including the Convention on the Elimination of All Forms of Discrimination against Women (CEDAW), gender-based violence, culture and the law, indigenous peoples, trafficking and migration, land and property rights, diversity and a life-cycle approach. Much of the conceptual work that informed these issues came out of a pan-Commonwealth Expert Group Meeting on Gender and Human Rights that took place at the Commonwealth Secretariat's Headquarters in London in February 2004. Participants came from all regions of the Commonwealth, and the experts included government policy-makers, judges, lawyers, academics, leaders of civil society organisations and specialists from multilateral agencies and the Commonwealth Secretariat.

This book comprises the papers commissioned for this Expert Group Meeting, together with some other key background papers that informed the discussion on these topics. Appendix 1 is a mini-report of the meeting – including the agenda, discussant notes, key recommendations made by the experts and a list of participants.

The purpose of this book is to contribute to current policy-making and programme action on gender and human rights. It is intended for a wide audience of policy-makers, members of the judicial system (judges, magistrates and lawyers), academics and civil society organisations grappling with these issues. In addition, its intention is to provide a conceptual/policy-oriented resource for those committed to implementing and supporting the human rights goals of the new *Commonwealth Plan of Action for Gender Equality 2005–2015*. It must be emphasised that this publication is a contribution of ideas, concepts and policy recommendations that served to inform the development of the human rights section of the *Plan of Action* and that it does not purport to address these issues in a detailed or comprehensive way; certainly each issue (e.g. gender-based violence, trafficking, etc.) could be – or has been – the subject of one or more books on its own. We hope this work will be useful for partners and stakeholders who are engaged in promoting and supporting the implementation of gender and human rights in the Commonwealth and globally.

We would like to express our sincere thanks to the Experts who contributed their best thinking, professional and personal experiences, time and energy to this effort. Thanks also to Cindy Berman, Gender, Human Rights and HIV/AIDS Programme Officer, who had primary responsibility for planning and chairing the Expert Group Meeting and for co-ordinating the production of this publication; to Rawwida Baksh, Deputy Director and Head of the Gender Section of the Secretariat's Social Transformation Programmes Division; to Justina Mutale, Musonda Mwila, Margarette Gittens and Greta Fernandez for their administrative support; and to Tina Johnson, not only for contributing an excellent expert paper on gender-based violence but also for her superb editorial skills on this publication overall. We also thank Rupert Jones-Parry for providing publishing support.

Nancy Spence
Director
Social Transformation Programmes Division
Commonwealth Secretariat

1 CEDAW: Achievements and Challenges

Progress, Achievements, Constraints and Key Priorities

Shanthi Dairiam

Introduction

CEDAW is a comprehensive bill of rights for women.

The United Nations General Assembly adopted the Convention on the Elimination of All Forms of Discrimination against Women (CEDAW) on 19 December 1979 and it came into force as a treaty on 3 December 1981. It is one of the most ratified conventions, with 177 States parties.[1]

CEDAW is a comprehensive bill of rights for women and combines concerns that had previously been addressed in an *ad hoc* manner throughout the UN system. It is monitored by the CEDAW Committee, which operates out of the UN in New York. States parties to the Convention have to report to the Committee one year after ratification, and thereafter every four years. On reviewing the reports, the Committee issues a set of recommendations for implementation, called Concluding Comments, to the countries concerned.

This paper looks at some of the achievements and challenges of CEDAW, drawing its examples from the Concluding Comments on selected States' reports.[2] It notes first of all that there is a lack of clarity on CEDAW as a human rights instrument. The Convention has not been made the basis of law or policy reform, and CEDAW principles are not integrated into domestic law; hence it is not directly applicable in the courts. The paper also draws attention to the lack of comprehensive and holistic plans to implement CEDAW. It points out that whatever reform is put in place suffers from weak implementation due to lack of monitoring, inadequacy of resource allocation, lack of capability and weaknesses of the institutions concerned. Discrimination therefore persists. In addition, almost all the reporting countries show a weak reporting record and lack of data collection for monitoring and report writing.

The paper further looks at the fact that, under the Convention, obligations must be fulfilled evenly for all, including minorities, overseas territories and even where there is devolution of powers. Hence there is a need for a unified strategy and policy for implementation of all provisions of CEDAW.

The Dynamics of Human Rights Treaty Law

In working with CEDAW, it is essential to understand the obligations of the State under international human rights treaty law. A treaty is a legal agreement between two or more countries and is a source of international law. Treaties can be entered into on a number of issues such as trade, delineation of borders, human rights, etc. Traditionally, international law used to be defined as the law governing relations between States (Buergenthal, 1988). Under this definition, international law did not regulate the human rights of individuals vis-a-vis the country of their nationality, which were deemed to fall within the exclusive domestic jurisdiction of each State (ibid). Over the years, however, the doctrine of humanitarian intervention recognised as lawful the responsibility of one State to stop the gross maltreatment by another State of its own citizens.

As a result, today it is an established principle of international law that a State may voluntarily limit its sovereignty by treaty ratification and thus internationalise a subject that would otherwise not be regulated by international law. For example, if one State concludes a treaty with another State in which they agree to treat their nationals in a humane manner and to accord them certain human rights, they have to that extent internationalised that particular subject matter (Henkin, 1977).[3]

Human rights treaty law imposes obligations that are legally binding on any State that is a party to it. In this regard, States parties to the treaties are voluntarily surrendering their sovereignty and submitting themselves to international scrutiny as well as committing themselves to reordering domestic law and policy, as it touches on matters that are the subject of the treaty concerned, according to universal and international standards.

Specific Obligations of the State Under CEDAW

The outcome that governments have to work towards under this Convention is to ensure that women will enjoy and be able to exercise all human rights and fundamental freedoms in the political, economic, social, cultural, civil or any other sphere on the basis of equality with men. This means that there must be both *de jure* and *de facto* equality rights for women (articles 1, 2a and 3).[4]

The norm of equality that the Convention imposes is that of substantive equality. This is a broad approach that requires equality in the substance of the law, equal protection of the law and equal benefit of the law. A related norm is that of non-discrimination, which requires the elimination of both direct and indirect discrimination. The latter means the elimination of laws and practices that have a discriminatory effect even though no discrimination was intended. All efforts to bring about equality between women and men need to be based on these understandings of equality and non-discrimination.

The means by which this is to be accomplished are given in articles 1–5. Obligations under these articles include the following:

1 To incorporate the principle of equality and non-discrimination of men and women in the legal system, abolish all discriminatory laws and practices, and adopt appropriate ones prohibiting discrimination against women (articles 2a, 2b, 2f and 2g);

2 To establish tribunals and other public institutions to ensure the effective protection of women against discrimination (mechanisms for enforcement) (article 2c);

3 To ensure elimination of all acts of discrimination against women by the public sector as well as by the private sector, including persons, organisations or enterprises (articles 2d and 2e);

4 To implement programmes and make relevant institutional arrangements and any other laws necessary that will enable women to exercise the equality rights given in the law (article 3);

The outcome that governments have to work towards under this Convention is to ensure that women will enjoy and be able to exercise all human rights and fundamental freedoms in the political, economic, social, cultural, civil or any other sphere on the basis of equality with men.

5 To accelerate the achievement of *de facto* rights by implementing temporary special measures such as affirmative action (article 4);

6 To eliminate cultural and traditional practices and attitudes, including stereotypical roles for women and men (article 5).

In conclusion, we could say that governments have to ensure the applicability of the norms and standards of the Convention at the domestic level.

Questions to ask on implementation

As a quick reference of indicators to assess the extent to which the Convention has been implemented, the following questions may be asked:

1 Has the Convention been incorporated at the national level? This step may be necessary, depending on the legal system and the provisions of the constitution. A treaty can be self-executing, in that no further legislation is required to make it applicable at the national level, or enabling legislation may be required to make treaty law applicable.[5] Legal opinion is that only then may the norms and standards of the Convention – should they be different from the existing norms and standards at the national level – be legally applied to provide equality rights for women.

2 Has the definition of substantive equality and the definition of discrimination as given in article 1 of the Convention been adopted in the constitution or other relevant laws?

3 Has any other appropriate legislation been enacted to make discriminatory acts in the public and private sectors actionable? Such legislation could take the form of an equal opportunities act or an anti sex discrimination act (article 3).

4 Has there been a review of all existing legislation and have all discriminatory provisions in the law been eliminated?

5 As a result of this review have any other relevant laws, such as laws to protect women against domestic violence or sexual harassment, been enacted and enforced?

6 Have policy directives been issued to the public and private

sectors to adopt codes of practice that will help to eliminate discriminatory practices and to develop equality plans for the acceleration of the *de facto* equality status of women?

7 Are there laws and programmes to combat violence against women, which is identified under the Convention as an extreme form of discrimination against women?

8 Has the Convention been translated and widely disseminated at all levels of the public and private sectors to raise awareness of the obligations under the Convention?

9 Have all relevant government officers in all sectors, as well as the judiciary and relevant legal personnel, been trained to carry out their obligations under the Convention?

10 Is the Convention applicable in the courts? In other words, has the Convention been cited in the courts to gain equality rights for women?

11 Has an intersectoral monitoring mechanism been established to gather data on compliance with the obligations under the Convention and to assess the effectiveness of laws and policies meant to promote women's equality?

12 Is there adequate data to assess progress made in the implementation of the Convention, such as data disaggregated by sex and data that needs to be collected to identify obstacles to the achievement of *de facto* rights for women and to assess the effects of laws and policies on women?

13 Is there a plan for implementation that sets out benchmarks for progress, contains proposals for special programmes to enable women to access rights given in the law, delineates responsibility, identifies intersectoral co-operation, allocates budgets and integrates capacity-building measures for the implementers, and is this plan integrated into mainstream national development plans?

... there are no examples of any Commonwealth country that has put in place a comprehensive and holistic plan to implement the Convention.

Weaknesses in Implementation

Lack of comprehensive and holistic plans

If the above set of questions is used to assess the status of implementation of CEDAW, then there are no examples of any Commonwealth country that has put in place a comprehensive and holistic plan to implement the Convention. For instance, we have no examples of any country that has taken steps to incorporate the principles of CEDAW into municipal legislation, so the Convention is not directly applicable – although definitions reflecting substantive equality or non-discrimination as provided for in CEDAW have been integrated into the respective human rights acts of Canada and New Zealand.

There are also examples from India, New Zealand and Nigeria where CEDAW has been cited in the courts. However, the use of international treaty standards in courts has been sporadic in many of the countries, and this has not been sufficient to change the culture of the courts so that arguments of obligation under treaty law become the norm. In other words, there has only been piecemeal achievement and no holistic law reform, much less a cohesive plan for CEDAW implementation.

CEDAW is not the basis of law or policy reform

Concerns in this regard include the fact that the principles of the Convention are not necessarily used to inform interventions such as law reform that could benefit women. An example is the adoption of the Human Rights Act 1998 in the United Kingdom. While the adoption of the Act is a positive move, the concern is that it is based on the European Convention on Human Rights and Fundamental Freedoms, which does not provide the full range of women's human rights incorporated in CEDAW. For example, it does not provide expressly for equality nor does it provide for positive obligations for governments to eliminate indirect discrimination and to implement temporary special measures.

Despite the existence of national plans of action for women and some gender-responsive budgeting, it is not clear that the norms and standards of CEDAW are being used as a framework. This is compounded by States parties' lack of understanding of the meaning of equality for women and so these efforts tend to be based on protectionist or welfarist approaches. In addition, they are not being monitored.

Lack of clarity on CEDAW as a human rights instrument

Further concern is the lack of appreciation of CEDAW as a human rights instrument. The Committee was particularly concerned with the replies of the UK expressing the view that it considers the obligation under CEDAW to be much more programmatic in nature than the European Convention on Human Rights and Fundamental Freedoms and thus difficult to introduce into common law.

The Committee commented on the processes in the UK to enable devolution of power to the Scottish Parliament, the Northern Ireland Assembly and the National Assembly for Wales. With regard to women, it was reported that detailed post-devolution arrangements would be worked out by each of the respective assemblies. But the Committee expressed concern that the devolution of powers might result in uneven protection for women. It urged the UK to ensure that there is a unified national strategy and policy for the implementation of all provisions of CEDAW so that all women can benefit equally as a result of the government's obligation under the Convention to fulfil their *de jure* and *de facto* rights.

Piecemeal law reform and weak implementation

Because of the lack of a holistic approach, law reform in one area is sometimes negated by conflicting laws. There may be dual or even triple legal systems – civil and religious or customary – as in the case of India, Sri Lanka, Malaysia and Nigeria. There may also be a lacuna in the law that has negative consequences in another area. In India, constitutional guarantees for equality do not regulate the private sector. The Committee has therefore recommended that India enact an anti sex discrimination act to make the standards of CEDAW and the guarantees of the Constitution applicable to non-state actors.

Even where there are good laws, implementation and enforcement is weak and the Committee has consistently pointed out the need for monitoring to see if there is de facto *enjoyment of rights by women.*

Even where there are good laws, implementation and enforcement is weak and the Committee has consistently pointed out the need for monitoring to see if there is *de facto* enjoyment of rights by women.

Persistence of discrimination

Basically there has not been much of an attempt to make a comprehensive inventory of discriminatory laws with a view to their revision or repeal, and in many countries discrimination in the law and practice remains. In Nigeria, the Constitution still contains discriminatory provisions, and social acceptance of harmful traditional practices – including widowhood practices, female genital mutilation (FGM) and child marriage – make their elimination difficult. In Trinidad and Tobago, the Committee noted that violence against women is deeply entrenched and perhaps tolerated by society. Other areas brought to the attention of the Committee are the need in India for a holistic health plan and the need to arrest maternal and infant mortality rates, which are among the highest in the world. The Committee also expressed concern at the lack of law reform with regard to the personal laws of different religious groups in India.

Rights not extended to minority women or throughout States' territories

The Committee has also drawn attention to the fact that, in spite of laws and policies to protect the rights of minorities, governments have been unable to fulfil these rights or to monitor and provide adequate remedies for the violations of the rights of women from minority and other disadvantaged groups such as the Dalits of India, the Maoris of New Zealand or the women of ethnic minorities in the UK. Besides legislation, more positive action is needed by governments to protect the rights of these women.

As noted above, the Committee was concerned that, with the devolution of power in the UK to national assemblies, the protection of women might not be even. They pointed out that the State must ensure that there is a unified strategy and policy for implementation of all provisions of CEDAW so that all women in the entire territory of the State party can benefit equally. Furthermore, the Committee pointed out that there was very little information in the report of the UK on the implementation of CEDAW in the Isle of Man, the Turks and Caicos Islands, the Virgin Islands and the Falkland Islands. The UK needs to pay serious attention to its obligations as a State party to CEDAW with regard to its overseas territories.

The Committee has consistently pointed out the weak representation of women in decision-making in almost all Commonwealth countries, both developed and under-developed.

Weak representation of women

The Committee has consistently pointed out the weak representation of women in decision-making in almost all Commonwealth countries, both developed and under-developed. Even in New Zealand, where women have held constitutional office, women are poorly represented in parliament and local government and do not hold adequate numbers of positions as chief executives in the public sector.

Weak reporting record and lack of data collection

Reporting is seldom on time and there is inadequate data collection for the purposes of monitoring the implementation of CEDAW. This means there is no monitoring of the effects of laws, policies and programmes, no indicators of *de facto* realisation of women's rights and no knowledge of obstacles to their realisation. There also do not seem to be plans to implement CEDAW's Concluding Comments.

Weak institutions

There are improvements in the infrastructure of the national machineries for women in all the countries concerned but these remain weak. Institutional arrangements for promoting women's rights lack the required technical capability or do not have the required influence to be taken seriously.

An example of this is India, which has put in place many initiatives for the protection of women's rights such as a National Commission on Women, with state-level commissions having the responsibility for developing action plans on gender and proposals for law reform. However, the CEDAW Committee and NGOs have observed that such plans adopt a welfarist approach and that the proposed law reform is not adopted by the Government.

Technically too the national machineries and plans of many countries suffer from a lack of resources, time-framed targets and/or monitoring.

Examples of Best Practices

CEDAW in the courts

CEDAW has been cited in the courts in India, New Zealand and Nigeria. The Committee commended the contribution made by the Supreme Court in India, in developing the concept of social action litigation and a jurisprudence integrating the Convention into domestic law by interpreting Constitutional provisions on equality between women and men. In the case of New Zealand it was pointed out that the courts had taken international treaties, including CEDAW, into consideration in domestic cases.

Law reform

There is considerable evidence of piecemeal law reform. For example, Canada has created Domestic Violence Family Courts. India has banned sex selective abortion. New Zealand has enacted the Employment Relations Act 2000 which, though not focusing explicitly on women, would benefit women. It has also established a Pay and Employment Equity Task Force, to make progress in the area of pay and equality in employment in the public sphere, and established paid parental leave.

Nigeria has put in place new federal laws supporting equality, the Trafficking in Persons Prohibition, Law Enforcement and Administration Act 2003 and the Child Rights Act 2003. There are also a number of state laws prohibiting discrimination against women in areas such as FGM, widowhood practices and early marriage.

Trinidad and Tobago has passed Equal Opportunity Legislation and in 2002 was awaiting the appointment of the

Equal Opportunity Commission and Tribunal. Legislation preventing employers from discriminating against women on the basis of pregnancy has been passed and marital rape is a crime.

Reform in the UK includes new legislation in areas such as the national minimum wage, the new outcome-oriented budgetary reform, the commitment to family-friendly employment and legislation for the protection of women, namely the Anti-Sex Discrimination Act 1996, the Protection from Harassment Act 1997 and the Sex Offenders Act 1997.

Policies and plans

There are a number of national policies for women, plans of action for women and initiatives for gender mainstreaming in budgeting, etc. Of interest is the UK's 1999 budget, which has a strategic orientation resulting in increased child benefit and family tax credit, and mainstreaming of the budget to benefit women.

Women in decision-making

In New Zealand, women have held four constitutional positions, namely those of the Governor General, the Prime Minister, the Attorney General and the Chief Justice, while the proportion of women Ministers of the Crown and the representation of women at all levels of the Ministry of Foreign Affairs and Trade has risen considerably.

Development assistance as part of States' obligations

Developed countries have an additional role: that of assisting developing countries. The obligation of States parties under CEDAW includes ensuring a gender dimension in any development assistance they may provide. New Zealand was commended for its policy of strengthening the promotion and protection of women's human rights and of integrating a gender dimension into development co-operation programmes, particularly in the Pacific region.

States must take steps to incorporate CEDAW into domestic law so that it is directly applicable in the courts. Capacity has to be built in all branches of government, vertically and horizontally, to use CEDAW as a framework for all interventions such as law reform, plans of action, programmes and services, gender mainstreaming as well as gender budgeting.

Conclusion

In many countries, while there is *ad hoc* reform of laws and creation of interventions for the advancement of women, such as plans of action or gender mainstreaming and gender budgeting, there does not seem to be a conscious application of CEDAW at the domestic level. States must take steps to incorporate CEDAW into domestic law so that it is directly applicable in the courts. Capacity has to be built in all branches of government, vertically and horizontally, to use CEDAW as a framework for all interventions such as law reform, plans of action, programmes and services, gender mainstreaming as well as gender budgeting. This will help introduce a rights-based approach into these interventions using the lens of CEDAW, focusing on substantive equality and non-discrimination. Special efforts must be made to train judges and lawyers to apply international human rights jurisprudence in court cases, with special reference to CEDAW jurisprudence. Capacity-building for all branches of government as well as for women's groups must focus on the creation of clarity on the meaning of substantive equality and indirect discrimination as embedded in the Convention. The capacity of women must be built to form constituencies for advocacy to claim their rights and to draw accountability from governments. Data collection must be consistent, sustained and refined to include indicators that will reveal the *de facto* situation of women and identify obstacles to *de facto* equality.

CEDAW report writing is a useful tool for a State to monitor itself and must be taken seriously. Reports must be submitted on time to ensure effective and progressive implementation of the Convention. Countries must draw up comprehensive plans to implement CEDAW, including incorporating the recommendations from the Concluding Comments, and special attention needs to be paid to disadvantaged groups of women. Adequate institutional arrangements, including mechanisms for intersectoral co-operation and budgetary allocation, must be put in place. States must form partnerships with NGOs for needs identification, data sharing and identification of obstacles to *de facto* equality.

Finally, a positive culture for human rights and women's equality must be created. CEDAW must be popularised and a plan put in place to eliminate negative elements of culture and stereotyping of women and men.

... a positive culture for human rights and women's equality must be created. CEDAW must be popularised and a plan put in place to eliminate negative elements of culture and stereotyping of women and men.

Notes

1 As of April 2004.
2 It is not the aim of this paper to provide a comprehensive assessment of CEDAW implementation in Commonwealth countries. Rather, what will be attempted is to provide brief snapshots of achievements and challenges in selected countries: Canada, India, New Zealand, Nigeria, Trinidad and Tobago and the United Kingdom. The information for this analysis is taken from the respective Concluding Comments of the CEDAW Committee. The years of the review and the reference to the Concluding Comments are as follows: Canada, 2003, A/58/38 (Part 1); India, 2000, A/55/38 (Part 1); New Zealand, 2003, A/58/38 (Part 2); Nigeria, 2004, A/59/38 (Part 1); Trinidad and Tobago, 2002, A/57/38 (Part 1); and the UK, 1999, A/54/38/Rev 1 (Part 2).
3 Cited in Buergenthal, 1988.
4 *De jure* and *de facto* – as a matter of law and as a matter of fact, i.e. in reality.
5 The lack of enabling legislation may be an obstacle for direct applicability of treaty law in the courts but, if there is political will, it should not be an obstacle to providing definitions of equality or discrimination or to amending legislation according to the norms and standards of the Convention.

References

Buergenthal, T (1988). *International Human Rights in a Nutshell*. St Paul, MN: West Publishing Company.

Henkin, Louis (1977). 'Human Rights and Domestic Jurisdiction'. In T Buergenthal, *Human Rights, International Law and the Helsinki Accord*. Montclair, NJ: Allanheld, Osmun.

Recent Key Trends and Issues in the Implementation of CEDAW

Feride Acar[1]

Human rights principles and standards such as the 'indivisibility' and 'universality' of rights, as well as the issues and concerns of the women's movement of the 20th century ranging from legal to economic equality, are incorporated in CEDAW

Basic Premises of CEDAW

The Convention on the Elimination of All Forms of Discrimination against Women has now been in force for over 20 years. To date, it has been ratified or acceded to by 170 States.[2] It is the only legally binding international instrument to set forth the human rights standards for women and girls in the full range of civil, political, economic, social and cultural areas of both public and private life. It sets the international standard of equality between women and men.

This unique instrument was drafted in the latter part of the 1970s, adopted by the General Assembly in 1979 and came into force in 1981. It was built on the legacy of decades of work going back to the inception of the UN itself. It is fair to say that the Women's Convention is the common offspring of the international human rights movement and the women's movement under the roof of the UN. The unique and almost 'revolutionary' text of this international legal instrument reflects the developments in both of these movements. Human rights principles and standards such as the 'indivisibility' and 'universality' of rights, as well as the issues and concerns of the women's movement of the 20th century ranging from legal to economic equality, are incorporated in CEDAW.

Thus, the Convention not only incorporates in itself provisions pertaining to all areas of human rights (i.e. political and civil as well as economic, social and cultural), and aims at their universal enjoyment by all women in all parts of the world, but it also elevates these broad-based human rights provisions to the level of a legally binding piece of international law.

Building on the gains of the second wave feminist movement, which emphasised the critique of patriarchy and the dichotomy of public versus private spheres, CEDAW approaches the human rights of women from a more sensitive and relevant perspective than any other international legal instrument. The Convention, by referring specifically to women's human rights in the private sphere, i.e. in the family and in marriage (article 16), operates from an awareness that the family, that most private of all private spheres and relations within it, need to be addressed in order to ensure respect for, promote and implement women's human rights.

It is in this sense that CEDAW has been called "an innovative and ambitious" treaty. This Convention not only covers a wide spectrum of rights but is also very aware of the systemic nature of violations of women's human rights. It clearly operates on the basis that all human rights of women are inextricably linked to one another (i.e. they are indivisible and interdependent).

Prior to CEDAW, human rights instruments often failed to bring to light violations of women's human rights no matter how serious these may have been. Because such violations often took place in the private sphere, they were not considered 'public concern' or 'state responsibility', or many violations were also thought to relate to the domain of traditions, culture and religion, which are areas that were all too often assumed to be impenetrable by or to have immunity from legal and policy intervention.

Today, around 20 years after the coming into force of CEDAW, one of the six core UN Human Rights Conventions, our perceptions and attitudes all over the world are significantly different. I believe, despite problems and challenges (to which I will be referring a little later), the fact that basic premises of CEDAW are accepted by the large number of States that have ratified this Convention is a gigantic step in the right direction for humankind. What, then, are these basic premises of CEDAW? Let me briefly underline them. First and foremost, this Convention does not operate with an abstract concept of equality. Instead, article 1 of the Convention provides a clear definition of discrimination and reflects the recognition that discrimination against women is a universal reality that is to be eradicated. In other words, this Convention is neither vague nor neutral with respect to it diagnosis and definition of gender-based discrimination.

... the State party that ratifies [CEDAW] should neither be passive nor neutral in the face of discrimination against women.

Therefore, the State party that ratifies it should neither be passive nor neutral in the face of discrimination against women. Specific forms and areas of discrimination against women are to be identified and made visible, and proactive and therapeutic measures as well as actions for redress of victims and punishment of violators are to be taken effectively and swiftly.

Through its substantive articles (articles 1–16) CEDAW transcends the traditional human rights framework by addressing both public and private realms. Through its reference (article 1) to discrimination of 'effect' and 'purpose', the Convention manifests a sensitive and comprehensive outlook that covers both 'direct' and 'indirect' or 'intentional' and 'unintentional' discrimination. Through its targeting of both *de jure* and *de facto* discrimination against women, the Women's Convention addresses legal norms as well as social norms, cultural practices, traditions and customs as possible bases of discrimination against women (article 5). Prejudicial and discriminatory traditions and cultural norms and practices are thus to be modified so as not to preserve or strengthen gender stereotypes that impede women's full enjoyment of their human rights.

This premise of CEDAW is certainly a very bold step that could only be built on the gains of the international women's movement. It nonetheless continues to constitute a major challenge to implementation worldwide (as the nature of so many of the reservations by State parties to CEDAW demonstrates). The issue of traditions and culture is inevitably raised, be it as an 'obstacle' or an 'excuse', during the CEDAW Committee's dialogue with State parties when they report. There is no doubt that discriminatory traditions and prejudicial cultural practices continue to be major impediments to women's human rights in most societies around the world.

Another very salient and radical aspect of CEDAW is the fact that this Convention clearly states (article 4.1) that affirmative action (called 'temporary special measures' in the language of the Convention) taken by States, political parties or employers to speed up *de facto* equality of women and men is not to be considered discriminatory. The Convention, at the same time, rules out very clearly the permanent maintenance of unequal and separate standards for sexes as discriminatory. This, I believe, is a critically important stand and most relevant to the realisation of gender equality in the world. In this very important article (article 4.1), the Women's Convention says that encouragement and incentive policies are needed to accelerate attainment of equality but that these cannot be allowed to turn into permanent standards of judgment, achievement, remuneration etc. separate for women and men. Our experience around the world testifies to the relevance of this approach.

We are now able to see clearly that, in societies with different levels of economic development and cultural backgrounds, 'temporary special measures' such as incentives and quotas have been uniquely effective in promoting women's participation in politics and decision-making positions as well as in the economy. In others, premature removal of quotas has resulted in a reduced number of women in such positions. We also observe that in the 21st century there are still countries where women are persistently denied the right to vote, let alone to be in positions of political decision-making, simply because they are women. Many women around the world do not enjoy their right to make decisions about personal and/or public aspects of their lives because cultural and social values and their reflections in laws of their countries have set permanently different standards for women and men. This is why we can confidently say that, if used as stipulated by the Convention (article 4.1), 'temporary special measures' are an indication of the 'degree' of a government's political will to improve the situation of women in a country.

Another very basic tenet of the Women's Convention is that it covers not only State and public actors but individuals, organisations and enterprises. Thus, this Convention holds the State responsible for prohibiting any discrimination against women by third parties. The State is to ensure through its laws, policies and monitoring mechanisms that such discrimination does not happen and to punish those who do discriminate against women.

Bearing in mind that discrimination against women often takes place in places and in contexts that are not formally 'state-controlled' and/or by people who are not official agents of the State, this is indeed a sine quo non for full implementation of women's human rights.

[CEDAW] *covers not only State and public actors but individuals, organisations and enterprises. ... The State is to ensure through its laws, policies and monitoring mechanisms that ... discrimination* [by third parties] *does not happen and to punish those who do discriminate against women.*

The Convention and the Beijing Platform for Action

Provisions of the Convention as set out in its 16 substantive articles and the 12 critical areas of the Beijing Platform for Action (BPFA) are closely connected. In fact women's human rights as enshrined under the Convention form the legal framework for and are central to the Platform.

Furthermore, the Convention's monitoring process enables the Committee on the Elimination of Discrimination Against Women (CEDAW Committee) to look for States' compliance with the Platform as well as the Convention itself. While it is the Commission on the Status of Women (CSW) that has the primary mandate for monitoring the implementation of the BPFA, the CEDAW Committee also has a salient role in this respect. The Platform specifically asks States parties to the Convention to include information on measures taken to implement it when reporting for CEDAW, and the Committee is tasked to take the Platform into account when considering these reports.

This is a responsibility that the CEDAW Committee takes very seriously and has been systematically carrying out through its review of State party reports since the Fourth World Conference on Women. Since that time the CEDAW Committee in its Concluding Comments has also routinely included a recommendation to the reporting State party to widely disseminate the BPA. In its review of State reports, the Committee has also often highlighted the commitments made by State parties at Beijing and in its Concluding Comments it noted if and where States have failed to address the BPFA in their reports. The Committee has often requested adoption of overall plans for implementation of the BPFA within a clear time frame, and in its 'constructive dialogue' with the States representatives it always inquires into the results of implementation of the Platform. Those issues and areas addressed more specifically by the Beijing+5 process, such as marital rape, crimes of 'honour', crimes of passion and racially motivated violence against women have also increasingly found their way into the Committee's review agenda in the years since 2000. Thus, the CEDAW Committee is accorded a unique opportunity to systematically observe and evaluate what is happening around the world with respect to the human rights of women.

Some Observations on Key Issues and Trends in Women's Human Rights

Looking out from the vantage point of CEDAW one is, first and foremost, struck by the fact that, despite significant progress, universal ratification of CEDAW – which was targeted for 2000 – has not been achieved, and there are still a large number of reservations to this Convention. In fact, CEDAW has the largest number of reservations of any human rights treaty. To me this shows that while most States may be willing to recognise the human rights of women on a general plane, many are still not ready to commit themselves to abide by these rights fully. It is also a fact that a good number of these reservations are entered on articles 2 and 16 of CEDAW and some, unfortunately, are stated in very broad, sweeping terms. Since articles 2 and 16 delineate the spirit and essence of effective implementation of women's human rights, the CEDAW Committee considers the presence of particularly very broad-based reservations to articles 2 and 16 as highly problematic and, in fact, incompatible with the Convention itself.

... despite significant progress, universal ratification of CEDAW – which was targeted for 2000 – has not been achieved, and there are still a large number of reservations to this Convention ... this shows that while most States may be willing to recognise the human rights of women on a general plane, many are still not ready to commit themselves to abide by these rights fully.

There are those who see ratification with such serious reservations to substantive articles as merely a political ploy by States who may want to jump on the band-wagon of international 'political correctness' without necessarily having a genuine political will to implement women's human rights. Perhaps some of the reservations to the Women's Convention give justification to these views. It is a fact that some States, contrary to international law, have placed reservations that are not only extensive in scope but also undermine the 'meaning and purpose' of the Convention. The Committee, as well as some other State parties and international women's voices (particularly the BPFA and Beijing +5), have expressed, time and again, serious concern over such reservations. I am pleased to say that in recent years there have been a few withdrawals of such incompatible reservations and/or limitation of their scope. Yet many such reservations still remain and some new ones have been added.

What is more, some States continue to indicate that they

have no intention of withdrawing incompatible and sweeping reservations that seriously impede the implementation of the Convention. This is a true dilemma not only for the Committee but also for all defenders of women's human rights around the world. One is left in the highly uncomfortable position of having to decide which is less damaging: ratification with reservations that may be contrary to the 'meaning and purpose' of the Convention, which seriously renders the instrument ineffective in terms of its impact on women in that country, or non-ratification, which means no reporting obligation and consequent absence of any international monitoring or scrutiny of women's human rights in that State. While the Committee's attitude has been to support the first option and hope to use the reporting process and the 'constructive dialogue' opportunity with the State party in a patient and determined manner to encourage and pressure for removal or trimming of such incompatible reservations, it is essential that the international community systematically press for a change of attitude on the part of State parties on this matter.

The progress in the world in the area of recognition and implementation of women's human rights is obvious. New legislation, growing awareness and sensitivity, strengthening of machineries at both State and civil society levels are universal phenomena. Yet there is also evidence that implies that the international community is still far from having reached a shared notion of women's human rights as contained in CEDAW, formulated into policy guidelines and programmes in the BPFA and further elaborated and updated in Beijing+5. National implementation remains as the bottleneck for human rights of women. Strikingly wide differences in political will, as well as actual capacity and resources available for national mechanisms, and, most importantly, the extent to which the harmonisation of principles of women's human rights into the social and cultural climate at the national level has been achieved, constitute fundamental axes along which national implementation varies among States.

Legal rights

It is true that legal frameworks for equality have been strengthened in most countries, and better mechanisms for redress for violations of rights (such as more informed and gender-sensitive courts and ombudsman mechanisms) have come into being in many countries. Some States have enhanced their constitutional principles of equality between men and women in the aftermath of Beijing. With respect to incorporation of CEDAW into domestic law there are variations. In some States international treaties take precedence over domestic legislation in which case, when ratified, CEDAW automatically becomes the law of the land. In others, specific legislation needs to be adopted to implement women's human rights as they are deployed in CEDAW. In countries that travel the former route, actual justiciability of women's human rights is often the problem. In the latter cases, on the other hand, enactment of the necessary legislation often takes a long time and is uneven with respect to the various types of rights protected under CEDAW.

There are still quite a few countries where the constitution does not refer to equality between women and men, and many others where the constitution does not incorporate a clear definition of discrimination such as that contained in article 1 of the Convention.

There are still quite a few countries where the constitution does not refer to equality between women and men, and many others where the constitution does not incorporate a clear definition of discrimination such as that contained in article 1 of the Convention. Generally speaking, while laws pertaining to civil and political rights are often enacted first and implemented more seriously, laws that protect women's economic rights in the areas of ownership and employment frequently lag behind.

At the national level, with regard to mechanisms, some countries have instituted specific gender ombudsman (notably the Nordic countries and some Eastern European States) and others have a deputy ombudsman and/or a women's rights commissioner in the Human Rights Commission to specifically respond to women's human rights issues. In most countries, however, women's human rights continue to be 'lost' in ombudsman or law commission structures and suffer from lack of sufficient attention at the national level. It is noteworthy that in several Muslim countries law reform measures, implementing the Convention and the Beijing Platform for Action, have included the revision of personal status laws, establishment of family courts, adoption of family codes and reform of citizenship laws. However, much more needs to be done in this area in order to make women's human rights, as they are depicted in CEDAW, 'real' for women at home in these countries.

In report after report, we in the CEDAW Committee observe that discriminatory laws, particularly those governing marriage, administration of marital property, divorce and the family, persist.

A relatively new area of law where women's human rights are increasingly being taken into consideration is migration and refugee legislation. Several States have recognised gender-based persecution in their refugee laws; provisions in immigration legislation to protect the human rights of immigrant women have also been adopted by a few. In report after report, we in the CEDAW Committee observe that discriminatory laws, particularly those governing marriage, administration of marital property, divorce and the family, persist. Many States also continue to have laws discriminating against women in relation to nationality whereby women cannot pass their nationality to their children on an equal basis with men. Blatant discrimination in penal law, particularly where prosecution of sexual crimes and rape and penalties for crimes committed in the name of 'honour' are concerned, can be found in many countries. Marital rape is recognised as a crime punishable by law in only a very small number of countries.

Discriminatory laws governing ownership and inheritance of land, access to loans and credits, and health, such as those requiring that a wife obtain her husband's consent for sterilisation or abortion, are maintained.

These observations provide sufficient evidence that at the national level even *de jure* discrimination is still far from being eradicated. It has also been the Committee's observation that women experience more discrimination as a result of the co-existence of multiple legal systems. In some countries, customary and religious laws, which govern personal status and private life, exist side by side with positive law. This situation often provides legal grounds for discrimination. Such laws sometimes prevail over the non-discrimination provisions of even the Constitution of the country and they often constitute a powerful foundation for non-implementation of women's human rights.

Violence against women

Having been drafted in the 1970s, when the State parties convened under the roof of the UN were not yet ready to admit to the reality of violence against women as a form of gender-based discrimination, the text of the CEDAW Convention makes no explicit reference to violence against women. Conceptually and theoretically, the Convention could readily accommodate it. So, since its establishment, the CEDAW Committee has taken it upon itself to make clear, in a number of General Recommendations, that gender-based violence falls within the meaning of discrimination against women. In 1989, the Committee adopted General Recommendation 12 on violence against women which recommended that States include information in their reports to the Committee on the incidence of violence against women. In 1990, General Recommendation 14 addressed 'female circumcision' and other traditional practices harmful to the health of women.

... in today's world there are still societies that fail to recognise violence against women as a public concern. In particular, violence that occurs in the home or is related to tradition or custom (such as female genital mutilation) presents a problem.

In 1992, the Committee adopted General Recommendation 19, which defines gender-based violence as violence that is directed against a woman because she is a woman or that affects women disproportionately, and declares it to be "a form of discrimination against women that seriously inhibits women's ability to enjoy rights and freedoms on a basis of equality with men". The general recommendation makes clear that "States may be ... responsible for private acts if they fail with due diligence to prevent violations of rights or to investigate and punish acts of violence, and for providing compensation".

Our examination of State reports reveals that significant progress has indeed occurred towards the elimination of violence against women in the world. This scourge is now widely recognised as a pervasive and unacceptable gross violation of women's human rights. It is, nonetheless, a fact that in today's world there are still societies that fail to recognise violence against women as a public concern. In particular, violence that occurs in the home or is related to tradition or custom (such as female genital mutilation) presents a problem. Many countries have passed legislation and introduced policies in this area. I am proud to say that alongside rising global awareness on the subject, largely owing to the Beijing process and other UN efforts, the CEDAW Committee's own review and recommendations have helped pave the way for domestic violence legislation in many States. The remaining questions in many national contexts are: how adequate are these laws and policies, and how well are they supported by measures to sensitise the police, judiciary, health professionals and the public in order to ensure their effective implementation?

One particularly relevant contribution to the elimination

I believe that women's NGOs worldwide that have played an absolutely indispensable role in bringing the Optional Protocol to life have now an equally critical responsibility in ensuring it a robust existence.

of violence against women through the more effective implementation of CEDAW worldwide can be expected via the Optional Protocol. This instrument, which entered into force at the end of 2000, allows individual women and groups of individual women to complain to the Committee of violations of their rights in the Convention. It also allows representative complaints where victims consent to representation, although this requirement can be waived where it is impossible to get such consent. The Optional Protocol also entitles the Committee to inquire of its own motion into "grave or systematic" violations of the Convention. No reservations are permitted to the terms of the instrument, but it is possible to opt out of the inquiry procedure. There is also a provision that obligates States to protect individuals from ill-treatment or intimidation as a result of using the Protocol's provisions. These impressive and progressive elements of the Optional Protocol should be taken advantage of by women around the world, particularly to combat all forms of violence against them.

The adoption and entry into force of the Optional Protocol – now with 49 State parties, and many more signatories – point to the improved and better-equipped capacity of the international legal framework to address the human rights concerns of women. Only time, however, will tell about its actual effectiveness. National level awareness-raising and capacity-building are once again critical for this instrument's effective utilisation. Like any other instrument it will only be as good as the way in which it is used.

I believe that women's NGOs worldwide that have played an absolutely indispensable role in bringing the Optional Protocol to life now have an equally critical responsibility in ensuring it a robust existence.

A critical emerging fact about the implementation of women's human rights in the globalised world is that, in a number of culturally or ethnically plural societies or in countries that have large immigrant populations (many of which are developed societies), what is called 'respect for traditions, culture or religion of minorities' appears to impede vigorous protection of women's human rights. This is particularly so with respect to the prosecution and punishment of perpetrators in religious and ethnic communities. This is an extremely grave situation because it adds a new dimension to an already existing serious challenge to women's human rights.

It is a fact that crimes that are committed against women in their communities, their workplace and in their own families are often excluded from the purview of much human rights protection, even if these violations are sustained by a State structure that tolerates or even encourages such action. But even more seriously, both *de facto* and *de jure* violations of women's rights – in areas such as family law, nationality, bodily integrity, freedom of expression, freedom of reproductive choice and liberty of movement – are also often overlooked, if not justified, by governments on the basis of respect for tradition, culture or religion. These are almost 'tolerated' due to a misguided notion of 'cultural relativism'. This not only obscures violations of the rights of women, but creates a dilemma and inhibits firm response to such acts from the international community. It is, therefore, a serious challenge which both the national governments and the international human rights community must be prepared to confront in the future.

We must all operate with the baseline assumption that not all traditions are good and are to be protected. Discriminatory traditions that violate women's human rights need to be changed.

We must all operate with the baseline assumption that not all traditions are good and are to be protected. Discriminatory traditions that violate women's human rights need to be changed.

Human rights are universal; women's human rights are also universal, which means they are the same everywhere and for every woman.

Our work in the CEDAW Committee bears witness to the rather disturbing and disappointing persistence of stereotypical attitudes towards the gender roles of women and men as a critical challenge to women's human rights worldwide. Prevalence of such attitudes is responsible for a whole range of violations in widely different contexts around the world. They form the social-psychological breeding ground of traditional practices and customs prejudicial to women, such as violence against women, polygamy, forced marriage, son preference and 'honour' killings. In many countries, stereotypical attitudes also create a pervasive climate of discrimination, incorporating rigid social codes that entrench the traditional role of women in the family and limit their participation in public life. In almost all regions of the world notions of appropriate work for women, which are often internalised by women themselves,

There is a growing recognition in the international arena that discrimination is multifaceted and complex, and that few individuals are affected by only one form of discrimination. The rise to prominence of women's issues had a significant role in drawing attention at the international level to multiple discrimination.

discourage women from entering public life and seeking non-traditional employment and seriously limit women's freedom to make choices about their individual roles.

Multiple discrimination

Last but not least, let me also point to a most relevant emerging issue. There is a growing recognition in the international arena that discrimination is multifaceted and complex, and that few individuals are affected by only one form of discrimination. The rise to prominence of women's issues has had a significant role in drawing attention at the international level to multiple discrimination. The multiple forms of discrimination that women may experience, indicating that cross-cutting factors such as age, disability, socio-economic position or belonging to a particular ethnic or racial group could combine with discrimination on the basis of sex and create specific barriers for women, gave visibility to the phenomenon and made clear that women so affected would experience multiple disadvantages. The BPFA emerges as a landmark document in that respect. The impact of multiple forms of discrimination in education and training, participation in decision-making, enjoyment of economic benefits and human rights, including in times of armed conflict as well as the right to be free from violence, was addressed in a number of the BPFA's critical areas of concern.

In this context, the CEDAW Committee has observed that while discrimination on the basis of sex has been slowly eroding, much more needs to be done with respect to the elimination of multiple and intersecting discrimination faced by women around the world. In recognition of this need, there is a growing tendency in the Committee in recent years to specifically inquire about and make recommendations to State parties with regard to women who are not only denied equality on the basis of their sex, but because of factors such as age, race and ethnicity. Other human rights treaty bodies are following suit, with the Human Rights Committee and the Social, Economic and Cultural Rights Committee increasingly integrating gender into their work. Over the years, through its consideration of States parties' reports, the CEDAW Committee has also seen that various types of discrimination do not always affect women and men in the same way. The Committee has observed that gender discrimination may be intensified and may occur concurrently with other forms of discrimination, such as racial, ethnic or religious discrimination. Women who are particularly affected by the multiple impact of discrimination are women belonging to minority groups in terms of race, ethnicity, nationality or caste, as well as migrant workers, women asylum seekers, refugees, displaced women and indigenous women.

The Committee has seen that discrimination against women of different ethnic and racial origins is often manifested in the most extreme and horrific forms of gender-based violence.

Armed conflict and extreme poverty, as well as natural disasters and catastrophes, which are often reflected by increasing violence against women in general, impact disproportionately on women from marginalised, racial and ethnic groups. Selective immigration controls, commercial sexual exploitation and cross-border trafficking of women are also contemporary phenomena where racial, ethnic or religious discrimination render women particularly vulnerable.

In its work, the Committee has also observed that contemporary phenomena such as neo-nazism and neo-fascism, resurgence of ethnic nationalism and religious fundamentalism, to the extent that these are phenomena based on ethnocentric values and xenophobic hostility towards out-groups, often target women of such groups as the prey of their oppression and aggression. Around the world, also owing to be spread of such movements, women's human rights have been severely violated in a variety of ways, ranging from limitation of their access to resources and basic services to their subjection to intimidation and physical violence by State agents and/or fellow citizens, all the way to their systematic rape and forced impregnation as a war tactic. At this critical juncture of history, when world politics once again appear to give way to armed conflict, it is particularly important that the lessons of the past are not forgotten. Women and girl children should not be rendered vulnerable to heinous crimes and violations of their human rights that the international community has often come to deeply regret and be ashamed of in the past.

Around the world ... women's human rights have been severely violated in a variety of ways, ranging from limitation of their access to resources and basic services to their subjection to intimidation and physical violence by State agents and/or fellow citizens, all the way to their systematic rape and forced impregnation as a war tactic

Conclusion

No country in the world has fully implemented the human rights of women, and full *de jure*, let alone *de facto*, equality has not been achieved anywhere in the world. There is, however, sufficient cumulative experience in combating different facets of discrimination against women in different countries. The globalised world, with the unprecedented communication opportunities it has, offers us a chance to benefit from each other's experience, to become aware of 'good practices' elsewhere and to share resources and, most critically, to avoid repetition of mistakes. I therefore insist that the challenge to confront the remaining obstacles can and should be taken up with a vision of a human condition based on full and equal enjoyment of human rights by all women and men as articulated by the Universal Declaration of Human Rights (UDHR) and a peaceful world free of all forms of discrimination against women.

Note

1 A written statement submitted by Feride Acar, Chairperson of the Committee on the Elimination of Discrimination Against Women, to the 47th session of the Commission on the Status of Women, New York, 3–14 March 2003.

2 At the time of writing. There are 177 States Parties as of August 2004.

2 Culture, Gender and the Law

Recent Thinking and Practical Strategies

Lisa Fishbayn

Conceptual Framework

The issue of the relationship between gender equality and the claims of culture has been identified as an important factor to be considered in Commonwealth efforts to improve the status of women (Coomaraswamy, 2000, para. 22). The conflict between women's human rights and some practices embedded in cultural traditions raises challenging questions. Does human rights discourse seek to impose universal values or culturally relative ones? Are conflicts over human rights indicative of an irreconcilable 'clash of civilisations'? Do human rights instruments like the Convention on the Elimination of All Forms of Discrimination against Women reflect a Western/liberal/Christian world-view that is inconsistent with Islamic/African/Asian/Aboriginal values? How can the claims of international human rights law and the claims of culture be reconciled? This paper will seek to provide an overview of recent thinking on the nature of this conflict and practical strategies for dealing with it. It provides no single criterion of analysis or plan of action. Rather, it argues for a complex, contextualised analysis to identify the role cultural claims play in a particular political context and for a subtle and wide-ranging array of strategies for building a new consensus on the relationship between culture and gender equality.

The issue of the relationship between gender equality and the claims of culture has been identified as an important factor to be considered in Commonwealth efforts to improve the status of women.

The paper is divided into five parts. Part 1 explores the nature of the notion of culture at play in legal debates. Part 2 considers the justification for cultural rights and the limits that may be put on them when they violate gender equality. Part 3 enumerates factors that make the eradication of traditional practices that impact on women particularly problematic. Part 4 develops the idea of using cross-cultural and inter-cultural dialogue to find ways in which human rights values are consistent with traditional cultural values. Finally, Part 5 identifies ways in which Commonwealth nations can use the law reform process to engage cultural communities in the process of reformulating traditional practices to conform with gender equality.

1 Unpacking the Notion of 'Culture'

The right to 'culture'

Article 15 of the International Covenant on Economic, Social and Cultural Rights (ICESCR) guarantees the right to participate in the cultural life of one's community. The right to pass on cultural beliefs to one's children through choosing their education is referred to in article 26(3). Article 27 of the International Covenant on Civil and Political Rights (ICCPR) provides that:

> In those States in which ethnic, religious, or linguistic minorities exist, persons belonging to such minorities shall not be denied the right, in community with the other members of their group, to enjoy their own culture, to profess and practise their own religion, or to use their own language.

This article has been interpreted to require not merely that governments do not impair minority cultural life but that they take affirmative steps to protect culture. It has been applied in relatively few cases and the scope of its potential application is not clear (Renteln, 2002).

Conversely, CEDAW requires State parties to "undertake all appropriate measures, including legislation, to modify or abolish laws, regulations, customs and practices" that discriminate against women. In particular, they undertake to "modify the social and cultural patterns of conduct of men and women, with a view to achieving the elimination of prejudices and customary and all other practices which are based on the idea of the inferiority or the superiority of either of the sexes or on stereotyped roles for men and women".[1] This construction suggests that where the rights to culture and gender equality come into conflict, gender equality should take priority.

Rights to the accommodation of cultural difference have been incorporated into domestic law in some Commonwealth countries. Several have drafted their national constitutions with a view to giving effect to article 27. For example, the South African Constitution substantially reproduces the rights in article 27 in sections 30 and 31.[2] A key difference is that while article 27 contains no limitations clause, the rights in the South African text are explicitly limited. Culture is only guaranteed to the extent that its enjoyment is consistent with the enjoyment of other provisions of the Bill of Rights, including the right to equality on the basis of sex and gender. Similarly, Section 27 of the Canadian Charter of Rights and Freedoms mandates that Charter rights be interpreted in a manner consistent with the preservation and enhancement of the multicultural heritage of Canada, but does not give cultural claims priority over those of equality.

Some Commonwealth nations guarantee multicultural rights in domestic legislation as well. Canada adopted a policy of official multiculturalism in 1971 and passed the Canadian Multiculturalism Act in 1985. This Act places Federal institutions under an obligation to recognise and promote multiculturalism, which includes ensuring that all individuals receive equal treatment and equal protection under the law while respecting and valuing their diversity (section 3(1)). The South African Promotion of Equality and Prevention of Unfair Discrimination Act 2000 clarifies that gender-based discrimination includes "any practice, including traditional, customary, or religious practice, which impairs the dignity of women and undermines the equality of women and men, including the undermining of the dignity and well-being of the girl child" (s.8).

Still other Commonwealth nations have chosen to exclude certain traditional practices or the regime of customary law from constitutional review. For example, the Constitution of Kenya prohibits discrimination based on sex but these protections do not apply to laws relating to marriage, divorce, inheritance and other aspects of customary family law. In essence, this means that these laws cannot be challenged as unconstitutional even if it is clear that they violate women's rights. A draft constitution released in 2002 abolishes some of these exemptions but would continue to exclude Muslim family law from the ambit of constitutional review (Human Rights Watch, 2003).

Culture defined

> Culture is a dynamic value system of learned elements, with assumptions, conventions, beliefs and rules permitting members of a group to relate to each other and to the world, to communicate and to develop their creative potential.
>
> (Canadian Commission for UNESCO, 1977)[3]

Debates over the impact of human rights norms on cultural practices often rely on two rival models of culture. In the first, the static model, a culture is understood as the way of life of a discrete people. The essence of the people is expressed in an integrated system of ideas and practices. Each element of this culture fulfils a necessary human function and is integrated with other elements in a perfectly balanced system (Bennett, 1991:16). A culture persists through history by reproducing itself through inserting individuals into their social roles in this system. The agency of individuals is shaped by and expressed through their social roles with little remainder. In this model, culture is a fragile, organic structure that flourishes if left alone but can be destroyed through even small changes. Such destructive change may come about through direct intervention from outsiders or through the abandonment of traditional ways by members.

The alternative conception is a more dynamic one. This sees a culture not as an organic whole but as a shifting set of texts, images and practices that has no central core features. The link between these materials and a particular people is wrought by history rather than by logical necessity. A cultural group maintains a sense of identity through acts of collaborative narration that organise changing materials into a story of identity and continuity. It is the capacity and desire to elaborate such stories that is key to the perpetuation of a culture:

> Groups negotiating their identity in contexts of domination and exchange persist, patching themselves together in ways different from a living organism. A community, unlike a body, can lose a central 'organ' and not die. All the critical elements of identity are in specific conditions replaceable: language, land, blood, leadership, religion. Recognised, viable [groups] exist in which any one or even most of these elements are missing, replaced, or largely transformed. (Clifford, 1998:338)

If we employ this more complex and dynamic notion of culture, it becomes apparent that change in cultural norms and practices is inevitable. The debate shifts from the legitimacy of any and all changes brought about by human rights to the substantive merit of the proposed changes and legitimacy of the mechanisms through which they are implemented.

The category of practices that are defended in the name of culture or tradition is quite broad and potentially unlimited because many practices can be defined or redefined as integral to cultural life.

The kinds of practices that are defended as part of culture or tradition

The category of practices that are defended in the name of culture or tradition is quite broad and potentially unlimited because many practices can be defined or redefined as integral to cultural life. Practices may always have seemed important or may have become so more recently in response to political struggles. There are, however, certain patterns of practices that appear frequently:

Marriage practices

Culture may be invoked to justify the marriage of girls under the age of 18. Early marriage is correlated with higher incidence of health problems in pregnancy and childbirth and higher rates of HIV infection. It is also linked with decreased economic development opportunities as young women tend to have more children, less power within their marriage, less education and less income earning power. Other marriage-related practices that may be challenged as violations of women's rights are polygyny (a husband taking more than one wife), levirate marriage (a widow being required to have sexual relations with and/or marry another member of her husband's family), bridewealth (payments made by the husband's family to the wife's family as part of the marriage contract) and abduction for purposes of rape which is then legitimised by marriage between the victim and perpetrator.

Traditional practices harmful to women's health

Culture is invoked to justify female genital mutilation,[4] dietary taboos in pregnancy that deny women and their growing babies nutritious foods, and ritual 'cleansing' of widows through sexual relations with men who may put them at risk of contracting sexually transmitted diseases.[5]

Property rights

Women may be characterised as incapable of owning property so that they cannot inherit or claim ownership of anything they produce. Inheritance practices may exclude women so that when a man dies, his estate passes to his eldest son or other male relatives, leaving his widow and daughters without property. Women's wages become the property of their husbands or guardians.

Permanent minority

The law may define women as perpetual minors who never become full legal persons. This means they cannot enter into contracts, sue or be sued in court, own property or act as guardians to other minors, including their own children. In particular, it means they cannot negotiate to enter into or to end their own marriages.

Violence

The authority of husbands and fathers to discipline women and children in the family is both defined as a key aspect of cultural tradition and an important means of allowing men to insure respect for cultural traditions. Such discipline may range from physical chastisement for perceived disobedience to murder to punish conduct that violates the family's 'honour'. The invocation of culture may prevent such conduct from being defined as a crime at all or may be accepted as a defence in court.

2 The Importance of Understanding and Accommodating Cultural Differences

The political challenge of accommodating cultural difference

Conflicts over culture and gender may emerge where the dominant values of the majority in a State, perhaps as embodied in law, conflict with human rights norms. They may also emerge where it is the practices of a minority cultural community that violate human rights norms, and perhaps also violate the norms of the general civil law. Philosophers of multiculturalism argue that "dealing with culturally-based claims is the greatest challenge facing democracies today" (Kymlicka, 1991).

Most Commonwealth States approach the problem of cultural toleration in the context of cultural pluralism. Cultural pluralism is a state of affairs in which participants in a variety of cultural communities live together within the borders of a single society. It is to be distinguished from cultural monism, a possibly imaginary situation in which all members of a political community share a single cultural identity.

Most Commonwealth States approach the problem of cultural toleration in the context of cultural pluralism. Cultural pluralism is a state of affairs in which participants in a variety of cultural communities live together within the borders of a single society.

The *Parekh Report on the Future of Multiculturalism in Britain* (the Commission on the Future of Multi-Ethnic Britain, 2000) identified four political strategies for coping with the fact of cultural pluralism:

1 Proceduralist

The State creates no national culture, only a neutral framework in which cultural groups go about their lives. Distinct systems of personal law allow people to live entirely within their own faith- or ethnicity-based community. Examples include the Ottoman Turkish 'millett' system and some forms of British colonial indirect rule.

2 Nationalist

In this model, cultural pluralism is seen as a source of insecurity, instability and potential for conflict and violence. The State has a duty to ensure that everyone assimilates into the national culture. Members of society should share a thick set of common values, i.e. they should speak the same language, learn the same history and values, enjoy the same artistic expressions and worship the same god.

3 Liberal

Liberals suggest we need a common civic and political culture in which political values like the rule of law and democracy, which make peaceful social interaction possible, are shared. Beyond this thin set of shared values, however, individuals are free to follow minority cultural practices in their private lives. The key point is that cultural difference is tolerated but the State remains entirely neutral between private cultures, treating minority and majority the same. This is the American ideal, if not the reality.

4 Multicultural/pluralist

In this model, ethnic culture and civic culture are seen to over-

... if culture is worthy of respect because it enables human flourishing, cultural practices that undermine the human flourishing of women cannot be preserved where challenged as violations of women's equality.

lap. It is acknowledged that the State cannot be neutral but always favours the ethnic culture of the politically dominant group and disables that of minorities. The law should alter public/civic culture to accommodate difference. The key difference from the liberal approach is that the law does not merely tolerate difference but celebrates and enables it. This approach informs Canadian policy and has increasingly guided recent British planning.

The significance of culture to human flourishing

Put very briefly, philosophers of multiculturalism argue that liberal democracies have a duty to respect and accommodate cultural differences because involvement in a cultural community is one of the basic necessities for a person to have a minimally satisfying life. Individuals need cultural communities or cultural structures in order to have a sense of personal identity, to have a sense of self-respect, to have a sense of belonging and to have a basis to critically evaluate their life choices (Kymlicka, 1989: 164–66).

However, it follows that if culture is worthy of respect because it enables human flourishing, cultural practices that undermine the human flourishing of women cannot be preserved where challenged as violations of women's equality. Cultural practices that undermine women's self-respect or express contempt for them, and cultural practices that deny women the opportunity to reflect upon and make important choices in their lives, are not entitled to toleration in a liberal State.[6]

3 Factors Complicating Arguments over Gender and Culture

Women as cultural defenders and cultural symbols

Women are often associated more intimately with the idealisation of cultural traditions than are men for a number of reasons.

i. Women may in fact be more traditional because they are excluded from the public sphere of work and politics and not exposed to other forms of life. Indian women may continue to wear traditional dress, for example, while the men in their families have adopted Western dress (Narayan, 1997:26). Patterns of migrancy to take advantage of employment opportunities may mean that women remain in less developed rural areas while men migrate to more cosmopolitan cities and abandon traditional practices (Walker, 1982:7).

ii. A key strategy for accommodating cultural pluralism in multicultural societies has been to develop national laws relating to crime and commerce while allowing religious and cultural communities to govern the family under regimes of personal law. In practice, this means that the cultural institutions over which the community retains control are centrally concerned with the regulation of women's conduct in marriage, divorce, custody, domestic violence and succession.

iii. Even if women are not in fact more traditional than men in their behaviours, they may play a symbolic role as defenders of cultural integrity. Women's conduct may be a repository of family honour.

iv. This role as symbols of cultural continuity is reinforced by women's involvement in child-bearing and child-rearing in which they reproduce and educate new members of the community. It may reflect women's involvement in political struggles on behalf of the community (Yuval-Davis and Anthia, 1989).

v. Women who are otherwise disenfranchised may cherish their association with tradition as a source of esteem in their own eyes and the eyes of the community.

vi. The equation of women with tradition may be a particularly important one to communities that understand themselves to be engaged in a nationalist struggle against a political majority in their own State or against other state or international bodies. Homi Bhabha describes the paradoxical relationship between two key elements in the identity of such groups. On the one hand, they want to see themselves as the logical development of a historically and geographically embedded culture. On the other hand, they

... human rights advocates need to be aware of the ways in which challenges to traditional practices may be co-opted by interest groups in order to serve ulterior purposes in the context of national or international conflict.

want to see themselves as a free and rational new generation capable of creating new forms of authentic cultural expression. How can one people both be artefacts unchanged through time and active unconstrained agents? Anne McClintock (1995:359) suggests that gender does the work of linking these conflicting demands:

> the temporal anomaly within nationalism – veering between nostalgia for the past and the impatient, progressive sloughing off of the past – is typically resolved by figuring the contradiction in the representation of time as a natural division of gender. Women are represented as the atavistic and authentic body of national tradition (inert, backward-looking and natural), embodying nationalism's conservative principle of continuity. Men, by contrast, represent the progressive agent of national modernity (forward-thrusting, potent and historic), embodying nationalism's progressive or revolutionary principle of discontinuity.

The centrality of gender as an organising principle in these communities makes transforming gender relations a complex task.

The legacy of colonialism

Parallels between contemporary women's rights legislation and colonial era attempts to extinguish customary law as repugnant to public policy may lead some to characterise these new laws as tainted with colonialism. For example, debates over the future of polygynous marriage in sub-Saharan Africa resonate with Victorian campaigns to eradicate polygyny for reasons of religious ideology and in order to undermine homestead farming to free up labour to work for European employers (Simons, 1968:21; Bozzoli, 1983:139, 158). The notion that women's rights legislation has been adopted in order to conform to the norms of international law may allow some to argue that they reflect a bowing to imperialist pressures. Indeed, some argue that human rights norms themselves are a form of modern imperialism, enforcing Western values on the developing world (Pollis and Schwab, 1980:7).

Conversely, human rights advocates need to be aware of the ways in which challenges to traditional practices may be co-opted by interest groups in order to serve ulterior purposes in the context of national or international conflict. Ratna Kapur's work has demonstrated how Hindu nationalists in India have used the language of human rights to argue for the rights of Muslim women as part of a conscious project to undermine the Muslim minority (Kapur, 1999).

Globalisation

"'Globalisation' refers to those processes, operating on a global scale, that cut across national boundaries, integrating and connecting communities and organisations in new space-time combinations, making the world in reality and in experience more interconnected" (Hall, 1993 *supra*: note 74 at 299). This may undermine one's capacity to take for granted the legitimacy of the practices of one's own culture by rendering visible the conscious choices that create and perpetuate them.

In a globalised world, people do not adopt and retain traditional practices uncritically. Their choices may be shaped by politics, law and demographics. The adoption of the veil is a good example. The veil may be adopted by Muslim women as a rejection of identification with Western values and assertion of Muslim nationalism as in revolutionary Iran (Haddad, 1985) or as a matter of convenience to avoid unwanted attentions from men in public places. It may also be adopted by individual young women as an act of rebellion against their more secular parents (Moghadam, 1993: 148–49). On the other hand, it may be supported by men as a means of fundamentalist renaissance and intensification of control of women. Those seeking to transform traditional practices must seek to understand precisely what role or roles the impugned traditional practice plays in its concrete contemporary context.

4 Responses to the Cultural Objection to Women's Human Rights

Patriarchy is a feature of all cultures

The argument that women's human rights are inconsistent with local cultural norms suggests that this situation is unique to traditional communities or societies. However, it is clear that cultural factors play a role in perpetuating discrimination

Those who oppose women's rights in the name of culture suggest that these rights are inconsistent with essential elements of their cultural traditions. However, those who make this argument elide the ways in which religious and cultural traditions undergo a process of interpretation, selection and refinement.

and hampering women's human rights everywhere. In the West, for example, Christian religious ideology is characterised as inconsistent with the recognition of women's rights to abortion and contraception (Cerna and Wallace, 1999:623, 639–40); values of family intimacy and solidarity are seen as threatened by women's rights to be free from physical and sexual violence in the family (Olsen, 1985); and women's employment opportunities are limited by gendered stereotypes that do not envision wage earners as having significant family responsibilities.

A related argument suggests that it is inappropriate to criticise traditional practices in other cultures while ignoring the exploitation of women in the West. Rather than disciplining the developing world, Western critics should ask, for example, why wearing the veil is a more exploitative form of dress than wearing a mini-skirt (Al-Hibri, 1999). Proponents of women's human rights are, or should be, seeking to alleviate women's disadvantage, whatever form it takes. This argument does, however, counsel openness and flexibility in identifying the nature and extent of discrimination entailed in traditional practices. Careful analysis of the precise harms of impugned practices may provide more tailored and effective remedies. For example, the South African Law Commission determined that the problem with polygynous customary marriage was not its inconsistency with English notions of civil marriage, which mimicked Christian marriage, but its impact on the economic well-being of prior wives who saw their share of family resources diminished when husbands took new wives. Rather than seeking to abolish the practice of polygyny, therefore, the Law Commission recommended that this precise problem be remedied by requiring that husbands divide their existing assets with their first wife before taking a second wife. In this way, the economic disadvantage to first wives was diminished, while the possibility of engaging in the traditional practice of polygyny, under new economic terms, was retained (South African Law Commission, 1998:90).

Human rights values are consistent with a wide range of cultural values

Those who oppose women's rights in the name of culture suggest that these rights are inconsistent with essential elements of their cultural traditions. However, those who make this argument elide the ways in which religious and cultural traditions undergo a process of interpretation, selection and refinement. There are very often counter-tendencies, alternative interpretations and insurgent schools of thought competing for dominance within the cultural community. Even where civil law purports to be the codification of customary or religious law, lawmakers have had to select from among competing schools of thought about its meaning and implications and about which revisions of the law would best implement this interpretation.[7] Codification does not end the debate either, a fact apparent to anyone who has read a judicial opinion in which judges disagreed on the interpretation of a statute.

A number of human rights theorists recommend encouraging the exploration of these dissonant voices in order to uncover ways in which human rights values can be seen as consistent with local cultural values. For example, Martha Nussbaum argues that human rights documents can provide the occasion and the template for dialogue about the norms of sexual equality within religious traditions and between religious groups. She also recommends involving religious communities by inviting them to submit plans for reform that articulate how they would integrate a commitment to equality and the perpetuation of their traditions (Nussbaum, 1999: note 36 at 217–8).

In the context of the South African customary law debate, Thandabantu Nhlapo argues that reliance on dialogue can enable the preservation of the substantive values of underlying customary law while changing the forms in which they are expressed (Nhlapo, 1998:625). In particular, he stresses that it is possible to find non-discriminatory means of expressing the values of respecting and providing for elders, commitment by the wider family to the well-being of children and the valorisation of the role of mothers (Nhlapo, 1991:141–45). Dialogue within and between cultural communities is an important part of this process:

> The importance of understanding these approaches is two-fold. In the first place, searching for the underlying principle encourages communities to engage in a little introspection: They may discover that they disagree less than they thought they did. Secondly, whatever the outcome, the communities concerned

> feel affirmed by taking charge of their own affairs and this undercuts any arguments about imposed changes in customary law. (Ibid: 626)

Indeed, including members of traditional communities in the process of identifying norms may often result in uncovering flexible egalitarian adaptations that are already in place but that are not reflected in formal accounts of customary law (Nyamu, 2000: 381–415).

A version of this strategy has been approved by the South African Constitutional Court in its judgement in *S. v. Makwanyane* (1995 (3) SA 391 (CC)). In addressing the permissibility of the death penalty, Justice Makgoro applied both the European notions of human rights to life and dignity and the customary notion of *ubuntu*, which she interpreted as expressing the values of group solidarity, compassion, respect, human dignity, conformity to basic norms and morality (ibid: para. 308). While they derive from different sources and are expressed in different ways, she suggested both conceptions repudiated the death penalty. She suggested that, in developing a constitutional jurisprudence for a unified and democratic South Africa, these commonalties should be identified and merged into an all-inclusive value system.

Abdullah An-Na'im suggests a discursive remedy that allows the integration of local and human rights norms to be explored. However, he emphasises that while participants in a cultural community can benefit from financial and moral support from outsiders committed to egalitarian change and from cross-cultural dialogue with them, significant voices within the community must be involved in order to legitimate these changes. He stresses the importance of supporting an internal discourse on the identification and legitimation of egalitarian themes and modes of redefinition within the culture (An-Na'im, 1994).[8] A recent account argues that successful interventions to alter harmful traditional practices have all involved the generation of an alternative internal discourse that can demonstrate authoritatively how women's rights fit within the existing cultural paradigm.[9]

Rhoda Howard objects that approaches that aim at identifying and developing egalitarian strands within the explanatory frameworks of illiberal cultural practices cannot solve the problem where there is in fact no indigenous norm that parallels important human rights norms (Howard, 1995:56). Indeed, reference to local norms plays an important legitimating role but cannot be the end of the story. In the context of debates over customary law in South Africa, there are some values, such as a commitment to patriarchal authority, that may not be able to be resolved into values consistent with women's human rights.[10] These views need to be heard, however, so that they may be examined and deconstructed through a process in which all parties participate. Appeals to rights will be unsuccessful if illiberal elites feel so marginalised that they give up trying to make themselves heard within law reform processes and choose instead to ignore mandates for legal change (Minow, 2002).

Equality norms must be given precedence in cases where the rights to culture and gender equality conflict. This balance between competing rights should be expressed in constitutional documents, human rights legislation, administrative regulations and rules and official government policy.

5 Policy Recommendations

1 Abolish cultural exceptions to laws protecting women's human rights

If liberal democracies have a duty to protect cultural structures to the extent that these structures foster human flourishing, cultural practices that deny women's full humanity cannot be justified as expressions of the right to culture. Equality norms must be given precedence in cases where the rights to culture and gender equality conflict. This balance between competing rights should be expressed in constitutional documents, human rights legislation, administrative regulations and rules and official government policy. However, attention should be paid to how this principle is implemented in order to ensure that it is legitimated and acted upon.

If oppressive forms of private law are to be retained, for example, under a plural family law regime, women must be able to opt out of private law into a general civil law regime (Coomaraswamy, 1997:24). Care must be taken to ensure that women can really access these exit strategies. For example, in the Indian case of Shah Bano the wife was allowed to opt out of the Muslim civil law regime that denied her claim and was awarded maintenance under the civil penal law. Riots ensued and the Rajiv Gandhi government amended the law to prevent such results in future (ibid). In other contexts, women who

It is clear that legislative change must be supplemented by educational programmes. It is also important to find occasions within the law reform process itself that can be used as educational opportunities by allowing members of the community to understand the need and justifications for particular law reforms measures.

have challenged their disadvantage under customary law complain that they have been ostracised from their communities.

2 Integrate education regarding the re-evaluation of traditional norms into the law reform process

Legislation to eradicate traditional practices that violate women's human rights has the advantage of being a public statement regarding the wrongfulness of a practice. It translates the claims of women from inchoate interests to justiciable legal rights. It moves women's disadvantage from the private sphere into that of public accountability.

Some argue, however, that legislation also creates a host of troubles that interfere with the implementation of human rights norms. As noted above, legislation may be perceived as a form of colonial or imperial intrusion by governments or international institutions or an attack on local minority ethnicity. Some argue that education is preferred to legislation because it allows the impetus for change to come from inside communities.

However, education about values on its own may be an excessively slow process. It is clear that legislative change must be supplemented by educational programmes. It is also important to find occasions within the law reform process itself that can be used as educational opportunities by allowing members of the community to understand the need and justifications for particular law reforms measures.

Education should aim to:

(a) Identify the ways in which cultural practices form part of a system that allows men to dominate women;

(b) Cultivate awareness that cultural practices are complex, contested and changing;

(c) Disseminate the history of particular local customs to show how they have waxed and waned in light of changing political circumstances;

(d) Disseminate awareness of variations in local customs to show how they adapt to local circumstances;

(e) Encourage inquiry into the purposes served, or believe to be served, by discriminatory practices and the design of new practices to serve the same function in a non-discriminatory way;

(f) Empower women to describe and value their own views regarding cultural practices;

(g) Encourage the expression of multiple views of traditional norms in public life.

3 Involve the community in identifying ways in which traditional practices can be made consistent with women's human rights

Involving the community can assist in effective law reform strategies for both theoretical and practical reasons. On a theoretical level, respecting the right to culture entails ensuring that cultural communities can continue to operate as discourses that are instrumental to autonomy. Eradicating discriminatory policies through legislative or judicial fiat may delegitimise participation in dialogue within minority cultural communities. It may also silence the diverse voices emanating from customary communities in public discourse. It follows from a notion of culture as a contested and changing product of dialogue and negotiation within communities that these processes of cultural articulation be enabled by law reform rather than silenced.

On a pragmatic level, legislation or judgements that impose policies that have not been developed and justified in terms that a significant number of members of these communities can understand and accept risk being ignored, constituting admirable 'paper law', but incapable of creating social change of use to disenfranchised women. An essential component to this process of legitimation is attempting to link contemporary developments in the civil law with already existing forms of social regulation in the customary sphere.

Sally Falk Moore identifies two factors that affect the success of attempts to implement legal change. Firstly, state-authored law is only one of many layers of social regulation. Legal change may be effective only to the extent that it imposes norms that are in fact accepted by participants in the

Even where the law has been changed, the cost of using it may be too high if the moral norms that govern women's everyday lives have not been changed.

social field subject to the regulation or where it can be manipulated to suit the interests of a powerful party within it (Moore, 1973:723, 744). Even where women are fully aware of their rights to be free from certain forms of discrimination or violence, they often choose on balance not to exercise these rights because their community is not persuaded that doing so is morally acceptable. So, for example, a woman might have the right to seek a divorce for her husband's adultery, but bringing this action would lead to her ostracism by her family and community. Even where the law has been changed, the cost of using it may be too high if the moral norms that govern women's everyday lives have not been changed (IRRRAG, 1998).

Secondly, those who enjoy power under the pre-existing social arrangement may continue to do so even where they are explicitly deprived of legal rights. For example, the wealth, status and networks of obligation that accrue chiefly to families are not immediately lost when the privileges of traditional leadership are formally abolished. On the contrary, these advantages may permit members of these families to successfully acquire positions of authority based on education, merit and political connections (Moore, 1973:740–41). Race and gender-based privileges built up under regimes of organised inequality also create entrenched forms of advantage and disadvantage that are not eradicated by the abolition of formal legal inequality (ibid:741).

Moore provides an example of changes to judicial administration that enjoyed more success when the new legal forms tracked pre-existing forms of normative regulation. The Tanzanian Government created arbitration tribunals in 1969 to attempt to resolve customary law disputes before they reached the formal legal system. These tribunals were used to a much greater extent where their jurisdiction tracked pre-existing political units rather than when they attempted to create new ones (Moore, 1985:165). Moore concludes that effective law reform strategies attempt to co-opt existing power structures rather than to supplant them. While courts or legislatures can make custom law, it is the semi-autonomous social field that can make law its custom (ibid).[11] Law reform must therefore attempt to legitimate egalitarian changes by involving existing authorities in developing, implementing and explaining the implications of these changes.

Communities can be included in exploring the way cultural practices should be developed to respect women's human rights by:

(a) Encouraging courts to adopt a complex notion of culture in adjudicating conflicts between gender and culture

Rather than finding that traditional practices and gender equality come into conflict, judges employing a dynamic conception of culture can explore the ways in which traditional practices are variously understood and practised. They can vindicate interpretations of tradition that best comport with human rights in their judgements. For example, in the South African case of *Mabena v. Letsoalo*, (1998) (2 SA 1068 per Du Plessi J) the court had to determine whether a valid customary marriage existed between Mrs Mabena and her deceased spouse. Her husband's parents argued that no valid marriage existed because the brideprice paid for her had not been received by a male guardian but by her mother. They argued that customary law could not recognise a female guardian. The judge begged to differ. Interpreting customary law in light of the Constitution's commitment to human rights, he found that patterns of migrancy, economic upheaval and family breakdown meant that some conceptions of customary law now recognised the female-headed householder and allowed her to negotiate valid marriage agreements on behalf of her children. The judge was able to integrate the preservation of customary law notions of marriage as an arrangement between families rather than individuals and the notion that women might sometimes act on behalf of their families.

Rather than finding that traditional practices and gender equality come into conflict, judges employing a dynamic conception of culture can explore the ways in which traditional practices are variously understood and practiced. They can vindicate interpretations of tradition that best comport with human rights in their judgements.

(b) Engaging in formal consultations with representative groups that include women in the development of legislation

The lengthy consultations undertaken by the South African Law Commission in its Project on the Harmonisation of Civil and Customary Law is an example of a process that engaged stakeholders in debate over the future of customary institutions in light of the Constitution's commitment to women's human rights.

(c) *Delegating deliberation and decision-making to local government structures that include women and are mandated to ensure women's rights are respected*

For example, as part of the process of land redistribution undertaken by the South African Department of Land Affairs, the Communal Property Associations Act 28 of 1996 requires that all communities seeking a grant of land or the return of land improperly appropriated by the apartheid regime must promulgate a constitution that details rules for entitlement to allocations. These rules may not discriminate on the basis of gender. Staff from the Department work with these communities to help them articulate the reasons for which gender has acted as a proxy.[12]

Appeals to women's alleged moral or intellectual incapacity can thus be translated into non-discriminatory rules. Men in some communities express fears that women will sell land rather than keep it in the community because their role in providing support to dependent family members leads them to be concerned with short-term sustenance rather than to share men's concerns for long-term welfare or social prestige annexed to land owning (Cross and Friedman, 1997). Rules could be developed that recognise these different priorities and strike some balance between them. Men also suggest that women should be denied allotments because they may follow husbands to other areas, leaving the land vacant. The propensity of women to move must be put in the context of their incapacity to provide land for their families under customary law. Having given women entitlements, rules could be developed to require that any allotment holder reside in and contribute to the welfare of the community or to require that only applicants with children be granted allotments (Claassens, 1996).[13]

(d) *Involving stakeholders in determining how courts should remedy violations of women's human rights*

In a recent decision, the Supreme Court of Canada found that a provision in the Indian Act that did not allow band members who lived off the reserve lands to vote in band elections violated the equality rights of non-resident band members. However, rather than simply declaring that the voting regulations were invalid and effectively re-writing them to allow all non-residents to vote, the court employed the remedial device of the suspended declaration of invalidity. They declared the rule invalid but stated that their declaration would not take effect for 18 months. During this time, the federal government would have time to consult with indigenous (First Nations) organisations on how these new rights should be administered and implemented in ways that would be most consistent with their culture. The eventual result reflected their own negotiation of the tension between cultural norms and constitutional rights mandates. The result was more subtle and perhaps more acceptable to the community because they had been involved in its development.[14] Caution should be taken in recommending suspended declarations of invalidity, however, to ensure that the government does undertake the consultations and does proceed with appropriate legislation before the time period lapses.

Education that gives women economic options so that they can avoid practices they have come to see as harmful is an effective tool in eradicating violations of women's human rights.

(e) *Giving women a stronger voice in developing cultural norms by giving them more economic and political clout*

Education that gives women economic options so that they can avoid practices they have come to see as harmful is an effective tool in eradicating violations of women's human rights (Gunning, 1999:669). For example, in South Africa, the Government's decision not to abolish polygyny flowed in part from their diagnosis of the problem as one of lack of economic options on the part of women. They found that urban women who had employment opportunities had largely turned their back on the practice. They addressed the problem by giving women within polygyny greater economic rights and by continuing to increase women's overall economic opportunities so that marriage was not the only means of livelihood open to them. The South African Law Commission commented that equalising women's proprietary capacity, contractual capacity and rights to be included in local decision-making would give women the bargaining power to refuse polygynous marriages.[15]

(f) *Training community leaders to initiate dialogue about harmful practices*

Train local experts within the community, such as health practitioners and midwives, to engage community members in discussion about the cultural legitimacy of impugned practices such as FGM. Encourage them to use their local legitimacy to help develop alternative practices.

(g) Funding research

Funding should be made available to support research into the changing nature of customary practices and to support the publication and discussion of results through conferences involving cross-sections of the relevant communities. The excellent work of Women and Law in Southern Africa (WLSA) is a prime example that has served to develop and support consensus about the need for changes to codified customary law.

Funding should also support research into the unexpected impacts of past law reform efforts. For example, the Canadian Government funds research into the impact of changes made in 1985 to implement international law by equalising the rights of First Nations' women to gain and retain their Indian status. A recent call for papers asks for an inquiry into the impact of these changes and "what policies can be put in place to promote women's right to full band life to best welcome off reserve Indian women returning to the band, while maintaining their culture?" (Canadian Status for Women website, Call for Proposals, 15 September 2003).

(h) Funding groups arguing for more egalitarian interpretations of traditional practices

Women's groups seeking to promote discussion of the ways in which human rights and traditional values can be integrated in their own communities should be funded. This funding should aim to support both direct educational efforts and programmes that engage in transformative discussion while delivering other services.

(i) Empowering women by educating children in a curriculum of civic values alongside cultural/ religious values so that they have a sense that they can choose to conform to or revise their traditions

The Ousley (2001) Report on community fragmentation in Bradford, UK, recommends a programme of citizenship education in schools that teaches shared values and anti-racist education in the workplace. Shared values include the rule of law, parliamentary democracy, the role of the free press, the role of individuals in effecting social change, the source of cultural pluralism and the importance of respecting diversity. A key objective should be to teach children skills of critical reflection and mutual respect for others.[16] On this view, a civic values curriculum has the dual purpose of including cultural minorities in the mainstream cultural dialogue and fostering respect for the choice of retaining or adopting minority cultural practices.

Conclusion

This paper has contended for a consciously complex approach to the problem of gender equality and traditional practices. On a theoretical level, advocates for women's human rights must adopt a dynamic and contextualised understanding of the notion of culture. In practical terms, they must seek to legitimate cultural conceptions that understand human rights values to be consistent with some revised forms of traditional practices. In these ways, customary communities and women demanding equality rights can arrive at consensus on remedies through consideration of what liberal right requires and through articulating with greater precision the functions that custom performs. Neither discourse is silenced by the interaction although both are reshaped. Feminist activist Gwendolyn Mikell urges for using such a 'dual strategy' of law reform and education in order to achieve social change. Legal reform is coupled with attempts to work through parallel institutions in civil society and to revive traditional institutions that have the potential to increase women's participation and power in culturally familiar ways (Mikell, 1995).[17] Women may thereby secure gender equality and exercise their right to culture on a basis of equality with traditionalists from positions within their own communities.

Notes

1 CEDAW articles 2(f) and 5(a). Similar commitments are contained in the Inter-American Convention on Violence against Women (article 7(e), the African Charter on Children's Rights (article 21.1) and the Convention on the Rights of the Child (article 24.3).

2 Constitution of the Republic of South Africa, No. 108 of 1996:
Section 30: Language and Culture
Everyone has the right to use the language and to participate in the cultural life of their choice, but no one exercising these rights may do so in a manner inconsistent with any provision of the Bill of Rights.
Section 31: Cultural, Religious and Linguistic Communities
(1) Persons belonging to a cultural, religious or linguistic community may not be denied the right, with other members of that community –
(a) to enjoy their culture, practise their religion and use their language; and
(b) to form, join and maintain cultural, religious and linguistic associations and other organs of civil society.
(2) The rights in subsection (1) may not be exercised in a manner inconsistent with any provision of the Bill of Rights.

3 As quoted in Renteln, 2002:195.

4 FGM is predominately practised in sub-Saharan Africa, although immigrant communities continue these practices to some extent in Europe and North America. Estimated prevalence rates range from over 90 per cent in Djibouti, Somalia and Sudan to 55 per cent in Nigeria, 40 per cent in Chad, Côte d'Ivoire, Kenya and Togo and 15–20 per cent in Cameroon, Ghana, Senegal, Tanzania and Uganda (Packer, 2002).

5 This practice may be associated with the spread of AIDS as the cleansing may be performed by a social outcast who is paid for his services and who performs the same service for many others. Condoms are believed to interfere with the effect of the cleansing (Human Rights Watch, 2003:4–8).

6 See generally, Okin, 1999, especially Nussbaum.

7 In the context of Islam, see An-Na'im, 2003; in the context of African customary law, see Channock, 1983.

8 An-Na'im (1990:162) also suggests that human rights norms and Islamic principles can be reconciled by looking for the common higher order principles on which they both rely.

9 Packer (2002) argues that the abolition of Chinese footbinding was successful because of the generation of an interpretation of Confucianism that repudiated mutilation of the body. Similarly, she argues that the abolition of suttee (wife burning) in India was

linked to acceptance of arguments that Hinduism did not approve of such conduct.

10 Mutua (1995) makes the well-intentioned but disingenuous argument that the African Charter could never be used to vindicate patriarchal values because it requires the individual 'to preserve and strengthen positive African cultural values in his relations with other members of society, in the spirit of tolerance, dialogue and consultation' in article 29. There are, however, those who view patriarchy as a one of these positive values. For example, see, Dlamini, 1991.

11 'Law reform often fails because while the government proposes, the people dispose differently' (note 27 at 744). See also Alott, 1981: 229.

12 Attention will need to be paid to the issue of ensuring that these staff members act as facilitators rather than as experts prescribing an appropriate remedy. My impression of reading some early accounts of landholding policy was that they were surprisingly similar to each other. See Tshabalala, 1996 (noting that the three communities assisted by CALS elected to use the household head as the unit of allocation).

13 A Department of Land Affairs study (1998) of the implementation of communal property association constitutions notes that the majority elect to use the household rather than the individual as the unit of allotment. They caution that this may mean that men, who continue to be seen as heads of households, will continue to be over-represented among decision makers with regard to land.

14 *Corbiere v. Canada* [1999] There was perhaps a gender element in this case as well because some band members may have lost their rights to reside on the reserve due to the operation of s. 12(1)(b) of the Indian Act. Even after Canada abolished this provision in 1985 in light of the decision under the ICCPR in *Lovelace v. Canada* 1981 that gender discrimination in granting Indian status violated article 27, many women and their descendants were prevented from moving back to reserves.

15 Report on Customary Marriages, 90.B.

16 See Gutmann, 1995:557; Rawls, 1994.

17 Describing activism in Nigeria and Ghana, she comments: "Culture may be dynamic in incorporating women's rights, as opposed to being devastated by legal change. In fact, given an opportunity, cultural integrity, while further reinforcing women's legal rights".

References

Alott, Antony (1981). 'Reforming the Law in Africa: Aims, Difficulties and Techniques'. In AJGM Sanders (ed.), *Southern Africa in Need of Law Reform: Proceedings of the Southern African Law Reform Conference, Sun City, Bophuthatswana, 11–14 August 1980*. Durban: Butterworths.

Al-Hibri, Azizah (1999). 'Is Western Patriarchal Feminism Good for Third World/Minority Women?'. In Okin, *op. cit*.

An-Na'im, Abdullah (1990). 'Towards an Islamic Reformation: Civil Liberties, Human Rights and International Law'. Syracuse, NY: Syracuse University Press.

—— (1994). 'State Responsibility Under International Human Rights Law to Change Religious and Customary Laws'. In Rebecca Cook (ed.), *Human Rights of Women: National and International Perspectives*. Philadelphia: University of Pennsylvania Press.

—— (2003). 'The Synergy and Interdependence of Human Rights, Religion and Secularism: Prospects for Islamic Societies'. Lecture at the Carr Center for Human Rights, Kennedy School of Government, Harvard University, 16 October.

Bennett, TW (1991). *A Sourcebook of African Customary Law for Southern Africa*. Cape Town: Juta.

Bozzoli, Belinda (1983). 'Marxism, Feminism and South African Studies', *Journal of Southern African Studies*, 9.

Cerna, Christina M and Jennifer C Wallace (1999). 'Women and Culture'. In Kelly D Askin and Dorean M Koenig (eds), *Women and International Human Rights Law (Volume I)*. Ardsley, NY: Transnational Publishers, Inc.

Channock, Martin (1983). *Law, Custom and Social Order: The Colonial Experience in Malawi and Zambia*. Cambridge: Cambridge University Press.

Clifford, James (1988). *The Predicament of Culture: Twentieth Century Ethnography, Literature and Art*. Cambridge, MA: Harvard University Press.

Claassens, Aninka (1996). 'Women and Tenure Reform'. In *Consultative Workshop on Women's Rights in Land*.

Commission on the Future of Multi-Ethnic Britain (2000). *The Future of Multi-Ethnic Britain – The Parekh Report*. London: Profile Books.

Coomaraswamy, Radhika (1997). 'Reinventing International Law: Women's Rights as Human Rights in the International Community', Harvard Human Rights Program, 1997.

—— (2000). *Critical Issues Confronting Commonwealth Women in the Area of Human Rights*, A Commonwealth Secretariat Paper, 6th

Commonwealth Ministerial Women's Affairs Meeting, New Delhi, India.

Cross, Catherine and Michelle Friedman (1997). 'Women in Tenure: Marginality and the Left Hand Power'. In Shamin Meer (ed.), *Women, Land and Authority: Perspectives from South Africa*. Cape Town: New Africa Books.

Department of Land Affairs (1998). *Communal Property Associations Review*.

Dlamini, CRM (1991). 'The Role of Customary Law in Meeting Social Needs', *Acta Juridica* 71.

Gunning, Isabel (1999). 'Women and Traditional Practices: Female Genital Surgery'. In Kelly D Askin and Dorean M Koenig (eds), *Women and International Human Rights Law (Volume I)*. Ardsley, NY: Transnational Publishers, Inc.

Gutmann, Amy (1995). 'Civic Education and Social Diversity', *Ethics* 105.

Haddad, Yvonne Yazbeck (1985). 'Islam, Women and Revolution in 20th Century Arab Thought'. In Yvonne Yazbeck Haddad and Ellison Banks Findly (eds), *Women, Religion and Social Change*. New York: State University of New York.

Hall, Stuart (1993). 'The Question of Cultural Identity'. In Hall et al (eds), *Modernity and its Futures: Understanding Modern Societies*. Cambridge, UK: Polity Press.

Howard, Rhoda (1995). *Human Rights and the Search for Community*. Boulder, CO: Westview Press.

Human Rights Watch (2003). *Double Standards: Women's Property Rights Violations in Kenya*. Kenya 15(5)A, March. *www.hrw.org/reports/2003/kenya0303/kenya0303.pdf*

International Reproductive Rights and Research Action Group (IRRRAG) (1998). 'Women's Wit over Men's'. In R Petchesky and K Judd (eds), *Negotiating Reproductive Rights*. London: Zed Books.

Kapur, Ratna (1999). 'The Two Faces of Secularism and Women's Rights in India'. In Courtney W Howland (ed.), *Religious Fundamentalisms and the Human Rights of Women*. Basingstoke: Palgrave Macmillan.

Kymlicka, Will (1991). *Liberalism, Community and Culture*. Oxford: Oxford University Press.

—— (1995). *Multicultural Citizenship: A Liberal Theory of Minority Rights*. Oxford: Oxford University Press.

McClintock, Anne (1995). *Imperial Leather: Race, Gender and Sexuality in the Colonial Context*. New York: Routledge.

Mikell, Gwendolyn (1995). 'African Women's Rights in the Context of Systemic Conflict', *Proceedings of the Annual Meeting, American Society of International Law*, 89.

Minow, Martha (2002). 'About Women, About Culture, About Them, About Us'. In Richard Shweder, Martha Minow and Hazel Marcus (eds), *Engaging Cultural Differences: The Multicultural Challenge in Liberal Democracies*. New York: Russell Sage Foundation.

Moore, Sally Falk (1973). 'Law and Social Change: The Semi-Autonomous Social Field as an Appropriate Subject of Study', *Law and Society Review*.

—— (1985). *Social Facts and Fabrications: 'Customary' Law on Kilimanjaro, 1880–1980*. Cambridge: Cambridge University Press.

Mutua, Makau wa (1995). 'The Banjul Charter and the African Cultural Fingerprint: An Evaluation of the Language of Duties', *Virginia Journal of International Law* 35:339–80.

Narayan, Uma (1997). *Dislocating Cultures: Identities, Traditions and Third World Feminism*. London: Routledge.

Nhlapo, Thandabantu (1991). 'The African Family and Women's Rights: Friends or Foes', *Acta Juridica* 135. (Also published as 'Women's Rights and the Family in Traditional and Customary Law' in Susan Bazilli (ed.), *Putting Women on the Agenda*.)

—— (1998). 'African Family Law under an Undecided Constitution: The Challenge of Law Reform in South Africa'. In John Eekelaar and Thandabantu Nhlapo (eds), *The Changing Family: International Perspectives on the Family and Family Law*. Oxford: Hart Publishing.

Nussbaum, Martha (1999). 'A Plea for Difficulty' in Okin, *op. cit.*

Nyamu, Celestine (2000). 'How Should Human Rights and Development Respond to Cultural Legitimization of Gender Hierarchy in Developing Countries?', *Harvard International Law Journal* 41.

Okin, Susan Muller (ed.) (1999). *Is Multiculturalism Bad for Women?* New Jersey: Princeton University Press.

Olsen, Frances (1985). 'The Myth of State Intervention in the Family', *University of Michigan Journal of Law Reform* 18.

Ousley, Herman (2001). 'Community Pride not Prejudice (Bradford Vision 2001)'. *http://www.bradford2020.com/pride/index.html*

Packer, Corinne A A (2002). *Using Human Rights to Change Tradition: Traditional practices harmful to women's reproductive health in sub-Saharan Africa*. Antwerp: Intersentia.

Pollis, Adamantia and Peter Schwab (1980). 'Human Rights: A Western Construct of Limited Applicability'. In Pollis and Schwab (eds), *Human Rights: Cultural and Ideological Perspectives*. Westport, CT: Praeger Publishers.

Rawls, John (1994). *Political Liberalism*. New York: Columbia University Press.

Renteln, Alison Dundes (2002). 'In Defense of Culture in the Courtroom'. In Richard A Shweder, Martha Minow and Hazel Marcus (eds), *Engaging Cultural Differences*. New York: Russell Sage Foundation.

Simons, HJ (1968). *African Women: Their Legal Status in South Africa*. London: C Hurst and Co.

South African Law Commission (1998). *Report on Customary Marriages*.

Tshabalala, Themba (1996). 'Experiences in Community Constitution Making Process within the Communal Property Associations Act', Working Paper, Centre for Applied Legal Studies.

Walker, Cherryl (1982). *Women and Resistance in South Africa*. New York: Monthly Review Press.

Yuval-Davis, Nira and Floya Anthias (eds) (1989). *Women–Nation–State*. London: Macmillan.

Reconciling Competing Rights

Catherine Muyeka Mumma

> In so far as these [human rights] standards are perceived to be alien to or at variance with the values and institutions of a people, they are unlikely to elicit commitment or compliance. While cultural legitimacy may not be the sole or even primary determinant of compliance with human rights standards, it is an extremely significant one. Thus the underlying causes of any lack or weakness of legitimacy of human rights standards must be addressed in order to enhance the promotion and protection of human rights in that society. (An-na'im, 1990)

Introduction

This paper will discuss the effectiveness of implementing international human rights principles in the context of culture. It looks at the definition of the principles of equality and non-discrimination, which are the focus of gender rights, and considers whether there are cultural definitions of these terms that are acceptable within the human rights context.

Background

Since the adoption of the Universal Declaration of Human Rights in 1948 and the International Conventions on Civil and Political Rights and Economic, Social and Cultural Rights in 1966, the human rights scene has been characterised by the formulation and drafting of more treaties that have addressed specific human rights issues, including the protection of women against discrimination,[1] the rights of the child[2] and many others. The implementation of the human rights in the various treaties is monitored by treaty bodies that are established for this purpose. Traditionally, monitoring is done by way of examination and analysis of state reports on the status of implementation of the said instruments in those States.

These bodies judge the progress in implementation by the level of incorporation of the provisions of these treaties in the domestic laws and practice on the ground.

Regional instruments have also been adopted, with organs that are specifically established to follow up on the implementation of these rights within those regions. In addition, Europe has gone further and established a functioning Court of Human Rights that helps shape a common understanding on the various concepts and complex human rights issues within the region. In Africa, the African Commission on Human and Peoples' Rights is the treaty body established to monitor the implementation of the rights in the Charter among the African member States. This system has so far not yielded the hoped for results in terms of information, guidance, precedent, decisions/comments and recommendations on the progress in implementing human rights in the African States. It was expected that the Commission would take a lead role in setting the pace on how to incorporate the observance of human rights in cultural situations. This has not happened, however, because the Commission still lacks the required support and the resources necessary to enable it to function fully and effectively. The African Court on Human and Peoples' Rights[3] is also about to be established, and it is hoped that it will be fully supported to enable it to deal with some of the uniquely African issues.

State reports under the various human rights instruments are the key measure by which the international community can judge the progress being made in the creation of enabling environments for the enjoyment of rights.

State reports under the various human rights instruments are the key measure by which the international community can judge the progress being made in the creation of enabling environments for the enjoyment of rights. However, the report-writing record of most developing countries is less than satisfactory, with many reports pending and those submitted being poor in quality. The ICCPR has generally received more attention in terms of inclusion in the agendas of human rights civil groups and also in terms of follow-up action, such as accountability and report-writing obligations. Economic, social and cultural rights, on the other hand, have been neglected by many States and the report writing under the ICESCR is poor. This is the case, notwithstanding the fact that most States from the developing world would prefer the international community to give more attention to the recognition of economic, social and cultural rights and the allocation of more global resources to facilitate the enjoyment of these rights.[4]

Cultural Rights in International Treaties

The definition/description of cultural rights is not very clear from the current treaties in force. The ICESCR talks of the right to 'cultural development', defined in terms of participation in cultural life made of art, moral interests, science and research.[5] The various treaty bodies' work has also not given clear guidance on the topic of culture and human rights. The Committee on Economic, Social and Cultural Rights, which has a direct responsibility in relation to this right, has not given enough comprehensive direction on the issue of culture. A look at the comments on some of the State reports by this Committee indicates that culture is usually limited to the protection of the rights of indigenous people (without a survey of their cultural practices in the context of human rights). Culture is also considered from the point of view of 'harmful traditional practices' and not as a medium through which human rights should be entrenched in society. The language of the Committee on these issues is often too general, indicating little effort in helping to develop the concept in relation to human rights.

The concept of culture in the African Charter on Human and Peoples' Rights (ACHPR) includes the right to freely take part in the cultural life of the community; the right to promotion and protection of morals and traditional values recognised by the community; and the concept of family.[6]

The Convention on the Elimination of All Forms of Discrimination against Women addresses the issue of culture from the point of view of its negative aspects. It focuses on the modification/abolition of customary practices that discriminate against women; the elimination of prejudices associated with the marital status of women; and the elimination of negative customary practices, including forced marriages.[7]

The Convention on the Rights of the Child (CRC) and the African Charter on the Rights and Welfare of the Child address culture from different perspectives: the former addresses the issue in relation to placing children separated from their families in culturally appropriate environments and urges State parties to abolish traditional practices that are prejudicial to health;[8] while the latter discusses culture very comprehensively. It recognises both the individuality of the child and the collective aspects of African communities, and pronounces both the rights and duties of the child and the community. It defines education as including the preservation and strengthening of positive African morals, traditional values and cultures. It does not discuss harmful practices in the context of the right to health; instead, it has an article on protection against harmful social and cultural practices, including those that are harmful to health, those that encourage discrimination and child marriages.[9]

The newly adopted Protocol to the ACHPR on the Rights of Women in Africa is perhaps the most elaborate instrument on issues relating to culture. It not only addresses the need to eliminate harmful practices and to discourage negative social and cultural patterns, including those that are based on stereotyped roles of men and women. It also moves the State's responsibility beyond the passing of laws by demanding that corrective measures be facilitated to also happen 'in fact'. In this regard the Protocol recommends that rights programmes include education and information communication strategies. It demands that the rights of women be equally protected in both the private and public spheres. The protocol talks of the creation of positive cultural contexts and participation by women in the formulation of cultural policies and in cultural decision-making structures. The right to protection and development of women's indigenous knowledge is also mentioned. In addition, the Protocol singles out as special the rights of the most vulnerable groups, whose vulnerability is usually linked to culture. These include widows, elderly women and the girl child. The protocol also obliges States to provide for practical implementation of these rights through budgetary and other resource provisions.[10]

The work of the treaty bodies under these instruments, and in particular that of the African Commission and now its Protocol on the rights of women, should contribute a great deal to making the connection between culture and human rights. For the majority of women whose lives are governed by cultural structures, it is important for this link to be made to enable the use of the positive aspects of culture and the negotiation for transforming and eradicating negative aspects of culture.

Fifty-two years after the adoption of the UDHR, the world

Fifty-two years after the adoption of the UDHR, the world needs to examine the progress made to facilitate the enjoyment of human rights by all. This audit also needs to look at the inclusion of cultural perspectives and the involvement of cultural structures in these efforts.

needs to examine the progress made to facilitate the enjoyment of human rights by all. This audit also needs to look at the inclusion of cultural perspectives and the involvement of cultural structures in these efforts. This paper argues that there are cultural perspectives on the various principles of human rights, and these should be recognised and included as valid perspectives that can also contribute to the enjoyment of human rights. It acknowledges that there is a link between culture and human rights and suggests the need for the implementation of human rights to go beyond domestication by way of legislation that is just derived from international instruments. It argues that true domestication includes the use of cultural structures without necessarily making radical changes to the cultural lives of those involved.

This paper recognises the role played by culture in the enjoyment and violation of human rights. It asserts that existing gender-related human rights concerns are largely attributable to culture; that the current focus of international and national human rights systems on State and public structures (and not on culturally-based structures) for the implementation of human rights has contributed to the slow pace of achieving universal enjoyment of human rights – in particular the rights of women. The paper recommends the need to factor in cultural perspectives when rights instruments are formulated and also in their implementation.

Culture, Gender and Human Rights

Culture is a combination of many ingredients shared by a group of people, including their traditions, beliefs (both customary and religious), rituals, moral values, system of knowledge, arts and many other factors that form their way of life. Human rights, on the other hand, are mainly concerned about systems that allow all human beings to live in dignity. This dignity is mainly described in terms of equality, equity and non-discrimination. It is about freedom and choice by human beings, aspects that distinguish the human from the other species of animals. The general definition of human rights is widely accepted; however, the focused interpretation of some of the terms and concepts may not be universal. For example, it has been argued that the definition of some of the terms – including 'dignity', 'freedom of the individual' and 'equality' – is not clear-cut. It has been suggested that the components of dignity, for instance, are determined by one's environment and the context within which the definition is being made. Those who believe in the universality of rights insist that the dignity of all beings is the same and cannot be measured using different scales. The effect of this debate is the common perception that culture is necessarily negative and a hindrance to the enjoyment of rights. This paper argues, however, that culture can be positive, though it also takes note of the fact that culture is often used as an excuse to violate human rights. Indeed, the dynamism of culture is such that when culture is not clearly pronounced and defined, the violator elects which bits to highlight in order to justify his/her violation. Official recognition of culture would therefore help in discussions on the various components, with a view to preserving the good and eliminating the negative.

... the dynamism of culture is such that when culture is not clearly pronounced and defined, the violator elects which bits to highlight in order to justify his/her violation. Official recognition of culture would therefore help in discussions on the various components, with a view to preserving the good and eliminating the negative.

Many of the States that have ratified human rights instruments and domesticated the principles therein, and developing countries in particular, have large populations of people whose lives are heavily influenced by traditional cultures. However, these States rarely see the need to work with cultural structures in their attempts to implement human rights. The result is that the policies and the laws seem to be human rights friendly on paper, but the practice on the ground is in accordance with a silent but powerful law that stems from culture. In countries where the economic and social well-being of the majority is dependent on community structures, resources and values, the enjoyment of human rights by most people heavily depends on the acceptance of these rights within the power structures of these communities. To measure human rights compliance on the basis of paper policies and laws alone is therefore not adequate and may indirectly condone the violation, within communities, of the human rights of the vulnerable.

This paper makes a few assumptions about culture and argues for a deliberate effort to address issues relating to culture in a specific manner. The first assumption is that culture is not universal. There are as many cultures as there are different communities even within the context of one State. Culture is a key component in the identification of different communities

Culturally constructed gender roles are ... responsible for most of the disparities and contradictions that command the day-to-day livelihoods of men and women in many parts of the world.

and often the basis upon which the ordering of these communities is based. In this regard, the day-to-day social and economic preoccupation of the individuals in a particular community is determined in accordance with that community's cultural construction of the issues at hand. This ordering includes the determination of roles and responsibilities of members of the community in terms of gender and sex; it is heavily influenced by years of practice of cultures that propagate such roles. In most African communities, the roles and responsibilities will be based on gender and different for men, women, boys and girls. Even though the individual is important, most traditional communities tend to emphasise the community as opposed to the individual. The enjoyment (or lack of enjoyment) of human rights within these communities cannot, therefore, be contemplated, designed or effected without taking into account these cultural perspectives.

Culturally constructed gender roles are, for instance, responsible for most of the disparities and contradictions that command the day-to-day livelihoods of men and women in many parts of the world. The expectation that all human beings must fit in a particular universal module therefore cuts out millions of world citizens, whose lives and styles are dictated by culture, from enjoying the benefits that they would obtain from marrying their cultural practices with human rights. The total disregard of cultural dynamics in the practice of human rights and the processes of monitoring implementation of human rights is therefore a big mistake.

It is also important to note that culture is dynamic. It is not static and can modify to suit environmental and socio-economic changes within any society. Working with cultural structures should therefore enable States to have some influence on any changes to culture and also to pick the aspects of change that may facilitate positive interaction with culture.

Compliance with Human Rights Treaties

States and state actors are traditionally viewed by the international community as the key institutions bearing the bigger responsibility to ensure the respect, protection, promotion and fulfilment of human rights. This is in keeping with the principles of international law. However, most violations of human rights, particularly gender-based violations, are perpetrated by non-state actors in the private sphere and in cultural settings. The focus of the international bodies monitoring compliance with human rights obligations on States and State actors has therefore contributed to neglect in examining the role of culture in the delivery or hindrance of the enjoyment of these rights. The traditional indicators of the domestication of human rights are laws and policy documents incorporating agreed-to norms. States parties that have ratified the key International human rights instruments are expected to take measures that will ensure the incorporation of the rights guaranteed in these instruments, into the domestic laws and practices.

It might be expected that evidence of implementation of international human rights will be indicated in the States' reports on their compliance status and the comments of treaty bodies on these reports. However, a look at the reports that have so far been received reveals very little reporting on cultural perspectives. For those States with communities that are heavily governed and influenced by their cultural beliefs and traditions, this must mean that their reports are only providing part of the full picture. Effective implementation of human rights must go beyond the mere inclusion of intentions in policy documents. The practice in many countries, especially developing countries, is that most policy plans are not usually implemented and the laws seeking to enhance human rights are also not known or accessible to the people who most need them. There is a need for more indicators and benchmarks to be developed as additional tools to policy documents and laws in the assessment of the level of compliance and implementation of human rights by State parties to human rights instruments. There are many good laws but they only benefit a very small fraction of the people they are supposed to protect. There are also good policy pronouncements on human rights that are hardly implemented because they lack recognition and are not known by the communities of the beneficiaries. It is for this reason that the argument for cultural relativism in the promotion of human rights must be seriously considered, not as a redefinition of human rights but as one of the approaches that is relevant in the efforts to have pro-rights practices within all communities.

There are many good laws but they only benefit a very small fraction of the people they are supposed to protect. There are also good policy pronouncements on human rights that are hardly implemented because they lack recognition and are not known by the communities of the beneficiaries.

Rights Enforcement within Judicial Systems

The judiciary is one of the state structures that is expected to enforce the human rights laws and international instruments that States are party to. It does this through the interpretation of the laws on these rights and the pronouncement of rulings that give direction in recognition of these laws. Courts usually focus on the provisions of the law and the circumstances of the matter in question when interpreting the law and making rulings. In systems that allow for the application of multiple laws, customary law may heavily influence the decision of the court. This part looks at a few cases relating to women's right to own and inherit family property. The choice of the cases in this subject area is deliberate because it helps to demonstrate the heavy influence that culture has in African communities and how this strongly defines gender roles. It also demonstrates that cultural perspectives are recognised and taken into account in most rulings in the region's courts.

In most African legal systems, customary law is one of the applicable laws. Most constitutions recognise customary law as the law applicable on personal matters, including marriage, divorce and maintenance. The laws governing land tenure are also multiple and they include customary law as well. In most African communities ownership of land was traditionally communal and the rights to land were vested in the community as a whole. The transmission of land from one generation to another and upon the death of the family trustee was clear. In patriarchal communities, land was passed through the eldest male son, and in matriarchal communities through the eldest daughter. Wives and children were guaranteed land use, access and ownership as members of the trust (Ojienda, 2003). The role of each individual in the community determined what connection would be made between the individual and the land. A first-born son would be a trustee; a wife would have permanent access; a daughter would have temporary access until she got married (all girls were expected to get married so their roles within their communities of birth were limited). Younger sons had temporary access until they married and became heads of households when they became trustees.

The change of the land tenure system by the colonial governments in many African countries disrupted the cultural and social order. It facilitated the absolute ownership of land rights by individuals, who are now able to defraud family members by abusing their positions of relative advantage as community trustees. Women are particularly vulnerable to this problem, given that their role does not allow them to be registered owners of family land. They also lose out on their customary right to access community land since these land registration laws facilitate the alienation of this right. The result is that, on balance, customs were more protective of women's right to access and benefit from land than the current land ownership laws that emphasise the rights of individuals against those of the community. Any monitoring of the implementation of rights to access property by women should thus not fail to look at the cultural perspectives.

... the practice of law and dispute resolution on matters of women's property rights [in Africa] *is unlikely to be based purely on international pronouncements on the human right principle on equality; it substantially listens to the cultural perspectives as well.*

The cases below demonstrate that the cultural/customary positions on land are still so strong in many African States that the focus on implementation of the succession laws that promote individual rights without due regard to customary law is often more academic than practical. In this scenario, it is important to determine whether most women in Africa can access family land more easily through the customary land tenure systems or through the system introduced by the colonial governments. An analysis of case law in Africa on this subject indicates that the practice of law and dispute resolution on matters of women's property rights is unlikely to be based purely on international pronouncements on the human rights principle on equality; it substantially listens to cultural perspectives as well. Where this happens, it is also important to emphasise the respect by the courts of the customary positions that protected the rights of women. Courts must not be allowed to implement only the cultural positions that favour one gender.

Most courts within the Commonwealth have tended to recognise customary law in judgments (although it is mostly in relation to determining ownership of land by individuals and not on the issue of access), thereby demonstrating the difficulty in fully relying on provisions of international human rights instruments and legislation that is based on these instruments. Judicial precedents that aim at radically changing the customary practices and attitudes do not seem to have an impact on the community at large. Their 'victory' tends to remain at the level of the particular individual involved in the case and of course the very few people who challenge traditional systems in the courts.

Some country examples

Kenya has laws that are intended to promote equal rights between men and women in the ownership of property. These include the contract law, the Registered Land Act and the Succession Act. These laws are hardly used by women, who are not aware of them.[11] Even if women understand the laws, many do not have the means to use them.[12] Others prefer not to use them in an effort to remain a part of the community in which they live and not disrupt the social order. Many women would like to be seen to be proud and supportive of their culture, and are prepared to give up a bit of what would be described as their rights in order to fit into society. Many educated and economically stable women will not, for instance, pursue their right to inherit property from their parents on equal terms. Customary law positions are still very strong and are the key determinants of what happens.

In the Zimbabwean case of *Magaya v. Magaya*,[13] a community court and the Supreme Court dismissed an applicant's claim to ownership of her father's estate on the basis that she was "a lady and therefore cannot be appointed to the estate when there is a man".[14] In dismissing the appeal, the Supreme Court took into account the fact that the Constitution of Zimbabwe stipulated an exception in the application of its non-discrimination rule and this includes the "devolution of property on death or other personal law, which in Zimbabwe, was to be governed by African customary law if the matter involved the estate of an African who was married according to African law and custom". The discrimination caused by this exception was not, in the opinion of the judge, based on the 'perpetual minority' of women but "on the nature of African society, especially the patrilineal, matrilineal or bilateral nature of some of them". He further cautioned on the need to be careful when trying to apply common law concepts to customary law situations.

In the explanation on the reasoning behind his ruling, Mr Justice Chechetere states that he took into account the patrilineal nature of the community concerned. He suggested that "allowing female children to inherit in a broadly patrilineal society such as in the present case, would disrupt the customary laws of that society". He also noted that the family in African society is the focus of social concern and the individual concerns are submerged under family concerns. The judge went further and stated that:

> ... women were always regarded as persons who would eventually leave their original family on marriage to join their husbands. The appointment of female heirs would be tantamount to diverting the property of the original family to that of her new family. Her property would be inherited by her children who would be members of the new family and this would be a distortion of the principles underlying customary law of succession and inheritance.

The opinion of Judge Chechetere in *Magaya v. Magaya* is not unique to Zimbabwe; it is more or less the position in the majority of communities in Africa. Indeed, it has been argued by many that the 'distortion' of the customary laws on inheritance also creates a potential for social disorder should a girl who is married in another family chose to settle with her husband on the property (usually land) inherited from her family and located in her parents' home area. This goes against custom by increasing the opportunities for 'taboo situations' to arise and risking the ruin of the usually respectful relationship between a man and his in-laws.[15] In practice, even where girls are given a portion of land as inheritance, they end up selling it or giving it up to their male siblings. Indeed most parents prefer to allocate to their married daughters portions of family land that are not strictly ancestral or clan land but family land acquired in addition to ancestral land. Most of the time this is physically located far from their home in case she chooses to settle there with her husband. The effect is that girls are still 'denied' (from the perspective of universality of rights) ownership of that family land. Many of the unmarried girls who are allocated family land end up in disputes with their male siblings and family members.

In *Ephraim v. Pastory* in Tanzania[16] the sale of clan land by a woman who inherited it from her father through a valid will was contested by a male relative (nephew to the respondent)

Most [women in Africa] *would like a balance between culture and rights to enable then to identify with their communities and their role therein but enjoy rights within that community.*

and a male clan member. The court of first instance recognised the customary position that 'females had no power to sell clan land'. The district court overturned the decision on appeal, and held that the sale was valid but that since it was made "without the clan's consent the nephew to the appellant was at liberty to redeem the land by paying back the purchase price to the buyer". This ruling was again contested at the high court. The high court upheld the district court's decision that the sale of the land by the woman was legal and went further to find as discriminatory the customary law provision that barred females from selling clan land. Justice Mwalusanya found this to be contrary to the constitutional provision that prohibits discrimination on the basis of sex.

The judge cited the provision of the Constitution of Tanzania,[17] which allows the interpretation of existing laws, including customary laws, "with such modifications, adoptions, qualifications and exceptions as may be necessary to bring it into conformity with the provisions of the fifth Constitutional amendment Act No 15/1984 – the Bill of Rights". He also made reference to relevant supportive international human rights instruments that Tanzania had signed or ratified.[18]

The judgement was seen as a victory for females all over Tanzania. Beyond the celebration of the judgment, however, not very many women's lives are likely to change as a result. It is also important to take note of the influence of culture on the decisions of the lower courts in this matter. Both courts chose to uphold the status quo in relation to the role and authority of the Haya tribe – to which the parties to the suit belonged – in accordance with the customary law of this tribe. This is of great importance because these are the courts that are usually approached first. Had the appeal not been lodged the positive ruling would not have been passed.

Many women in Africa value their cultural backgrounds and agree with some of the customary arrangements but are afraid to speak up on this because it is not politically correct in the world of human rights. Most would like a balance between culture and rights to enable then to identify with their communities and their role within it, but to enjoy rights within that community.

Sharia Law

Sharia law, which is closely linked with the Islamic religion and culture, is another example related to the subject of human rights and relativism. The sharing in succession property by women under Islam is determined by Sharia law, which stipulates the portions of entitlement. The division of property allocates women lesser portions than men. This is seen by some as discriminatory. Many Moslems disagree with this view and have defended the retention of this in the laws. They argue that those who see discrimination in the different portions have no appreciation of Islamic traditions and the way in which duties and responsibilities are allocated between men and women, i.e. the woman is allocated a lesser portion but is not given any responsibility in terms of provision for the family and herself. Looked at from the common understanding of the term 'equality', Sharia law is discriminatory, but when other issues relating to the practice are considered, then one may not make the judgement so rapidly. Moslems try to protect this law within the legal systems in the various States. In Kenya, for example, Moslems have included a clause in the draft constitution excepting Moslem women from the provision on equality when comes to matters such as succession rights.

Should the Islamic Sharia conceptualisation of the principle of gender equality in the context of property inheritance matters be considered as a violation of human rights? Does it necessarily show a conflict between human rights and culture/religion or could it be another acceptable variation of right to equal enjoyment of property? Should the practice of human rights be concerned with the transformation of different cultures into one universal culture or should it operate in the context of different cultures?

Other Cultural Practices

There is a danger in defining the 'do's' and 'don'ts' of human rights out of the cultural context and attempting to implement them outside cultural structures. It is likely to make implementation of the rights more difficult.

This is well demonstrated by the continuation of cultural practices such as female circumcision despite the laws and

... culturally-based issues on human rights need to be addressed with more than legislation and judicial precedents.

huge campaigns against the practice. In Kenya, as in some other countries, the practice of female circumcision on children is prohibited by law.[19] This law is difficult to implement by way of carrying out prosecutions against the parents of children involved and the circumcisers because jailing them would disrupt families socially and economically, and penalising by fining is not a deterrent. In Kenya, a Magistrate's Court recently sentenced three women to two years probation for circumcising 26 girls (as reported in *The Nation* in December 2003). The complaint was brought by the parents of one of the girls. Although the magistrate found the women guilty, he considered their plea in mitigation and sentenced them to two years probation. The mitigation was that "the girl was not forced into the ritual but joined her peers who she found being circumcised at a relative's house".

Attempts to introduce educational programmes with a focus on alternative symbolic rights to female circumcision are also increasingly meeting resistance, with some families opting to get their children circumcised even after the education. Some parents have interpreted the argument that the surgery is harmful to health to mean that it can be done in hospitals (*The Nation*, 2003). There is definite hesitation within the communities about recognising this law and there is clear defiance in complying with the law by communities, and a reluctance by the law enforcement mechanisms to seriously enforce it. This supports the argument that culturally-based issues on human rights need to be addressed with more than legislation and judicial precedents.

HIV/AIDS and Gender

HIV/AIDS, which has reached disastrous proportions in Africa, has made the impact of culture on women more visible. It is now acknowledged that gender considerations have substantially contributed to the spread of the epidemic. The gender disparity between men and women, together with the consequent economic marginalisation and gender-based violence, has clearly manifested itself through the different effects of this scourge on men and women. The vulnerability of women and girls has made them suffer more in terms of infection rates and, although they have limited access to economic and social opportunities, they are still expected to continue to undertake their various social tasks as assigned by the cultural orders within their communities, including the bulk of the care of the infected.

The management of the AIDS pandemic in Africa has largely and unfairly been left in the hands of women without the necessary structural support for them.

Much of the development planning and the planning for HIV/AIDS management focuses on working with the formal or government-recognised care systems and spending most of the available resources here (even though they are taking care of less than 40 per cent of their populations), while giving token support to the rural women who are taking care of more than 60 per cent of those infected and affected by HIV/AIDS. The management of the AIDS pandemic in Africa has largely and unfairly been left in the hands of women without the necessary structural support. It further fails to recognise that the women need extra care because they are more vulnerable to infection; statistics show that more of them are infected than men, and yet they are expected to continue providing care for all in the society, particularly children. Africa is burying many of its citizens daily partly because the women are 'collapsing' under the weight of HIV/AIDS-related burdens.

The failure to plan with the cultural structures and the communities means that the support needs of these women are not properly factored into the different interventions. Since HIV/AIDS strikes at the economic, social and cultural aspects of life, the planning for HIV management needs to be done in the context of all these aspects.

Government Planning

The scale for measuring 'progressive achievement' of economic, social and cultural rights is not very well developed. As a result of this, most government economic policies and planning processes hardly factor in human rights perspectives. It has taken a deliberate effort by UNIFEM, for example, to persuade governments to mainstream gender in their policies and programmes. Human rights treaty monitoring bodies need to specifically require governments to come up with pro-rights policies.

Resource allocation and use should target structures that

There is a need for the concepts of human rights to be injected into culture, and for cultural perspectives to be incorporated in the processes of monitoring implementation of human rights.

can enhance the enjoyment of economic, social and cultural rights. States must facilitate community participation in policy formulation and implementation. National human rights institutions, together with civil society, should develop tools to track pro-rights components in policy and public expenditure documents. The tools should deliberately help to track gender and cultural issues. These will help to give attention to the needs of men, women, boys and girls, factoring in the needs of the more vulnerable, such as people with disabilities.

Conclusion

The true enjoyment of human rights by all the people/s of the world requires, in the view of this paper, the recognition that there is no universal or standard formula on how to implement and enforce the practice of human rights. Human rights are not just about the individual. The individual lives in an economic, social and cultural context. The individual's rights can either be recognised in isolation or in the context of the individual's group or community (Mutua, 1995).

Some of the solutions to the human rights problems that are linked to culture can only be derived from the internal cultural structures in the communities concerned. The international and national structures for monitoring and implementing human rights should therefore shift from emphasising the protection of the individual's rights to looking at the context in which the individual is living. Unless they do this, the opportunity to enhance individuals' enjoyment of human rights in their environment will be lost. The right to retain culture and the right of individuals to free themselves from culture or some cultural practices is in fact a conflict between competing rights. The resolution of this conflict must therefore look at both the individual and her or his community.

The tendency to design human rights education and advocacy programmes that concentrate on the empowerment of the individual or the possible 'victims of abuse' also helps a smaller number of individuals and misses the opportunity to hasten the pace on a wider practice of human rights. There is a need for the concept of human rights to be injected into culture, and for cultural perspectives to be incorporated in the processes of monitoring the implementation of human rights. The acceptance of cultural perspectives in addressing human rights will necessarily mean that broadened definitions of some human rights principles be accepted. The meaning of gender equality may, for instance, include the Sharia law definition in the context of succession law. The term 'dignity' may include the kind of dignity that derives from the collective rather than the individual.

There is a need for the international efforts and processes for the enforcement of human rights standards to acknowledge that human rights are about day-to-day activities and practices. Culture and socialisation largely determine the enjoyment or violation of rights. Any standards set need to take note of this.

Notes

1 In the Convention on the Elimination of All Forms of Discrimination against Women.
2 In the Convention on the Rights of the Child.
3 Set up under a Protocol of the Charter that came into force in February 2004.
4 As has been the case in the arguments for 'the right to development'.
5 Articles 6, 10 and 15.
6 Articles 17 and 18.
7 Articles 2, 5, 9, 11, 14 and 16.
8 Articles 2, 20 and 24.
9 Articles 1, 11,12,18, 21 and 31.
10 Articles 2, 4, 17, 18, 20, 21, 22 and 26.
11 The operative law in most rural areas is customary law. Issues of concern usually arise when a family member elects to register and sell some family land without due regard to the needs of the other family members.
12 To seek redress in the courts is a costly exercise for many people, particularly women. Many give up before they are able to get a remedy.
13 Supreme Court of Zimbabwe 1999 Judgement No. SC 210/98 (1999) 3LRC 35.
14 As was stated by the presiding magistrate.
15 It is customary in most African cultures for a son-in-law to be expected to display the highest level of respect before his parents-in-law. Interaction between men and their in-laws is often

restricted to formal scheduled visits that ensure that both parties are on their best behaviour. Impromptu visits are usually limited to emergency situations, such as where a married daughter needs medical care and the sons in the home are not able to take on the responsibility. To expect a daughter to inherit ancestral land and use it in a way similar to that of a son, including settling in with her husband, is likely to cause a lot of social disharmony in most African communities.

16 Tanzania High Court, 1990, 87 ht. L Rep. 156 91992.

17 Section 5 (1).

18 The UDHR, CEDAW, ICCPR and ACHPR.

19 Under the Children Act.

References

An-na'im, Abdullah Ahmed (1990). 'Human Rights in the Moslem World: Socio-Political Conditions and Scriptural Imperatives', *Harvard Human Rights Journal* 3, Spring.

Mutua, Makau (1995). 'The Banjul Charter and the African Cultural Fingerprint: An evaluation of the language of duties', *Virginia Journal of International Law*, 339.

The Nation (2003). 'Parents defy female cut ban' and '4 girls seek permit to get circumcised', 5 December.

Ojienda, TO (2003). 'Customary law perspectives in land law in Kenya'. In Law Society of Kenya, *The Dawn of a New Political Era.*

3 Gender and Human Rights in the Life Cycle

Taking the Life-cycle Approach to the World of Work

Lin Lean Lim

Overview

Globalisation and recent demographic and labour market trends are having a different impact on girls and boys, women and men. Gender roles and relations are being affected as are the gender differences in the inter-generational transmission of both opportunities and disadvantages over the life cycle for decent work and livelihoods for women and men – including the feminisation of poverty and the vicious cycle of poverty from one generation to the next. The changes that are happening in the world today are having important impacts – all with gender implications – for:

1 Fertility decisions, including sex preference and the value attached to daughters and sons;

2 Educational opportunities and types of education and training for girls and boys;

3 The school-to-work transition and the opportunities and barriers to entry into the labour force for young women and men;

4 Employment in the formal or informal economy and the types of employment relationships;

5 The nature of working life and careers, including, importantly, how women and men balance paid work and care work;

6 The returns from work, the working poor and the poor who are excluded from work;

7 Age at marriage, marriage patterns and family formation;

The processes of globalisation ... are benefiting some but disadvantaging others.

8 Family structures and dynamics, including intra-household decision-making and the economic and social roles of different family members;

9 Labour mobility – within and between countries;

10 Access to different forms of security and social protection;

11 Who is socially excluded and falls into poverty, whether the voices of the poor are heard or not heard and new forms of insecurities.

The processes of globalisation – including trade liberalisation, the trend towards a single borderless economy, the changing organisation of production and employment, developments in information and communications technologies (ICTs) and the changing roles of the state, business sector and civil society – are benefiting some but disadvantaging others. Who is benefiting and in what context? Why and how are others being disadvantaged? How is discrimination against women throughout life, from birth to old age, contributing both to the feminisation of poverty and the perpetuation of poverty from one generation to the next? What are the cultural and socio-economic class variables?

Why are young girls often outshining boys at school yet still finding it harder to enter the labour market? Has there been a reversal of inter-generational care, and can older women who have already spent their lifetime looking after other people expect to be cared for in their twilight years? Is there a trend away from gender-based discrimination and disadvantage to age-based discrimination and disadvantage? Or is sexist *and* ageist discrimination in the world of work affecting people at younger ages, so that women over 35 years are finding it harder to get hired or rehired and to get out of poverty? How is discrimination and disadvantage by gender *and* age evolving over the life cycle of women and men, and what are the links with other forms of discrimination, such as class and race?

Parallel to the processes of globalisation, various demographic changes are taking place. Populations everywhere are ageing. The number of persons aged 60 years or older is currently estimated to be nearly 600 million and is projected to grow to almost 2 billion by the year 2050, at which time the population of older persons will be larger than the population of children for the first time in human history. Of this two billion, a much higher proportion will be women. Today, the developed world is already experiencing gender differences in longevity, with women accounting for a higher proportion of the older and oldest old population. In the United States, for example, women now account for 56 per cent of the over-60 population. In Japan, over a quarter of the female population is already over 60. But the feminisation of later life is occurring at a much faster rate in the developing rather than developed regions, so that within the next 25 years, nearly three-quarters of the world's older women are expected to work and live in the developing world, particularly in the Asian region. Although, women outnumber men in old age around the world, they generally have lower pension and social security entitlements. As widows, heads of households or living in single-member households, older women are highly vulnerable without income support.

Populations everywhere are ageing. The number of persons aged 60 years or older is currently estimated to be nearly 600 million and is projected to grow to almost two billion by the year 2050 .... Of this two billion, a much higher proportion will be women.

At the same time, HIV/AIDS is having a devastating effect on some populations, especially in Africa, cutting down those in the prime of their working lives and changing the inter-generational pattern of care. The implications are not just in terms of those who are infected with HIV/AIDS but also those – often the oldest and the youngest – who have to provide care for the infected and who are left without their breadwinners.

These demographic, economic and social changes in the global economy help to explain the importance of adopting a life-cycle perspective to the promotion of gender equality in decent work and poverty reduction.

International Perspectives

At the United Nations Millennium Summit in 2000, the community of nations committed to "make a real and measurable difference to people's lives in the new century" through a concerted and co-ordinated drive to achieve eight Millennium Development Goals (MDGs). These are to: eradicate poverty and hunger; achieve universal primary education; promote gender equality and empower women; reduce child mortality; improve maternal health; combat HIV/AIDS, malaria and other diseases; ensure environmental sustainability; and develop a global partnership for development. The MDGs provide a

Equality between women and men and the elimination of discrimination is a fundamental right throughout all stages of life – from childhood to old age.

context in which the life-cycle approach to the promotion of gender equality in decent work and poverty reduction is all the more significant and relevant.

The Report of the Director-General to the International Labour Conference 91st Session clearly explains this:

> Today's girl child is tomorrow's older woman worker, and it is her opportunities and experiences now that will shape her ability to obtain and maintain decent work throughout her adult life, and enjoy security and protection in her old age. If girls, compared to boys, face negative cultural attitudes and practices and discrimination from birth, they will grow up to be women with greater constraints and few choices and opportunities. In turn, they will be less able to influence positively the lives of their daughters and sons, so that poverty is likely to be passed on from one generation to the next. The links between a vicious cycle of poverty and gender discrimination against the girl child start at the earliest stages of life within families. Throughout life, from birth to old age, gender discrimination contributes both to the feminisation of poverty and to the perpetuation of poverty from one generation to the next. (ILO, 2003:26)

Equality between women and men and the elimination of discrimination is a fundamental right throughout all stages of life – from childhood to old age. This life-cycle approach to the promotion of gender equality is at the core of the International Labour Organization 'decent work' approach (see Figure 1). The concept of decent work is best expressed through the aspirations of individuals and families, through the eyes of people. It is about your job and future prospects; your working conditions; your ability to earn enough to feed, clothe and educate your children and give them a childhood rather than put them into labour. If you are a woman, it is about equality with men; about being able to compete on a level playing field; about receiving equal pay for work of equal value; about being able to balance your work life and family life; about having your care work and domestic chores acknowledged and valued; about having a say about whether your daughter has the same opportunities as your son; and about having a voice in your community. Decent work is at the heart of family life and society – work that offers possibilities for personal creativity, expression and fulfilment, and that provides a sense of self worth and secures human dignity.

Figure 1: Decent Work in the Life Cycle

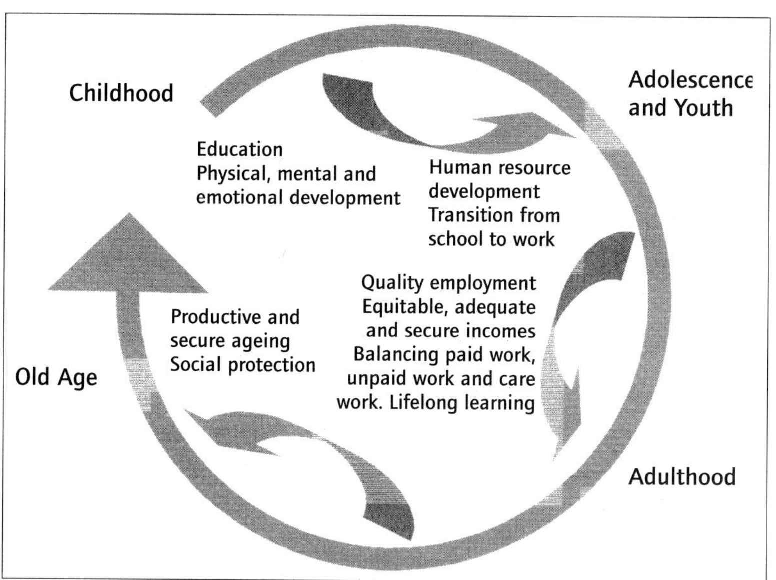

The Vulnerability of Children – Especially Girls

Every child should have the right to health, nutrition, literacy and education, and protection from exploitation and abuse as child labour. The estimate is that some 120 million children between the ages of 5 and 14 years are engaged in full-time work, and another 130 million work as a secondary activity. Of these 250 million child workers, about 110 million are girls. Girls are much more likely than boys to face negative cultural attitudes and practices, beginning within their own families; start working at an earlier age; be paid less for the same work; work longer hours; work in hidden and unregulated sectors where they are particularly vulnerable to exploitation and abuse; be excluded from education; or suffer the triple burden of housework, school work and economic work. Since the work that girls do is often 'invisible', they are especially vulnerable to the worst forms of child labour, including child prostitution, child slavery, sale and trafficking, debt bondage and serfdom.

Since the root causes of child labour are poverty and socio-cultural attitudes towards the value of sons and daughters, actions are needed to target parents. Between parents, there is substantial empirical evidence that mothers tend to have a greater influence than fathers on children's education, health and welfare, and that women tend to use their income, however, meagre, for the benefit of the family more than men do. Programmes need to improve the quantity and quality of employment for women and at the same time ensure, for example through awareness-raising and training, that decent employment translates into empowerment and greater decision-making power for women within their families and communities and improved welfare for their families, especially their children.

Poverty leads many households in developing countries to survival strategies that can have the effect of accentuating gender inequalities. One survival strategy, for instance, is to withdraw children from school so that they can work and contribute to family income. While often born out of desperation, such a strategy can further discriminate against the girl child. Families are likely to take prevailing gender prejudices as given in their economic decisions and thus choose to invest their limited resources on, for example, boy's education and health since returns to girls' education in labour markets tend to be much less. Economic security is thus vital for families.

The Importance of Education and Training

Where girls have improved access to education, their labour market opportunities have also improved. An important gain in recent years has been the narrowing of the gender gap in education. In higher education, women's enrolment now equals or surpasses that of men in many countries. Yet the school-to-work transition is still harder for young women than for young men. The pathways to decent work for young women tend to be very difficult to negotiate, with many obstacles, setbacks, exits and re-entries. Unfortunately, at the end of the process, many young women, particularly those in developing countries, still do not find decent work. They may already be married, already mothers or pregnant, and desperately looking for whatever work they can find so that they and their children can survive. The available data also indicate that there are many more young women than young men living with HIV/AIDS. And even those that are not thus affected still face stereotypical prejudices and discrimination in trying to enter the labour market.

From a life-cycle perspective, education is a first step to decent work. Employment opportunities are a next step. Unfortunately, however, employment opportunities tend to be limited, especially for those 15 to 24 years of age. Worldwide, some 60 million young people are looking for work but cannot find any. Unemployment rates for youth are more than twice the corresponding rates for the economically active adult population in all regions of the world, and young women have much greater difficulty than young men in entering the labour market and retaining their jobs in periods of economic downturn, especially in Latin America, the Caribbean and South Asia.

From a life-cycle perspective, education is a first step to decent work. Employment opportunities are a next step.

Access to education and training is fundamental for enabling young women to compete on the basis of objective criteria for recruitment and promotion. But, increasingly, it is the type, rather than the level, of education and training that is critical. Young women are still not going into some fields of study traditionally dominated by men. Gender-based stereotypes survive and role models that could lead young women to challenging, better-paid careers are still scarce. Importantly, girls are much less likely than boys to enrol in mathematics and computer science courses. It is true that more and more women are having access to the new ICTs that are dramatically changing the world, but the next essential challenge is for women to enter these new and powerful media as producers. If women do not participate in designing the content and modes of use of ICTs, they will be doubly excluded.

Women and Work

More and more women are spending their child-bearing and child-rearing years in paid employment. The increasing participation of women in paid work has been driving employment trends, and the gaps between male and female labour force participation rates have been shrinking. For example between 1980 and 1996, the annual growth rate of the labour force was over 4 per cent for females and 1.2 per cent for males in Latin America, and 2.2 per cent and 1.8 per cent respectively in Asia. While women have become more economically active, the male labour force participation rate has been declining in

... there is still a long way to go to achieving gender equality in decent work. With 54 per cent of working age women in the labour force as compared to over 80 per cent male participation, the world is still not making the most of its female talents and potentials.

most regions, albeit slowly; an important reason is a tendency toward earlier retirement. In the developed countries, East and South-East Asia, the Caribbean and sub-Saharan Africa women now account for close to half the labour force.

Growing numbers of girls and women with ever-higher educational qualifications have been breaching glass walls and ceilings. The share of women in administration and middle management has increased. More women are also creating their own enterprises. In the United States, the number of firms created and managed by women has grown twice as fast as those set up and managed by men. In Japan, the percentage of women entrepreneurs increased from 2.4 per cent in 1980 to 5.2 per cent in 1995. In several Organisation for Economic Co-operation and Development (OECD) countries, women-owned small and medium-sized enterprises have been growing at a faster rate than the economy as a whole and have been an important source of employment generation, innovation and economic development.

But there is still a long way to go to achieving gender equality in decent work. With 54 per cent of working age women in the labour force as compared to over 80 per cent of men, the world is still not making the most of its female talents and potentials. Gender remains a ubiquitous source of labour market inequalities and inadequately utilised human resources. More jobs for women have not necessarily meant better jobs. Worldwide, women hold only 1 per cent of chief executive positions. The majority experience the effects of the so-called 'sticky floor' – on the bottom rungs of the occupational hierarchy.

Quantitative increases in employment have not been matched by qualitative improvements in working conditions and social protection. After all this time, about half of the world's labour remains in sex-stereotyped occupations, with women dominating in clerical and secretarial jobs and low-end service occupations that tend to be outside the scope of labour legislation and social protection. In occupations where many women but few men work, pay levels remain low. With so many women concentrated in low-paying jobs, it is no surprise that despite the increasing adoption of equal pay legislation, a large gap persists between male and female earnings. Although real manufacturing wages have been rising faster for women than for men in recent years, women continue to earn 20–30 per cent less than men.

Women's working lives are greatly determined by the presence of children in the family. In order to achieve equality of treatment, measures must be taken to ensure that women's specific role in reproduction has no adverse effect on their employment. These measures include: health care for pregnant women and mothers; cash benefits and maternity leave; arrangements to better reconcile family and occupational responsibilities, and give fathers the opportunity to play a recognised role in raising children; and other types of collective responsibility such as family allowances, taxation arrangements and childcare systems.

... societal perceptions of work and family have not changed; the division of labour is still based on the 'man breadwinner, woman homemaker and caregiver' idea.

Balancing Paid and Unpaid Work – for Women and Men

Women now constitute almost half the global labour force and account for the tremendous rise in dual-income families and single parent households. But societal perceptions of work and family have not changed; the division of labour is still based on the 'man breadwinner, woman homemaker and caregiver' idea. Some facts are illustrative:

1 Women work more hours than men, more than half their working time being spent on unpaid work. Because women continue to have primary responsibility for housework, childcare and unpaid work in general, women's increase in paid employment has in many instances simply meant that women work extra long hours. In Bangladesh, for instance, women working in the formal sector devote another 31 hours per week to unpaid work, as compared to only 14 hours by men.

2 Small children greatly increase women's unpaid work, not men's. Part-time work can offer women an effective way to divide their time between paid work and looking after young children and other dependents. There has been a substantial increase in part-time employment over the past two decades, with women accounting for up to 80 per cent of all part-timers. In the United Kingdom, for instance, over 40

Lifelong learning and continuous training are also particularly important for women because ageist and sexist discrimination in the world of work appears to be occurring at earlier and earlier chronological ages.

per cent of all women workers are part-time, as compared to only 8 per cent of men workers. However, the problem is that part-timers earn lower hourly wages than full timers, lose out even more on benefits than on hourly pay and have little prospects for career advancement, training or skills enhancement.

3 The available evidence shows that where women lack quality childcare, they take their young children to work with them and often expose them to the hazards of their work place; and also that child victims of various forms of violence tend to have both parents working away from home.

4 The pressures are especially great for a sandwich generation of women who are marrying later and having children later – because they have been investing in their own human resource development – but then end up struggling to juggle career advancement, care of young children and care of elderly parents, all within the same time span of their lives.

For most, if not all, of our history, there has been a care deficit – mainly a deficit in the care provided to women who spend most of their time caring for other people but have little time to care for themselves. Nowadays, men and children are also beginning to experience a care deficit, as more and more women enter the labour force and the pressures of the double burden of paid and unpaid work become too much for women and men do not take on more of it. What we need is not only a better balance between paid and unpaid work for women but also a change in attitudes and responsibilities on the part of men. Until and unless men assume their fair share of family responsibilities, the social order will not change.

Gender Concerns around Ageing

Over their life course, women are likely than men to move in and out of the labour force several times as they seek to combine work and family responsibilities. There is thus a need for lifelong learning and continuous training to enhance employability and flexibility for women at different stages of family formation and care. Lifelong learning and continuous training are also particularly important for women because ageist and sexist discrimination in the world of work appears to be occurring at earlier and earlier chronological ages. In a growing number of countries, women over 35 years of age are finding it increasingly difficult to get jobs or to be rehired.

Ageing raises important gender concerns. As noted earlier, nearly everywhere women live longer than men. At 60 years and above, there are 99 males to every 100 females. At the age of 80 and over, there are just 69 males to every 100 females. So the ageing world is also a female world. Older women account for the majority of single person households. Older women are often living alone, neither cared for nor able to productively contribute their knowledge and experience to society. Particularly in developing countries, where public assistance is meagre, women are even more likely to end up in poverty in their old age. Growing numbers of today's older women are left unsupported by formal social protection. In addition, public expenditures on social security and health care have been cut, often based on the mistaken belief that families and communities will take care of their aged. The sad fact is that there has been a reversal of inter-generational care. Older women who have already spent their lifetime looking after other people increasingly cannot expect to be cared for in their twilight years. In many least developed countries, the impact of the HIV/AIDS pandemic has left older women with responsibility for caring for their infected children and, later on, their children's children. Thus, AIDS now provides a further distortion of gender inequalities both at the beginning and end of a woman's life cycle.

The progressive ageing of the populations compels us to rethink the conventional concept of a simple three-stage life cycle of education, employment and retirement. As the vitality of our societies increasingly depends on active participation by older people, we must foster economic and social conditions that allow people of all ages to remain fully integrated into society, to enjoy freedom in deciding how to relate and contribute to society and to find fulfilment in doing so. The central challenge is to promote a culture that values the experience and knowledge that come with age. A wider basket of policy tools, strongly oriented to ease and support participation in economic and social life by older workers, is needed.

Discrimination against older women workers needs to be

... we can achieve what people are asking for in their daily lives – work, security and human dignity – only if there is equality of opportunity and treatment for women and men from childhood to old age ...

addressed at all stages of the employment process, including recruitment, selection, training, promotion, redundancy and termination. This may involve reviewing recruitment and training policies and procedures (e.g. banning job advertisements that not only specify sex but also age and physical characteristics), redesigning jobs (e.g. by providing seating and better lighting) and analysing social security and pension arrangements from the perspective of the older woman worker.

Conclusion

The life-cycle approach focuses not just on the individual but on the family. No matter the culture or country it is family goals that determine life and work strategies; the family that assigns economic and social roles for girls and boys, women and men; the family that ultimately decides on issues such as education, consumption, gender and employment. There needs also to be recognition of the fact that, unlike the standard pattern of the 20th century, more and more women (and men) will be having flexible working lives, moving in and out of the labour force at various times of their lives and changing work status more often. Thus, their need for lifelong learning and social protection to deal with such changes is greater than ever.

In summary, the message of the life-cycle approach is that we can achieve what people are asking for in their daily lives – work, security and human dignity – only if there is equality of opportunity and treatment for women and men from childhood to old age; if discrimination encountered at one stage of life is not perpetuated at later stages or gains made at one stage are not lost as one ages; and if there is better harmonisation of work and family responsibilities for men and especially women.

Reference

International Labour Organization (2003). *Working out of Poverty.* Report of the Director-General to the International Labour Conference 91st Session. Geneva: International Labour Office.

Older People

Fiona Clark

> Each and every one of us, young and old, has a role to play in promoting solidarity between generations, in combating discrimination against older people, and in building a future of security, opportunity and dignity for people of all ages.
>
> UN Secretary General, Kofi Annan,
> *Foreword to the Political Declaration and Madrid International Plan of Action on Ageing*, 2002

In order to ensure that progress and gains made in one stage of life are not negated by adverse experiences and discrimination based on age in a later stage, people need support in the transitions from one stage of life to another.

Introduction

The issue of gender and human rights has to be understood in the context of the multiple and complex factors that intersect gender roles and identities and the ability of citizens to claim their rights. One of these factors is age and these issues must therefore necessarily be approached from the basic understanding that:

1 Discrimination is experienced by virtue of people's age, and this is especially the case for older women and men.

2 Age cross-cuts other forms of discrimination and disadvantage throughout the life cycle, to fundamentally determine people's health and well-being throughout life and into old age.

A life-cycle approach is based on the recognition that people are faced with different opportunities and obstacles throughout their lives that determine their development, well-being and status. In order to ensure that progress and gains made in one stage of life are not negated by adverse experiences and discrimination based on age in a later stage, people need support in the transitions from one stage of life to another. Similarly, one cannot understand or address issues of older people without knowing the trajectory of their lives and the opportunities and constraints they faced to place them in their current situations.

Public policy options to counter discrimination need to begin by recognising that there is age discrimination in the first place, and take affirmative action in all fields to ensure that older people's rights are upheld ...

Age-based Discrimination

A life-cycle approach to gender and human rights must take account of existing, if unacknowledged, age-based discrimination and the violation of the rights of older persons of both genders that this entails. Advancing age is connected to social exclusion and social distancing from policy processes. In poor communities poverty only serves to exacerbate this exclusion. Stripping older people of assets is common, as is rationing of services and support to old people when resources are scarce. This is the case in developed as much as in developing countries. Poor health and dependence on family for material well-being and physical security in old age enhance the potential for discrimination, where older people may be dependent on the very people who are discriminating against them.

'Being old' is not an identity people are too keen to promote, and yet age is a defining feature in our identity, our access to resources and claiming our rights, and can cross-cut gender, ethnicity, religion, and geography to increase disadvantage and discrimination. A gender analysis therefore necessarily has to acknowledge that older women, for example, experience high levels of disadvantage by virtue of their age and cumulative gender disadvantage over the life course. Poor access to education, the labour market, economic assets and health services over their lives leave women doubly or triply disadvantaged in old age. Illiteracy, economic insecurity, discriminatory laws and practices mean that older women suffer from violence (including gender-based violence such as rape), property grabbing and disinheritance, denial of access to justice and participation in decision-making.

However, it is important to realise that gender and age also intersect with negative consequences for older men. Very often the reduced capacity of older men to make economic or other contributions to the households and family leave them isolated as their role is perceived to lessen and their burden seen to increase. Therefore human rights approaches to gender equality from a life-cycle perspective need to consider and put in place actions in favour of older men too, who are discriminated against socially and in the household (Beales, 2000; Clark and Laurie, 2000).

Public policy options to counter discrimination need to

begin by recognising that there is age discrimination, and take affirmative action in all fields to ensure that older people's rights are upheld and that older people's perspectives are included in national and international plans for poverty reduction, gender equality, tackling the HIV pandemic, as well as dealing with emergency and conflict situations.

Secondly, efforts must be made to measure the impact of policies and programmes on people of all ages. There is a need for concerted efforts to collect and disaggregate data by age and undertake age disaggregated research and policy work.

… UN principles for older persons and the Madrid International Plan of Action on Ageing are not well known. They still need to find their way into the body of legislation at national and international level and be connected with existing poverty reduction and human rights instruments …

The MIPAA

There is now an opportunity for affirmative action on ageing with the agreement in 2002 on the Madrid International Plan of Action on Ageing (MIPAA). The plan commits UN Member States, including Commonwealth countries, to the inclusion of older people in poverty and human rights agendas, and to tackle negative attitudes to older people to ensure an enabling environment for a society of all ages.

Principles underpinning the MIPAA include:

1 The full realisation of all human rights and fundamental freedoms of all older persons;

2 The achievement of secure ageing, which involves reaffirming the goal of eradicating poverty in old age and building on the United Nations Principles for older persons;

3 Ensuring the full enjoyment of economic, social and cultural rights, and civil and political rights of persons and the elimination of all forms of violence and discrimination against older persons; and

4 Commitment to gender equality among older persons through, *inter alia*, elimination of gender-based discrimination.

The problem remains that the UN principles for older persons and the MIPAA are not well known. They still need to find their way into the body of legislation at national and international level and be connected with existing poverty reduction and human rights instruments, including gender-related instruments such as CEDAW.

Best Practices: HelpAge International

HelpAge International (HAI) is a global network of not-for-profit organisations with a mission "to work with and for disadvantaged older people worldwide to achieve a lasting improvement in the quality of their lives". Its core aim is to integrate an understanding of a life-cycle approach and the needs and rights of older women and men into policy at local, national, regional and international levels, via the perspective of older people.

Including the voices of older people

HAI brings the voices of older people into development and decision-making processes that affect their lives, through their own participation, through its publications and through its policy and advocacy work. For example, in 2001 HAI and its partner organisations undertook a large number of consultations with older people around the world in preparation for the 2nd World Assembly on Ageing in 2002. HAI informed older people and their groups about the existence of the plan, asked them to put forward their views and demands as to what should be in the plan, and helped them to attend the Assembly and engage with their own national government delegations who would be representing them. The outcomes of these consultations are presented in the report *State of the World's Older People 2002* (HelpAge International, 2002), launched in Madrid at the time of the Assembly.

Direct practical work with older people

On a practical level, HAI supports older people and their groups to get involved in processes working for poverty reduction and the achievement of the Millennium Development Goals at a national level. In Tanzania, HAI is now actively involved in the Poverty Reduction Strategy Review. It is undertaking programmes to support older people who are caring for people living with AIDS and orphaned grandchildren. However, it is also stressing the risk of older people becoming infected with the virus. International statistics on prevalence rates refer to those between the ages of 15 and 49, making those above this age totally invisible. Yet, recent data from Uganda show that of those over 50 who presented at Voluntary Counselling and Testing Centres, 20 per cent were HIV positive. Older people are sexually active and are at risk of HIV infection through their own sexual behaviour, as well as from contaminated blood transfusions.

International statistics on prevalence rates refer to those between the ages of 15 and 49, making those above this age totally invisible. Yet ... older people are sexually active and are at risk of HIV infection through their own sexual behaviour, as well as from contaminated blood transfusions.

HAI's Regional Rights Programme in Africa works to raise awareness about the rights of older people, and supports older people and their organisations in launching legal challenges in the courts. In Mozambique and Tanzania, HAI has been undertaking work on civic education with older people at community level. A widowhood and inheritance project co-ordinated by HAI-Tanzania trains older women as paralegal advisers to act as resource persons for local community members, to understand the statutory and customary laws and the implications they have for widows and inheritance issues, and to refer people to the local justice system as and when required (HAI, 2003).

Changed policy environment for older people

HAI is also campaigning for improved social protection measures as a right for older people and as a means of cushioning the most vulnerable against the shocks and obstacles they encounter over the life course, and especially nearer the end of it. It is working to promote the feasibility of a basic universal income transfer to be integrated into Poverty Reduction Strategy Papers (PRSPs) and national development plans. Few countries in the world have adequate social security for their older citizens. One country that does is South Africa and HAI research there shows that the state pension, although small, provides an important part of household economy and survival. Older women, especially, spend their pensions largely on school fees and uniforms for their grandchildren, on health care, rent and other vital elements of family livelihood strategies.

Recently, HAI has been working at EU level with members of the gender movement, the disability movement and Minority Rights Group to promote what has been termed an "inclusive approach to development". This is a reaction to the widely held cynicism about the failure of mainstreaming efforts, especially gender mainstreaming, and the need for development policy to be inclusive of all those who are poor and marginalised. It is hoped that these efforts will help HAI to push for EU development co-operation to be focused on reaching the very poorest and those off the margins of mainstream development, including older people.

In the UK, HAI is involved with the 'Grow-up free from poverty' coalition for international action against child poverty. HAI has been successful in integrating an inter-generational, cross-sectoral and inclusive approach into the work and advocacy of this coalition, which is concerned with child poverty within the achievement of the Millennium Development Goals.

Similarly, HAI is involved in the UK Consortium on AIDS and International Development, and has worked hard with others to ensure that the Consortium's focus is not only on access to treatment and ARV therapy for those infected with the virus, but also support for those affected as carers, family members and breadwinners for households affected by AIDS. HAI is making some headway ensuring that the impact of AIDS on older people is recognised within the Consortium, its membership and its work.

Finally, HAI is also involved in the UK Gender and Development Network. Interestingly, the current debates about 'diversity', and especially EU legislation on diversity, have lead to the women's movement feeling that gender is under threat of being diluted. These defensive (if justified) reactions of the gender movement have hampered attempts to broaden debates within the movement about the heterogeneity of women and men and to see diversity as an opportunity to strengthen discussions around discrimination and difference.

HAI seeks to embrace diversity and to promote an inclusive approach to development based on the fundamental freedoms and rights of all people and a focus in development co-operation on the poorest and most disadvantaged.

References

Beales, S (2000). 'Why we should invest in older women and men: the experience of HelpAge International'. In 'Gender and Lifecycles', *Gender and Development* 8(2), July.

Clark, FC and N Laurie (2000). 'Gender, age, and exclusion: a challenge to community organisations in Lima, Peru'. In 'Gender and Lifecycles', *Gender and Development* 8(2), July.

HAI (2003). 'Widowhood and Inheritance: Reducing the poverty of older women', Programme summary leaflet. London: HelpAge International.

—— (2002). *State of the World's Older People 2002*. London: HelpAge International.

United Nations (2002). 'Political Declaration and Madrid International Plan of Action on Ageing, 2002'. In *Report of the 2nd World Assembly on Ageing*. New York: United Nations.

The Life Cycle: Adolescent Girls[1]

From the Report of the Expert Group Meeting on Adolescent Girls and Their Rights

The international community has acknowledged that the equal rights of girls and the equal participation of women in the social, cultural, economic and political life of societies is a prerequisite for successful and sustainable development.

The issue of the girl child was firmly placed on the international agenda by the 1990 Declaration of the World Summit for Children, which accorded priority attention to the girl child for survival, development and protection.

The Programme of Action adopted by the international community at the International Conference on Population and Development (ICPD) in Cairo in 1994 highlighted the need to improve the situation of the girl child, to eliminate all forms of discrimination against her and to increase public awareness of her value. The Regional Conference on Women, held in Dakar in November 1994 in preparation for the Fourth World Conference on Women, adopted the African Platform for Action, which clearly identified the crucial link between the well-being of today's girls and the status of tomorrow's women. Consequently, the Beijing Platform for Action, adopted at the Fourth World Conference of Women, included the girl child in its 12 critical areas of concern.

The international community has acknowledged that the equal rights of girls and the equal participation of women in the social, cultural, economic and political life of societies is a prerequisite for successful and sustainable development. For those countries which have ratified CEDAW and the Convention on the Rights of the Child, the achievement of equality between girls and boys and the elimination of discrimination against girls are legal obligations.

The Beijing Platform for Action seeks to promote and protect the full realisation of the human rights and fundamental freedoms of women throughout their life cycle. The Platform identifies 12 critical areas of concern in which major actions are designed to overcome the existing obstacles and to advance the status of women. The chapter on the girl child, one of the critical areas of concern, recognises that in many countries the girl child faces discrimination in all stages of life, from birth, through childhood and into adulthood, despite the progress in advancing the status of women worldwide. The Platform argues that due to this discriminatory environment, girls often receive limited opportunities for education and consequently lack knowledge and the skills needed to advance their status in society. The Platform underscores the responsibility of governments to protect and promote the rights of girls and recommends eliminating all barriers in order to enable girls to develop their full potential and skills through equal access to education and training, nutrition, physical and mental health care and related information. The Platform also notes that girls are encouraged less than boys to participate in and learn about the social, economic and political functioning of society, and urges governments to take action to provide access for girls to training and information to enable them to articulate their views, and to promote the equality and participation of girls in society.

Adolescent girls have needs that differ significantly from those of boys because of their expected biological and social roles, and are often discriminated against on the accounts of both their age and their sex.

Since the Fourth World Conference on Women, greater attention has been paid at all levels by governments, the United Nations system and other international institutions and NGOs to the needs of girl children. However, not enough action has been taken to redress the discrimination and difficulties they face, in particular during adolescence. Adolescents are caught between childhood and adulthood in terms of their social status and physical development. Adolescent girls have needs that differ significantly from those of boys because of their expected biological and social roles, and are often discriminated against on the accounts of both their age and their sex.

The Expert Group Meeting identified the following predisposing and determining factors that contribute to the vulnerable situation of adolescent girls:

1 The slow pace of dissemination and implementation of the CRC and CEDAW;

2 The low and unequal status accorded to girls and women from birth resulting in low self-esteem among girls;

3 Poverty in the high proportion of female-headed households and poor access to basic services;

4 Lack of social policies that recognise the situation of adolescent girls and the girl child in general;

5 Urbanisation, the social impact of globalisation and structural adjustment policies.

The Expert Group Meeting noted that the rights of adolescent girls should be seen as an integral part of human rights and that girls should be enabled to develop fully and contribute to all spheres of life. They need to be given the skills and knowledge that contribute to their self-esteem in order to become more self-reliant and be active participants in society. The Meeting focused on the following critical aspects relevant to improving the situation of adolescent girls:

1 Adolescent girls in need of special protection;

2 Health, including reproductive and sexual health and nutrition;

3 Creating an enabling environment for the empowerment of adolescent girls.

1 Adolescent Girls in Need of Special Protection

CEDAW and the CRC contain mutually reinforcing principles that, if fully implemented, would ensure the protection and fulfilment of the rights of girls and put an end to gender-based discrimination. Although adolescent girls have special needs, and face many especially difficult circumstances on the way to womanhood, their specific situation and needs remain largely ignored and neglected.

While some 191 countries have ratified the CRC and some 166 countries have ratified CEDAW, there remains a large gap between the State obligations resulting from those Conventions and their reflection in national legislation and effective implementation. The increasingly important role of NGOs in supporting implementation of these instruments has been noted.

Globalisation, poverty and erosion of values and family and community ties make adolescent girls increasingly exposed to the sex industry, child pornography and trafficking in women and children. These phenomena are neither confronted with adequate legal and political measures at national and international levels, nor sufficiently addressed by civil society.

Although the situation varies greatly from region to region and even within countries, a common thread seems to be the lower value ascribed to girls in relation to boys in virtually all countries. In addition, rapid urbanisation, growing economic disparities between rich and poor, and especially between the resources women and men control, gender-based violence and armed conflict exacerbate the already distressing situation of adolescent girls.

Although the situation varies greatly from region to region and even within countries, a common thread seems to be the lower value ascribed to girls in relation to boys in virtually all countries.

For many girls, discrimination often starts within their families and extends to affect their educational opportunities and all other spheres of their lives. Their powerlessness to protect themselves from sexual assault, early child-bearing, exploitation and abuse, and the effects of war and armed conflict rob them of the chance to enjoy their childhood and develop their full potential. The extent of their individual suffering is often hidden by the overwhelming numbers of those affected.

The rapid transmission of HIV/AIDS is a new threat to millions of adolescent girls around the world, especially those who are exploited in the sex industry. An even greater number of girls are losing their parents and primary care givers to HIV/AIDS and also find themselves forced to assume responsibility for younger siblings.

Attention was given to adolescent girls who worked at home and were often exploited and deprived of their rights, benefits and opportunities which other adolescent girls enjoyed such as access to education, training and social interaction.
There are many groups of adolescent girls in need of special protection. They include:

1 Girls with disabilities, further exacerbated as they become adolescent and often neglected in favour of younger siblings;

2 Girls in armed conflict, including combatants and refugees;

3 Orphaned girls through AIDS, maternal mortality or conflict and who lack any care giver;

4 Girls subject to sexual abuse whose mothers are abroad as migrant workers;

5 Girls in conflict with the law;

6 Sexually abused girls including victims of incest, rape, forced prostitution and sexual harassment;

7 Girls subjected to female genital mutilation or suffering from fistula, often subsequently ostracised, and devalued if they are not able to be wives or mothers;

8 Girls obliged to marry too early and consequently bear children at a young age who are more likely to suffer from maternal morbidity or mortality as well as a curtailment of other opportunities;

9 Girls affected by the dowry or 'bride price' systems;

10 Girls abducted by men, including soldiers, for marriage or sexual exploitation;

11 Girls used as subjects of child pornography, which may cause them lasting damage;

12 Girls working under hazardous and exploitative conditions;

13 Migrant girls who cross international borders.

Violence against adolescent girls is often hidden. Yet there is evidence to indicate that it is widespread, and some young people even assume it to be the norm. The need for proper legislation, awareness-raising and education on the rights of girls and young women is not sufficiently recognised by planners and policy-makers.

2 Health of Adolescent Girls Including Reproductive and Sexual Health and Nutrition

Health is a state of complete physical, mental and social well-being, and not merely the absence of disease and infirmity. The health of adolescents is intimately linked to their development. Changing global conditions are placing greater strains on young people and modifying their behaviours and relationships, which are increasingly exacerbating some health problems. These health problems often fall on the young girls who are disadvantaged due to their age, gender and low economic status.

Adolescent girls who are no longer children, but not yet women, are denied rights and protections available to adult women. Because of their gender, they often suffer culture-bound violations and are exploited, abused and denied opportunities more available to adolescent boys. When they live in impoverished settings, they lack access to health services, education and gainful employment, all issues that have an impact on their health and well-being.

When [adolescent girls] *live in impoverished settings, they lack access to health services, education and gainful employment, all issues that have an impact on their health and well-being.*

Building on the international standards set by the CRC and CEDAW, and the consensus reached in the ICPD Programme of Action and the Beijing Platform for Action, which have recognised the rights of adolescent girls to reproductive and sexual health, including information, counselling and services, attention was drawn to the responsibilities of parents, communities, governments and international organisations in this regard. The importance of the active involvement of men and boys in this process was emphasised.

In the light of systematic discrimination against girls in many societies, as well as the conditions that force girls into early marriage and child-bearing, emphasis was placed on the critical need for self-reliance and empowerment of adolescent girls. It is also necessary that girls are helped to resist pressure to provide sexual favours in exchange for material goods, and to challenge the attitudes to adolescent girls as 'sex objects'. The need for relevant in- and out-of-school programmes and open, informed discussion of adolescent girls' reproductive and sexual health was recognised as an important way to reduce their problems with peers, parents and medical personnel. Programmes are needed to raise their self-esteem, develop support networks and re-examine the roles and impacts of existing institutions and country-based organisations.

Particular concerns expressed with regard to some health problems that particularly affect adolescent girls include:

1 Malnutrition and anaemia;

2 Sexual and reproductive health, including FGM, too early and unwanted pregnancy, adolescent maternal morbidity and mortality, unsafe abortion, sexually transmitted diseases (STDs) and HIV/AIDS;

3 Violence, including sexual abuse and incest;

4 Mental health;

While some progress has been made in putting the needs of adolescent girls on the agenda of governments, international organisations and NGOs, much more needs to be done.

5 Substance abuse including the use of tobacco, alcohol and other drugs.

While some progress has been made in putting the needs of adolescent girls on the agenda of governments, international organisations and NGOs, much more needs to be done. Many programmes have been effective while others have failed, but even the successful ones tend to be small scale. The need for new, effective means to address those issues was stressed.

The Meeting identified critical obstacles to adolescent girls' health, including nutrition and reproductive and sexual health:

1 The reluctance of society at large to address adolescent girls' reproductive and sexual health;

2 The lack of knowledge, information and skills among young people;

3 The lack of health provisions, including counselling services in all sectors designed for adolescents;

4 The lack of training for service providers and educators who interact with young people, especially in sensitive areas such as sexuality, which require skills in confidential counselling;

5 National policies, laws and practices that can be restrictive and/or inconsistent, or those of which the general public is not aware, or those that are inefficiently implemented and/or those that often limit the access of young people to services and information, for example by requiring the consent of another party;

6 Absence of national strategies for the health of young people, which could provide a framework for health care;

7 Inadequate support from the donor community.

It was recognised that interventions are needed in five major areas to improve the situation, as indicated in the WHO/ UNFPA/UNICEF document, *Action for Adolescent Health: Towards a Common Agenda*, drawn from the Study Group on Programming for Adolescent Health. These are:

1 The provision of information;

2 Strengthening skills;

3 Access to quality health services;

4 Provision of counselling;

5 A safe and supportive environment.

3 Creating an Enabling Environment for the Realisation of Human Rights and Empowerment of Adolescent Girls

Despite the critical importance of the adolescent period in a woman's life, until recently little effort has been made to accurately address and analyse the specific situation and needs of adolescent girls with an aim to realise their rights. Following the United Nations Decade for Women, 1976–1985, when data on women began to be increasingly collected and disaggregated by sex, children continued to be profiled as a collective entity, with the exception of data on schooling. Lack of sex- and age-disaggregated data on adolescent girls was a limitation to analysis, making it difficult to accurately define and assess their status. Later developments in regard to realising the human rights of women and children have not sufficiently helped to give priority to issues concerning adolescent girls. It was noted that very few States parties reporting on the CRC or CEDAW analyse or discuss adolescent girls. There is an urgent need for research in this area and the compilation of sex- and age-disaggregated data will help to deepen the understanding among the international community of the situation of adolescent girls, their status and the achievement of gender equality.

... the compilation of sex- and age-disaggregated data will help to deepen the understanding among the international community of the situation of adolescent girls, their status and the achievement of gender equality.

Accurate information is particularly important when analysing the enabling environment for the empowerment of adolescent girls to exercise their rights, as it encompasses a wide range of aspects, including education, socialisation, mass media, human rights and preparation for participation in social and political life as full citizens.

Girls continue to be under-valued both by society and by themselves and suffer from low self-esteem which prevents them from realising their full potential. This could lead to the detriment, not only of themselves, but of society as a whole.

There are many contributing factors to these problems, including poverty, social policies that are inadequate for

The male-female relationships in the family need to be redressed to serve as role models for girls and boys.

addressing the development of adolescent girls, stereotyping of adolescent girls in negative images in the mass media that tend to portray girls as passive, as victims or as sex objects. Teachers, textbooks and educational materials often perpetuate these same stereotypes of girls as passive and destined to serve others. Girls are not given sufficient opportunity for full education and training to equip them for a wide variety of potential roles in life. They are not provided with opportunities for non-traditional jobs and are not prepared for responsible decision-making and participation in matters that affect their lives or the community.

Girls are often forced to drop out of school because of pregnancy or violence or for economic reasons. These problems sometimes lead parents to stop them continuing in school or to disrupt their education.

Laws are often contradictory and derived from different sources in society. Commonly the law that is least favourable to the girl is applied. Even in countries with legal systems that provide for *de jure* equality, *de facto* discrimination of adolescent girls prevails.

The family, including male family members, has a crucial role to play. Gender roles are predisposed from birth and perpetuated in the family. The male-female relationships in the family need to be changed to serve as role models for girls and boys. However, one of the difficulties that needs to be overcome is reaching families to help them appreciate the value to them and to society of investing in the complete education and training of girls as well as boys.

Note

1 Extracted from the *Report of the Expert Group Meeting on Adolescent Girls and Their Rights*, Addis Ababa, Ethiopia, 13–17 October 1997. This meeting was held by the UN Division for the Advancement of Women in preparation for the 42nd session of the Commission on the Status of Women (CSW). The full report is available online at: *www.un.org/documents/ecosoc/cn6/1998/gchild/egmagr1997-rep1.htm*

4 Gender-based Violence

Meeting the Challenge to End Gender-based Violence

Tina Johnson

> Violence against women is an obstacle to the achievement of the objectives of equality, development and peace. Violence against women both violates and impairs or nullifies the enjoyment by women of their human rights and fundamental freedoms. The long-standing failure to protect and promote those rights and freedoms in the case of violence against women is a matter of concern to all States and should be addressed.
>
> (United Nations, 1995: para. 112)

Gender-based violence is violence that is directed at individuals on the basis of their gender, with women and girls making up the vast majority of victims (though boys and men can also be the target). It is indiscriminate, cutting across racial, ethnic, class, age, economic, religious and cultural divides.

Conceptual Framework

Gender-based violence: an overview

Gender-based violence is violence that is directed at individuals on the basis of their gender, with women and girls making up the vast majority of victims (though boys and men can also be the target). It is indiscriminate, cutting across racial, ethnic, class, age, economic, religious and cultural divides. Gender-based violence takes place throughout society: in the home, in the community and in state institutions (including prisons, police stations and hospitals). It can be grouped into five main, though not exclusive, categories:

1 Sexual violence – e.g. rape, incest, forced prostitution and sexual harassment;

2 Physical violence – e.g. wife battering and assault, 'honour' killings, female infanticide, child assault by teachers and gay bashing;

3 Emotional and psychological violence – e.g. threats of violence, insults and name calling, humiliation in front of others, blackmail and the threat of abandonment;

4 Harmful traditional practices – e.g. female genital mutilation,

denial of certain foods and forced and/or early marriage;

5 Socio-economic violence – e.g. discriminatory access to basic health care, low levels of literacy and educational attainment, inadequate shelter and food, economic deprivation, armed conflict and acts of terrorism.

Violence against women "is a manifestation of historically unequal power relations between men and women, which have led to domination over and discrimination against women by men and to the prevention of the full advancement of women," and is "one of the crucial social mechanisms by which women are forced into a subordinate position compared with men" (United Nations, 1993). Women's lack of social and economic power, accepted gender roles and the low value put on women's work perpetuate and reinforce this subordinate position. Early marriage, inheritance of widows and male control of property encourage female dependency, particularly in regions with high under- and unemployment of women and poor access to social welfare services, and limit women's ability to escape violent situations.

Intimate partner violence

The most widespread form of gender-based violence is physical abuse of a woman by a present or former intimate male partner. Thirty-five studies from a wide variety of countries show that, in many of them, one-quarter to more than half of women report such abuse (Heise et al, 1994). Forty per cent of all female homicide victims are killed by their intimate partners in the UK; while every year thousands of women suffer dowry-related deaths or are disfigured by acid thrown in their faces by rejected suitors in Bangladesh, India, Nigeria or Pakistan (UNIFEM, 2003). There is also considerable overlap between physical, emotional and sexual violence. Sexual abuse or rape by an intimate partner is experienced by between 12 and 25 per cent of women at some time in their lives (WHO, 2000). This is not considered a crime in most countries, since it is assumed that a marriage contract provides a husband with the right to sex with his wife whenever he chooses (UNICEF, 2000).

Violence against girls

A growing number of studies, particularly from sub-Saharan Africa, indicate that girls' first sexual experience is often unwanted and frequently forced (Garcia-Moreno and Watts, 2000). Research has shown that 36–62 per cent of all sexual assault victims are aged 15 or less (WHO, 1997). In addition, cross-cultural data from rape crisis centres reveal that 40–58 per cent of the sexual assault cases they deal with involve girls aged 15 and under, including girls younger than 10 or 11 (Heise et al, 1994). In fact, the younger a girl is at first sexual intercourse, the more likely that sex is forced. The abusers are frequently male relatives, family friends or other men in influential positions, such as teachers.

A growing number of studies, particularly from sub-Saharan Africa, indicate that girls' first sexual experience is often unwanted and frequently forced.

Harmful traditional practices

It is estimated that some 130 million women and girls, mainly in Africa, the Middle East and Asia, have undergone some form of FGM, which has both immediate and long-term negative health and psychological effects (UNFPA, 1999). Early marriage also exposes girls to physical violation and trauma, as well as greater health risks during pregnancy and childbirth.

Sex work and trafficking in women and girls

Women often take up sex work because they have no other way of supporting themselves or their children, or their entry into sex work may itself be as a result of violence. They are then at risk of further physical violence and rape, especially where this work is against the law, as the police may assault instead of protecting them. In a survey of prostitutes in Bangladesh, for example, 83 per cent had been raped and 91 per cent had been beaten by the police (WHO, 1997). In addition, trafficking is now among the fastest growing criminal activities worldwide and within countries (Sauerbrey, 2002). The International Organisation for Migration estimates that 700,000 women are transported, mostly involuntarily, across international borders each year for the sex trade (Binder, 2002). Two million girls between the ages of five and 15 are introduced into the commercial sex market each year (UNFPA, 2000).

Violence against women in armed conflict

In situations of armed conflict, currently experienced in some 30 countries, women and girls are often systematically targeted

Gender-based violence adversely affects victims, family members, perpetrators, communities and nations on profound emotional, physical, psychological and economic levels.

for abuse, and rape and sexual assault are widespread. Rape has been used as a deliberate weapon of war in many conflicts, including in Central Africa and the Balkans. Women and girls make up 75 per cent of the world's 22 million refugees, asylum seekers or internally displaced persons, putting them at particular risk of gender-based violence.

Gender-based violence and HIV/AIDS

Gender-based violence and HIV/AIDS are intersecting epidemics. Women's relative lack of control over their sexual lives and methods of preventing HIV and other sexually transmitted infections due to violence or fear of it is one of the main factors behind the spread of AIDS (Johnson, 2002). This lack of control is experienced not only by women who are sexually assaulted, but also by those in relationships where they are unable to negotiate condom use with their partners. Violence both exposes women to HIV infection and limits their ability to participate in and benefit from HIV/AIDS prevention methods and treatment.

Consequences of gender-based violence

Gender-based violence adversely affects victims, family members, perpetrators, communities and nations on profound emotional, physical, psychological and economic levels. It accounts for more death and ill health among women aged 15–44 worldwide than cancer, obstructed labour, heart disease, respiratory infections, traffic accidents or even war (World Bank, 1993).

Some of the consequences of gender-based violence are feelings of hopelessness and isolation, guilt and depression, or suicide. The more severe or longer term the abuse and violence, the greater the impact on women's autonomy, sense of worth and ability to care for themselves and their children. In concrete terms, it may lead to bruises, cuts, broken bones or limbs, unwanted pregnancies, sexually transmitted infections (including HIV/AIDS), permanent disabilities or death. Rape and domestic violence are major causes of disability and death among women of reproductive age in both developed and developing countries. In the latter, it is estimated that gender-based violence accounts for 5 per cent of the healthy years of life lost to women of reproductive age (World Bank, 1993).

Victims may also suffer from a loss of human potential and wages, resulting in personal economic hardship and depressed overall development. Violence – and the threat of violence – reduces women's and girl's opportunities for work, their mobility and their participation in education and training, community activities and wider social networks. In addition, there are direct economic costs to the country as a whole. For example, the direct annual cost of violence against women in Canada has been estimated at Canadian $684 million in the criminal justice system and $187 million for police. Counselling and training in response to violence is an additional $294 million, making a total of over Canadian $1 billion a year (Buvenic et al, 1999). The Governor of the Reserve Bank of Fiji Islands estimated the costs to that country to be $300 million, or 7 per cent of the gross domestic product (GDP).

Gender-based violence on the international agenda

The 1989 Convention on the Elimination of All Forms of Discrimination against Women does not refer specifically to gender-based violence. However, lobbying and advocacy work undertaken primarily by women's NGOs have led to increasing international understanding of this as a human rights issue. In 1992, the CEDAW Committee adopted General Recommendation 19, which identifies gender-based violence as a form of discrimination against women that seriously inhibits their ability to enjoy rights and freedoms on a basis of equality with men.

At the 1993 UN Conference on Human Rights in Vienna, governments signalled their recognition that this was an urgent issue to be addressed by calling for the drafting of the UN Declaration on the Elimination of Violence Against Women, adopted unanimously by the General Assembly in December of the same year. Violence against women was one of the Critical Areas of Concern of the Beijing Platform for Action, the document agreed to by governments at the UN Fourth World Conference on Women in 1995. This outlines three strategic objectives: to take integrated measures to prevent and eliminate violence against women; to study the causes and consequences of violence against women and the effectiveness of preventive measures; and to eliminate traffick-

Commonwealth governments ... agreed in the 1995 Commonwealth Plan of Action on Gender and Development that women's human rights and the elimination of violence against women, the protection of the girl child and the outlawing of all forms of trafficking in women and girls would be priority areas for action.

ing in women and assist victims of violence due to prostitution and trafficking.

Commonwealth governments further agreed in the 1995 Commonwealth Plan of Action on Gender and Development that women's human rights and the elimination of violence against women, the protection of the girl child and the outlawing of all forms of trafficking in women and girls would be priority areas for action. Eliminating gender-based violence is also integral to the achievement of the Millennium Development Goals adopted by 189 governments across the world in September 2000, and formally endorsed by Commonwealth Heads of Government in the Coolum Declaration of 5 March 2002.

Overview of Achievements

As noted above, the international community, regional bodies and national governments have in recent years affirmed their commitment to eliminating gender-based violence. It has been recognised as a human rights issue and as essential for the empowerment of women and for poverty eradication and equitable, sustainable development. Significant efforts have been made to update legal frameworks and initiate law reforms. A number of countries have adopted integrated approaches to tackle gender-based violence, and there are numerous examples of good practice in areas such as regional co-operation, public education and gender-awareness training for the police and judiciary.

Legislative changes

Substantial progress has been made to develop and put in place laws that address family violence and abuse, rape, sexual assault, FGM, trafficking and other gender-based violence. UNIFEM (2003) reports that at least 46 nations now have laws that explicitly prohibit domestic violence and 13 more are drafting new laws to do so, while in many others criminal assault laws have been amended to cover domestic violence. Marital rape is now recognised as a crime in 45 countries.

In the Caribbean, the Commonwealth Secretariat and the

Caribbean Community (CARICOM) Secretariat have collaborated on the development of model legislation on women's human rights. The legislation covers eight areas: domestic violence, sexual offences, sexual harassment, equal pay, inheritance, citizenship, equality for women in employment and maintenance. National governments in nine Caribbean countries have used the model legislation to introduce new legislation and/or revise existing laws. Guyana, Jamaica and St Lucia, for example, have enacted new domestic violence legislation. The Domestic Violence Act (1999) of Trinidad and Tobago widens the definition of 'domestic abuse' found in the 1991 Act to include psychological, emotional and financial abuse, as well as physical and sexual abuse. It also recognises that many couples in the country are part of 'visiting' or 'cohabitating' relationships rather than being married, and gives the police greater powers to take the perpetrators of violence into custody.

In Asia, under Malaysia's Domestic Violence Act (1994), domestic violence is attached to the Penal Code under definitions and procedures for hurt, criminal force and assault. This enables it to be classified as 'criminal behaviour' under federal jurisdiction (rather than coming under the Sharia jurisdiction of the states) and ensures its applicability to all Malaysians. A recently-added section in the Indian Evidence Act (section 114A) makes it an offence for persons in a custodian role (policemen, public servants, managers of public hospitals and remand homes and wardens of jails) to have sex with people for whom they are responsible.

In Southern Africa, Mauritius, Namibia, Seychelles and South Africa have passed legislation to deal specifically with domestic violence. Under the Protection from Domestic Violence Act, passed in Mauritius in 1997, for example, victims may report cases of domestic violence to enforcement officers who provide a range of services from transport to help with preparing an affidavit for presentation to a magistrate. The magistrate can issue an interim occupation or protection order to protect the victim while the case is being heard. Botswana, Seychelles and Tanzania have each amended their laws to allow evidence to be given *in camera*, to widen the definition of rape, to deny bail to persons charged with rape and to provide for stiffer sentences for convicted rapists. Malawi and Tanzania have amended their penal codes to address the

National plans of action to tackle violence against women have been instituted in many countries.

issue of people running businesses for prostitution and/or transporting or trafficking women for the purposes of prostitution. In a landmark judgement in 1999, the High Court of Malawi ruled that arresting a woman for prostitution but leaving her male partner free was discriminatory and unconstitutional. Mauritius has adopted provisions for severe penalties for trafficking in children.

In the Pacific, the criminal code in Papua New Guinea has been amended to include domestic violence as a criminal offence, and the Enticement Act and Adultery Act have also been amended. Legislation on sexual violence has also been passed and an amendment made to the Evidence Act to make it easier for victims of sexual violence to testify and to win justice.

Government policies

National plans and systems

National plans of action to tackle violence against women have been instituted in many countries. In East and Southern Africa, these plans were developed at national workshops on gender-based violence held in ten countries. The plan of action that emerged from the Mauritius workshop, for example, later endorsed by Cabinet, committed government and non-governmental stakeholders to undertake concrete legislation, services and preventative programmes to assist victims in a co-ordinated and efficient manner, and to sensitise the public on the law and procedures for its use.

The National Family Violence Networking System was developed in Singapore in 1996 to integrate the management of family violence. This system links police, prisons, hospitals, social service agencies, the courts, prisons and the Ministry of Community Development and Sports (MCDS) in a web of assistance for victims and perpetrators of family violence. Programmes include mandatory counselling for victims and perpetrators, training of social workers, and police, public education and court, police and community programmes.

More victim-friendly courts

A number of different approaches have been taken to making the courts more accessible to the victims of gender-based violence. For example, there is growing support in the Caribbean for family courts, which have been established in Belize, Grenada, Jamaica, St Lucia and St Vincent and the Grenadines. This is in line with a suggestion in the CARICOM model legislation that domestic violence cases should be heard at the magisterial level and decentralised. The courts are staffed by trained judiciary and supported by social services.

In the Pacific, the Chief Magistrate of Vanuatu introduced new rules in the Magistrates Courts in 2001 which provide for the granting of domestic violence protection orders and the provision of some security for survivors of domestic violence, as well as penalties for breaches and faster tracking of cases. In Papua New Guinea, good behaviour bonds, implemented by the Magisterial Service, assisted the victims of domestic violence.

Sexual harassment policies

The Fiji Islands Ministry of Women and the Fiji Women's Rights Movement are developing a policy on sexual harassment in the workplace. In Botswana, the Public Service Act was amended to include sexual harassment as misconduct.

Examples of good practice

Integrated approaches

Several countries have developed integrated approaches. For example, the Partnerships Against Domestic Violence Programme is a collaborative effort between the Australian Government and the States and Territories, and the business sector, NGOs and the community. Key projects include: community education campaigns; national competency standards for workers dealing with domestic violence; prevention workshops for young people; a clearing-house for information and best practices; and perpetrators' programmes. In Bangladesh, the Multi-Sectoral Programme on Violence Against Women is a government project led by the Ministry of Women and Children's Affairs with the participation of several related ministries. Naripokkho, a women's NGO, provides technical assistance in detailed project formulation, implementation and evaluation.

Although NGOs are the foremost providers of shelter to the victims of violence, Project Haven in the Philippines shows how governments and NGOs can pool their resources to respond to the needs of victims and survivors. The project is hospital-based and offers medical services, crisis intervention and healing, referrals, education and training, research and documentation for women victims of violence. The Women's Crisis Center (WCC) trains hospital staff on gender-sensitive handling of survivors and provides the psycho-social component and referrals to other agencies and institutions.

Similarly, Malaysia's WAVe (Women Against Violence) Campaign was launched at the federal and state levels in July 2001. The Ministry of Women and Family Development coordinates the initiative and fosters co-operation between government agencies, NGOs and the private sector. Training of volunteers is conducted in collaboration with NGOs and includes management of domestic violence, rape and sexual harassment cases by hospitals, police and the welfare department. Once trained, the volunteers are placed in the Ministry where they handle telephone calls and make appointments in the Ministry's counselling unit.

In Papua New Guinea, the Family and Sexual Violence Action Committee meets on a regular basis to review progress and identify ways forward. Its members come from government agencies, the private sector, NGOs, community groups and donor agencies.

Regional co-operation and agreements

One example of regional co-operation is the model legislation mentioned earlier that was developed by the CARICOM Secretariat and the Commonwealth Secretariat. This has been used not only by governments but also by NGOs and intergovernmental agencies in their research and advocacy work. UNIFEM also brought together other UN agencies and NGOs from Latin America and the Caribbean to develop an awareness-raising campaign, launched in 1998, around the theme 'A Life Free from Violence: It's Our Right'. The campaign was subsequently replicated in other regions.

Model legislation was also developed in the Asia-Pacific region, where the first Regional Ministerial Conference on People Smuggling, Trafficking in Persons and Related Transnational Crime was held in Bali in February 2002. It was intended to assist governments in drafting domestic laws criminalising people smuggling and trafficking in persons.

In 1998 Member States of the Southern African Development Community (SADC) agreed to an Addendum (to the SADC Declaration on Gender and Development) on the Prevention and Eradication of Violence Against Women and Children. This commits them to take urgent measures to prevent and address violence against women and children through legal, social, economic, cultural and political means and to adopt legally-binding instruments to ensure that these commitments are translated into action. More recently, the 2003 Protocol on the Rights of Women in Africa supplemented the provisions of the African Charter on Human and Peoples' Rights by requiring State parties to take appropriate measures to prohibit all forms of violence against women, identify the causes, punish the perpetrators and ensure effective rehabilitation and reparation for victims.

Governments in the Pacific region adopted the Pacific Platform for Action in 1995, which identified violence against women as a critical area of concern and urged the Pacific to work towards its elimination. At the NGO level, the Pacific Women's Network Against Violence Against Women, established in 1992, has played a key role in developing the skills and organisational capacity of NGOs working to end violence against women across the region. With 23 members in ten countries, it provides an important mechanism for sharing successful approaches and strategising to overcome resistance and constraints in work to end violence against women.

A number of regional workshops – in Southern Africa, Asia and the Pacific – have been held to strengthen partnerships for eliminating gender-based violence, jointly organised by the Commonwealth Secretariat and key national, regional and international stakeholders.

A number of regional workshops – in Southern Africa, Asia and the Pacific – have been held to strengthen partnerships for eliminating gender-based violence, jointly organised by the Commonwealth Secretariat and key national, regional and international stakeholders.

Using international law at the national level

National courts are increasingly looking to international norms for the purpose of deciding cases "where the domestic law – whether constitutional, statute or common law – is uncertain or incomplete" (Bart, 1997:117). In 1999, for example, the Supreme Court of India stated that international instruments – CEDAW, the International Convention on Economic, Social and Cultural Rights, the Beijing PFA – "cast an obligation on the Indian State to gender sensitise its laws, and the Courts are under an obligation to see that the message of international instruments is not allowed to be drowned" (Chinkin, 2000:60). In East Africa, the International Women Judges Federation has been working with universities and judiciaries to promote the use of international human rights instruments in national settings.

Improving the police response

Several countries have set up special units in the police force with a specific mandate on violence against women. For example, trained women police officers in the Victim Support Unit in Barbados provide counselling to victims of rape and child abuse, helping them to cope with their experience and preparing them to testify in court. In addition, a Regional Training Programme for Police Officers and Frontline Workers dealing with domestic violence is being co-ordinated by the Caribbean Association for Feminist Research and Action (CAFRA).

In the Philippines, Women and Children Protection Desks (WCPD) have been created by the police to improve their level of response to women and children who are victims of gender-based abuse, exploitation and discrimination. In Bangladesh, the Centre for Women and Children's Studies (CWCS) has brought together NGOs and police to design a training manual for law-enforcement personnel on gender-based violence, and have trained more than 400 police officers in 12 regions.

An integrated Community Safety Strategy for safer homes, streets and schools has been developed by Cook Islands. Important aspects of this include working with the police "from the inside out"; challenging police leadership and organisational culture; and collecting, analysing and sharing information with key partners.

Gender-awareness training for the judiciary

Gender Judges and Equality is a regional project in Asia that was conceived and initiated by Sakshi, an NGO in New Delhi. Workshops are held to sensitise senior members of the judiciary to women's issues and help them view matters from a woman's perspective. The strategy is to allow judges to exchange views and points of law as well as initiate debates with their peers on issues related to violence against women. As a result of the workshops, the conveners have received requests for materials from participants and there have been several positive rulings by the sensitised judges on cases related to violence.

At the national level, workshops were held in Jamaica in 1998 to sensitise justice system personnel – including judges, police, clerks of the court, lawyers, probation officers and social workers – to a gender perspective. In Canada, the Western Judicial Education Centre (WJEC) organises continuing education programmes for judges from the west and northwest. While a key element is 'peer leadership' (i.e. judges are trained by other judges), other interested people, including women and members of racial minorities, can participate in the sessions. At a workshop on gender equality, for example, survivors of sexual assault and crisis centre workers gave judges first-hand information about violence against women.

Several countries have made an effort to make the law accessible to more people.

Advocacy and public education

There are numerous examples of advocacy and public education initiatives from many different countries. Among the more innovative is the series of Grade 1–10 textbooks produced by the Simorgh Women's Resource and Publication Centre in Pakistan to promote equality and equity in gender relations as well as to teach children about violence in the context of power relations. The NGO carried out teacher training to familiarise teachers with the whole process and methodology of participatory teaching. It started with four schools but is now supplying books to over 30.

Other public education activities from various regions include a national 'One Act Play' competition by women at the grassroots in Mauritius; the development, production and distribution by fem'LINKpacific in Fiji Islands of media materials as community education tools to bring violence issues into the public sphere, particularly in rural areas; and the use of radio and television programmes, school and community discussions, information pamphlets and leaflets in St Vincent and the Grenadines to promote public awareness.

Several countries have made an effort to make the law accessible to more people. In Botswana, for example, after a review of the Children's Act to harmonise it with the Convention on the Rights of the Child, the Act was translated into Setswana, the local language. The Government of Bangladesh has attempted to popularise and disseminate CEDAW by translating it into Bangla.

Men's initiatives

In Malawi, the Network on Violence Against Women and the Malawi Human Rights Resource Centre (MHRRC), which co-ordinate non-governmental activities within the country, hold an annual Men to Men Symposium that gets more men involved in the issue. UNIFEM's End Violence Campaign encouraged men to demonstrate against violence in Kenya and South Africa, and helped to increase the involvement of men worldwide in the White Ribbon Campaign working to end men's violence against women. Other initiatives led by men include Men Against Abuse and Violence in Mumbai, India, focused on ending domestic violence, and Men Against Violence Against Women (MAVAW) in Trinidad and Tobago, which runs community-based programmes and produces leaflets on anger management and bumper stickers against battering.

Monitoring and indicators

The Third Ministerial Meeting on Women, convened by the Economic Commission for Latin America and the Caribbean (ECLAC) and the Caribbean Development and Co-operation Committee (CDCC) Secretariat in 1999, identified the need for ongoing review, monitoring and implementation of legislation to counteract and eradicate violence against women. ECLAC subsequently conducted a study to evaluate the implementation of domestic violence legislation in Antigua and Barbuda, St Kitts and Nevis, St Lucia and St Vincent and the Grenadines.

International Women's Rights Action Watch (IWRAW) Asia Pacific has developed a framework to monitor governments' implementation of CEDAW. The Asia Pacific Research and Resource Centre for Women (ARROW) has developed a framework of indicators for monitoring violence against women.

At the national level, the NGO Naripokkho in Bangladesh monitors the incidence of violence against women in the country through scanning national newspapers, collecting nationwide information on reported cases from Police Headquarters, and from reports from members of Naripokkho's networks. In addition, 22 police stations in Dhaka Metropolitan Area, two public hospitals and the Special Court trying cases under the Repression of Women Act are monitored regularly on handling of cases of violence against women. Partner organisations in 30 small towns are being trained and provided with technical assistance to carry out similar monitoring at district level. Findings are regularly shared in workshops with police, health-care personnel, lawyers and public prosecutors.

Providing accurate data

In order to collect data on violence against women, the World Health Organization (WHO) started a Multi-Country Study on Women's Health and Domestic Violence Against Women in 1997. The aims include: obtaining reliable estimates of the prevalence of violence against women in different countries in a standardised manner that allows for inter-country comparisons; and using the findings nationally and internationally to advocate for an increased response to gender-based violence. The study teams co-ordinate with research institutions, ministries of health, other government entities and NGOs. As of 2003, data collection had been completed in Bangladesh, Brazil, Japan, Namibia, Peru, Samoa, Tanzania and Thailand.

The Economic Commission for Latin America and the Caribbean (ECLAC) is also working on a gender statistics and indicators model to measure the incidence of and trends in violence against women.

Gaps, Constraints and Opportunities

National policy and institutional and legal frameworks

National policy and institutional and legal frameworks are still often inadequate, and co-ordination among different parts of government is lacking. Women's human rights have not been fully realised due to non-harmonisation of laws, lack of domestication of international treaties and the absence of a human rights framework for planning and programming. Stakeholder

National policy and institutional and legal frameworks are still often inadequate, and co-ordination among different parts of government is lacking. Women's human rights have not been fully realised due to non-harmonisation of laws, lack of domestication of international treaties and the absence of a human rights framework for planning and programming.

interventions generally remain fragmented, poorly co-ordinated and isolated.

According to UNIFEM (2003), only 17 nations have distinct legislation referring to sexual assault, while as few as three have legislation that specifically addresses violence against women as a category of criminal activity in itself. Laws tend to focus on domestic violence and rape and not deal with other violence such as sexual harassment and traditional practices such as FGM (only 14 countries have adopted laws on sexual harassment and nine have specific legislation outlawing FGM). Moreover, many countries do not recognise spousal rape in domestic violence laws, and those that do have laws against it often provide exemptions.

Civil laws that may appear to have little to do with violence may also limit women's ability to protect themselves and to leave violent situations – for example, if they have no legal access to divorce. Discriminatory laws on inheritance and the ownership of property also mean that women lack the economic ability to leave abusive relationships. There is a tendency in some countries to require mediation or other forms of alternative dispute resolution for family law matters, leaving women open to further abuse. Laws against trafficking may punish women for being illegal immigrants rather than prosecuting the traffickers.

Model laws have been developed that can be replicated or adapted to local situations. Commonwealth Law Ministers expressed their support in May 1999 for Commonwealth co-operation around the UN Convention to combat transnational organised crime (including its Protocols on preventing, suppressing and punishing trafficking in women and children, and on the illegal trafficking of migrants). An opportunity was also identified for co-ordinated, collective action to fight the commercial sexual exploitation of children using existing Commonwealth schemes for mutual assistance and co-operation in criminal matters.

Law enforcement

Criminal law is not enforced effectively and is therefore limited as a deterrent. Where women are offered no protection by the State, they are frequently afraid to bring charges. The majority of cases of violence against women are thus not reported. Those cases that are reported often do not result in successful prosecutions. Law enforcement officers, medical officers and judicial personnel can be insensitive to the needs of threatened and abused women and children. Despite the prevalence of violence against women, research from many countries – including Australia, Bangladesh, Canada, India, New Zealand and the UK – has shown that it tends to be treated less seriously by the police than crimes against men or property. There continues to be a perception of domestic violence as a private matter. Victims of gender-based violence may face further abuse in the judicial system due to a continuing tendency to think that women call sexual abuse or harassment on themselves by the way they dress or act. The issue of appropriate treatment as well as adequate punishment for perpetrators has not been a focus.

The dissemination of judicial decisions from other jurisdictions and shared understanding by judges can be important tools in addressing gender-based violence.

The dissemination of judicial decisions from other jurisdictions and shared understanding by judges can be important tools in addressing gender-based violence. For example, judicial colloquia held in the Commonwealth that focused specifically on the promotion of the human rights of women and the girl child through the judiciary produced recommendations that recognise the duty of an independent judiciary to interpret and apply national constitutions and laws in conformity with women's human rights. Gender sensitivity training for all levels of the court system and for the police have had encouraging results. Reforms of criminal justice systems may require evidence on the woman's past history to be inadmissible (as, for example, in the Bahamas and Barbados) and aggressive questioning and harassment in court to be prohibited (Chinkin, 1999).

Women's knowledge of and access to the law

Laws are of limited use if women do not know that they exist or are unable to take advantage of them. Due to economic, religious, social and cultural constraints, women's legal literacy and consciousness about their rights is generally low in developing countries, particularly among rural women.

Without access to legal information or legal aid, women may stay in abusive relationships or fail to apply for protection orders or maintenance for their children. A study in the Eastern Caribbean found that applicants and respondents in domestic violence matters were generally under-represented by lawyers, who did not consider such cases financially viable. A lack of legal assistance has a marked effect on success in court, and the personal and financial consequences for women can be far-reaching.

There is a need for legal aid and advisory services. Government-funded specialist women's legal services could play an important role in providing advice, information and referrals on legal matters that affect women. They could also help in overcoming the attitudinal barriers that women confront in the legal system, and help courts dominated by male judges and lawyers to understand female perspectives. National women's machineries (NWMs) could be instrumental in the systematic dissemination of information to women about their rights.

Human and financial resources

Support (as measured in budgetary allocations) for programmes addressing gender-based violence is limited. There are serious gaps in service provision, particularly for the victims of rape and other sexual violence, and services are not widespread enough to cover rural communities. Those services that do exist are handicapped by a chronic shortage of human and financial resources.

Governments have largely depended on women's groups and other NGOs for the provision of services and programmes, yet NGOs in many countries do not receive financial support from governments. In addition, NGOs often depend on donors, which threatens the viability and sustainability of their programmes.

There is inadequate participation by women in the formulation of policies, strategies and activities designed to ensure their economic empowerment. Capacity and information to engage the political leadership, as well as to support structures for women in power, are inadequate. NWMs are often under-resourced and have little clout within government. In the absence of high-level political commitment they face difficulties developing policy frameworks and action plans, let alone co-ordinating other key ministries.

It is important for gender-based violence to be seen as a national issue, not a 'women's issue'. The problem is not so much that resources are scarce but the manner in which they are allocated. Gender-responsive budgets provide an opportunity to examine the effects of government expenditure and revenue policies on women and men. They can also reveal the gaps between policy and budget.

It is important for gender-based violence to be seen as a national issue, not a 'women's issue'. The problem is not so much that resources are scarce but the manner in which they are allocated.

Traditional norms, beliefs, practices and attitudes

In a statement to the 2001 session of the UN Commission on Human Rights, the Asian Legal Resource Centre noted that progress to stop violence against women in Asian countries was seriously hampered by governments' failure to recognise that cultural values and traditional patterns had not changed (UNIFEM, 2003). This problem is not limited to the Asian region but is widespread.

Such customs and traditions may lead to a high level of acceptance of and justification for gender-based violence, particularly that occurring in the home. Women as well as men often perpetuate stereotypical gender roles and adhere to a belief in women's inferiority. Practices such as early marriage and FGM that attempt to control women's sexuality may continue even if formally legislated against. Judges in many countries in sub-Saharan Africa continue to apply discriminatory customary laws with regard to women's inheritance or ownership of property despite law reforms that give women equal rights. Traditional systems of conflict reconciliation, such as *bulubulu* in Fiji Islands, may be used to protect the honour of perpetrators of crimes rather than to bring justice for female victims.

States parties to CEDAW are obliged to "modify the social and cultural patterns of conduct of men and women, with a view to achieving the elimination of prejudices and customary and all other practices" based on ideas that one sex is superior or inferior to the other or on stereotyped gender roles (article 5). One important entry-point is education about gender equality from an early age. Another is community-based work and advocacy to influence attitudes and customs. A workshop in Southern Africa, for example, identified elders – as traditional advisors or marriage counsellors – as a special target for

A major obstacle in the search for solutions to violence against women has been the lack of reliable data on the root causes, magnitude and consequences of the problem.

community-based education programmes to prevent the perpetuation of gender-based violence. NGOs in Kenya have successfully introduced alternative rituals to FGM to celebrate the passage of girls into womanhood. They have also involved men and boys as advocates for change.

Inadequate data

A major obstacle in the search for solutions to violence against women has been the lack of reliable data on the root causes, magnitude and consequences of the problem. Countries will not be able to eliminate gender-based violence until they identify the true incidence and causes of types of violence that are most prevalent in their own society. It is currently difficult to compare data between countries because statistics are not collected in a standardised way. Countries may have looked at different populations, and abusive acts are differently defined and/or are considered crimes in some countries but not others. Police records may include gender-based violence under a general heading such as assault, making it difficult to extract the number of incidents involving women. In addition, sexual crimes tend to be under-reported, making it difficult to come up with accurate figures. While women's groups may be able to collect more data, UNIFEM (2003) points out that few of them have the means to provide the level of statistical evidence that is needed to build a valid record.

Conclusion

Despite legislative, administrative, judicial, educational and other efforts by governments, regional and inter-governmental agencies, and non-governmental and civil society organisations to address gender-based violence, it remains endemic throughout the Commonwealth and other parts of the world. Clearly, a different approach is needed to tackle this cross-cutting and complex phenomenon on all fronts.

The Commonwealth Integrated Approach to Eliminating Gender-based Violence was developed as a guide to government planning and action at the national level, and also involves collaboration with NGOs and civil society. It includes enactment of laws, co-ordination of key government ministries and the setting up of government systems. An integrated approach is intended to respond to the needs of all, while ensuring that those of the victim – whether to trained medical attention, counselling or legal recourse – are paramount. It enables different stakeholders to work in a co-ordinated manner to understand the problem, develop strategies to address it and take joint action at the local and national level. It promotes efficiency and adequacy of services and service delivery so that women are facilitated at all levels through a variety of organisational networks. The resource base is increased and the expertise and experience of the organisations involved are maximised.

Stakeholders include victims and their families, communities, institutions such as the police, cultural and religious leaders, employees, educational institutions and perpetrators. Within each category there are those interested in maintaining the status quo and those who wish to change it. Often, agencies and support systems work in isolation from each other, resulting in duplication and fewer achievements as well as wasting limited resources. The criminal justice system is generally punitive rather than preventive, and while women need the protection of the law, "the limitations of a predominant reliance on the legal system to eradicate violence against women has been pointed out repeatedly" (Clarke, 1998). Gender-based violence is not a 'women's issue'. It is a human rights violation as well as "an obstacle to the achievement of the objectives of equality, development and peace" (United Nations, 1993). Addressing it within a holistic framework can change the societal values, attitudes and behaviours that condone or encourage it, and eventually bring about its elimination.

References

Binder, David (2002). 'In Europe, Sex Slavery is Thriving Despite Raids', *New York Times*, 20 October, p. 8.

Buvinic, Mayra, Andrew Morrison and Michael Shifter (1999). *Violence in Latin America and the Caribbean: A Framework for Action, Technical Study*. Washington, DC: Inter-American Development Bank.

Chinkin, Christine (2000). *Gender Mainstreaming in the Legal and Constitutional Sector*. London: Commonwealth Secretariat.

Clarke, Roberta (1998). Violence Against Women in the Caribbean: State and Non-State Responses. New York: UNIFEM.

Committee on the Elimination of Discrimination against Women (1992). 'Violence Against Women', General Recommendation 19, UN Doc. A/47/38.

Coomaraswamy, Radhika (2003). 'Integration of the Human Rights of Women and the Gender Perspective: Violence against Women', Report of the Special Rapporteur on violence against women. E/CN.4/2003/75, 6 January.

Garcia-Moreno, Claudia and Charlotte Watts (2000). 'Violence Against Women: Its Importance for HIV/AIDS', *AIDS* 14 (supplement 3), pp. S253–S265.

Heise, Lori with Jacqueline Pitanguy and Adrienne Germain (1994). *Violence Against Women: The Hidden Health Burden*. Washington DC, World Bank Discussion Paper #255.

Johnson, Tina (2003). 'Sex, Violence and Death – The intersection of two global epidemics: HIV/AIDS and gender-based violence', MA thesis, Columbia University, February.

Piot, Peter (1999). 'HIV/AIDS and Violence against Women', presentation at the panel on Women and Health, 43rd Session, UN Commission on the Status of Women, New York, 3 March. *www.unaids.org/whatsnew/speeches/eng/ny3march99.html 21/05/02*

Rwezaura, Bart (1997). 'Protecting the Rights of the Girl-Child in Commonwealth Jurisdictions'. In Byrnes, Andrew, Jane Connors and Lum Bik (eds), *Advancing the Human Rights of Women: Using International Human Rights Standards in Domestic Litigation*. Hong Kong and New York: Commonwealth Secretariat.

Sauerbrey, Ellen (2002). Statement by the US Representative to the UN Commission on the Status of Women, at the 3rd Committee, 9 October. USUN press release #148 (02). *http://www.un.int/usa/02_148.htm 10/11/02*

United Nations (1993). 'Declaration on the Elimination of Violence against Women', General Assembly resolution 48/104, 48 UN

GAOR Supplement (No. 49) at 217, UN Doc. A/48/49.

—— (1995). *Platform for Action and the Beijing Declaration*, Fourth World Conference on Women, Beijing, China, 14–15 September. New York: UN Department of Public Information.

United Nations Children's Fund (UNICEF) (2000). 'Domestic Violence Against Women and Girls', *Innocenti Digest* (6), May.

United Nations Development Fund for Women (UNIFEM) (2003). *Not a Minute More: Ending Violence Against Women*. New York: UNIFEM.

United Nations Population Fund (UNFPA) (1999). *Population Issues*. New York: UNFPA.

—— (2000). *The State of the World Population – Lives Together, Worlds Apart: Men and Women in a Time of Change*. New York: UNFPA.

World Bank (1993). *World Development Report 1993: Investing in Health*. New York: Oxford University Press.

World Health Organization (1997). 'Violence against Women Information Pack: A Priority Health Issue'. Geneva: WHO. *http://www.who.int/frhwhd/VAW/infopack/English/VAW_infopack.htm 21/05/02*.

—— (2000). *Violence Against Women and HIV/AIDS: Setting the Research Agenda*, meeting report, Geneva, 23–25 October. Geneva: WHO.

5 Trafficking in Women

Trafficking in Women: Causes, Consequences and Responses

Meena Shivdas

Introduction

Trafficking in human beings has, historically, taken many forms, including slavery and slavery-like practices. The International Labour Organization (2003) suggests that the term 'trafficking' came to be used in its current form – referring to the illicit movement of humans – in the late 20th century. Although there are varying definitions of trafficking, it is acknowledged that it is a complex series of states and events that involves the movement of human beings under coercion or deception which leaves them in vulnerable situations without recourse to their human rights.

Trafficking in women and children has come under increased scrutiny since the early 1990s with perspectives from NGOs and feminists gaining currency with interventionists and donors. According to Williams and Masika (2002), the factors that define the coercive and exploitative practices characterising current trafficking trends include inequality and oppression based on gender, age, caste and poverty. Many analysts have identified the globalisation of economies, with its facilitation of human movement and opening of national borders, on the one hand, and stringent immigration laws of developed countries, on the other, as leading to a climate conducive to the trafficking of women and children. It is within the framework of competing discourses on trafficking and the complex nature of interventions that Jordan (2002) identifies the various reasons for inappropriate or inadequate responses. These include denial of the problem, the objectification of victims and consequent failure to consider their human rights, conflation of trafficking with undocumented migration and an improper or ambiguous 'criminal' definition of trafficking.

... it is clear that trafficking leads to a denial of human rights of individuals and ... the outcomes of being trafficked involve more than just forced sex work.

Although most trafficking discourses tend to frame the trafficking of women and children from the standpoint of sexual exploitation and coercion, trafficking can be seen as an outcome of a process through which:

- Individuals are recruited and moved within and across national borders without informed consent and eventually forced to 'work' against their will;
- The trafficked individual then loses control over her/his life (Jana et al, 2002).

From the above definition it is clear that trafficking leads to a denial of human rights of individuals and that the outcomes of being trafficked involve more than just forced sex work. This paper provides a brief background on trafficking, including definitions used and the conceptual distinction between trafficking, migration and people smuggling, and identifies the various outcomes of being trafficked. It then offers a brief summary of the trafficking situation in certain Commonwealth countries. A review of international instruments is covered before turning to policy gaps and best practices, and the paper then raises a number of points about the conceptual categories used in definitions of trafficking to show how these lead to the recommendation of interventions that may or may not benefit trafficked women. The final part of the paper elaborates on a human rights approach to combat trafficking.

Situating Processes and Outcomes, Identifying Actors and Causes

Main features of trafficking

The process of trafficking and its various outcomes have been identified as complex and difficult to delineate. However, certain salient features can be made out:

At the point of origin, these include:

1 Coercive or persuasive processes that lead to the movement of people with promises of 'work' that they are often misinformed about;

2 The participation of certain actors who could be agents,

recruiters, acquaintances, friends or family members;

3 The exchange of money at the initial stage of the journey, which places people under debt, threat and insecurity.

At the point of destination, these include:

1 Being met by people who may confiscate the trafficked person's travel documents and/or take them to the workplace or place of residence;

2 The trafficked person may realise that the picture is not what it was made out to be and that more debts have been incurred;

3 The work engaged in could involve long hours in the construction, agriculture, garment/sweatshop, food processing, domestic work, manufacturing and sex sectors;

4 There would be no formal contract, and no regulation over wages, holidays, benefits and access to services;

5 There could be undue control exercised over the trafficked persons through threats, violence, reprisals back home and fear of being reported to authorities and facing deportation.

... trafficking can be defined as the illegal movement of people made under coercion and/or deception, which places the trafficked persons in vulnerable, indebted and insecure positions in work sectors that do not guarantee them safety of personhood and access to rights and benefits.

Trafficking, migration and people smuggling

From the above, trafficking can be defined as the illegal movement of people made under coercion and/or deception, which places the trafficked persons in vulnerable, indebted and insecure positions in work sectors that do not guarantee them safety of personhood and access to rights and benefits. Migration, on the other hand, is the voluntary movement of both skilled and unskilled persons in search of economic and social improvement to situations that are generally not exploitative or oppressive. Migrants can be both documented and undocumented. People smuggling has elements of both migration and trafficking. While people are smuggled using illegal channels akin to trafficking, those smuggled may have volunteered/agreed to being smuggling (much like the choice to move made by migrants).

Although we can make such analytical distinctions, in real-life situations these can become blurred. For example, according to Doezema (2000), the differences in the way feminist groups perceive sex trafficking causes current anti-trafficking campaigns to become split along ideological lines defining sex work, which make distinctions between voluntary and forced sex work problematic. The first position, or the abolitionist perspective (Barry, 1995), views trafficking and sex work as a violation of human rights. The second position, or the sex workers' rights movement's perspective (Skrobanek et al, 1997), makes a distinction between voluntary and forced sex work, i.e. they are against trafficking of women for sex work but recognise that choice in sex work exists. These two positions, however, do not consider the range of states between victims and agents where trafficked women's lives can be situated and which would have implications for the way interventions are planned.

Causes of trafficking

It has already been pointed out that complex interacting socio-economic and political structures that marginalise people on the basis of class, caste, gender and ethnicity create the climate for trafficking. Factors on the supply side, such as natural disasters, vulnerabilities arising from personal problems, discriminatory cultural practices and gender-based discrimination, may place women seeking physical and economic security at risk of being trafficked. On the demand side, restrictive immigration laws and policies, the need for cheap labour and the presence of trafficking rings with connection to corrupt public officials facilitate the entry of trafficked women into work sectors that may endanger their health (e.g. exposure to sexually transmitted infections, including HIV/AIDS) and also leave them socially stigmatised.

A Commonwealth Secretariat report (2003) has elaborated on new dimensions of trafficking given the forces of globalisation at play, including liberalisation of services and the spread of information and communications technologies. We know that, increasingly, economic migrants are educated and highly skilled and seek economic opportunities outside their countries. At the same time, we also know that developed countries source for a cheaper labour force to cut costs and still meet demands for products and services. The ILO (2003) asserts that if sensible migration policies were in place in both origin and destination countries, then there would be a chance of orderly labour migration. However, with the closure or even severe restrictions on migration channels, the climate for trafficking is created. While men may be able to legally migrate to work in, for example, the agriculture and construction sectors, women may be excluded from using legal migration channels and are particularly vulnerable to being trafficked for other kinds of work. Analysts and activists also point out that women tend to be excluded from the migration policies of their countries on the basis of gender, and this type of discrimination may also extend to destination countries.

While men may be able to legally migrate to work in, for example, the agriculture and construction sectors, women may be excluded from using legal migration channels and are particularly vulnerable to being trafficked for other kinds of work.

Trafficking and criminal networks

While considerable attention is paid to the situation in sending countries, it is in countries of destination that most of the human rights violations of trafficked persons take place. Most of these are developed countries and most trafficked persons end up in the unorganised and invisible sectors like domestic services or the sex sector. Attempts to facilitate the realisation of trafficked persons' labour and human rights are fraught with problems, given the involvement of crime syndicates. Bruggeman (2002) from EUROPOL argues that organised criminal networks are increasingly becoming involved in the trafficking of people as huge profits are at stake and there is evidence to show that criminal networks are closely linked to sex trafficking (ICMDP, 1999). Current estimates peg profits from trafficking at US$12 billion a year as criminal networks are able to hire out the systems and structures that they use for the movement of other contraband, such as drugs and vehicles, for the movement of humans as well (ILO, 2003).

According to the Commonwealth Secretariat (2003), traffickers manipulate legal migration channels in many ways including:

- using legal entry mechanisms such as work visas, student permits and business and transit visas to facilitate unlawful and extended stays for trafficked persons; and
- using stolen or counterfeit travel documents and avoiding border controls in the course of transporting people.

... trafficking networks often enjoy political patronage and/ or rely on corrupt public officials to facilitate their work.

The report further states that trafficking networks often enjoy political patronage and/or rely on corrupt public officials to facilitate their work. Research in the South Asian context bears this out (D'Cunha, 1991; Shivdas, 2003). Trafficking networks are extensive, with links between points of origin and points of destination. They involve a wide slew of actors, from women and men at village and town levels to those who operate in border areas and agents to recruiters at different areas in destinations, including workplaces and safe houses.

Some outcomes of trafficking

What are the outcomes of trafficking? In addition to women and girls being trafficked into the sex industry, some specific examples often cited include cases of young boys from Bangladesh being trafficked to the Gulf States to become camel jockeys and young girls in India being trafficked for domestic work overseas. Nepali girls are trafficked into the Indian circus industry. Cases of women being trafficked for marriage have been recorded by human rights groups. Two hundred and thirty-eight women from Sri Lanka ended up in a factory in the Middle East and worked for a pittance till the factory closed before their 'contracts' expired. Despite being promised full wages and benefits, they received token wages and were deported after being given US$100 each (GAATW, 1999). The International Organisation for Migration (IOM) has also recorded cases of old women, handicapped persons and children being trafficked for begging.

An ILO report (2003) asserts that people of all ages are trafficked across South Asia and into carpet workshops, garment factories, street hawking, begging, brick kilns, construction projects and tea plantations. The report also suggests that children are trafficked within and across the borders of Central and South America and West and Central Africa for domestic service. In the Middle East and North Africa, Asian men are trafficked for manual and construction work and women find themselves exploited and oppressed in domestic services.

Examining the Trafficking Situation in Various Regions

Africa

In Africa, Sita (2003) identifies two main types of trafficking: trafficking in children mainly for domestic work and farm labour across and within national borders; and trafficking in women and children for sexual exploitation mainly outside the region. Ghana has been identified as a country of origin where 'connection men' or traffickers are sighted frequently at border crossings; a corresponding increase in fake visas has also been noted (IOM, 2001). The immigration services in Ghana estimated that 3,582 women were trafficked between 1998 and 2000, while 535 trafficked women were repatriated to Ghana during 1999–2000. Ghanaian women are trafficked to Belgium, Côte d'Ivoire, Italy, Lebanon, Libya, the Netherlands, Nigeria and the US. Belgium, Côte d'Ivoire, the Netherlands and Spain are also destination points for trafficked Nigerian women. IOM notes that in Central and Western Africa, women are trafficked as domestic workers to Kuwait and Saudi Arabia from Mali. Children from Benin are exploited as workers in plantations, in the sex industry and as domestic helpers in Burkina Faso, Côte d'Ivoire and Nigeria. Young women and girls in Uganda are trafficked by the Lord's Resistance Army to neighbouring Sudan and sold as sex slaves.

Sita (2003) notes that not all of the countries of the Economic Community of West African States (ECOWAS) have specific legislation that criminalises trafficking in women and children, as current penal codes focus on kidnapping and abduction. Significantly, under these provisions parents and guardians are exempt but there is evidence of family collusion in trafficking. Makkai (2003) reports that initiatives to address trafficking include the Western African region's action plan to combat trafficking, a bilateral arrangement between Côte d'Ivoire and Mali for the prevention of trafficking for child labour and an agreement on a Platform for Action by West and Central African States.

... not all of the [ECOWAS] countries ... have specific legislation that criminalises trafficking in women and children, as current penal codes focus on kidnapping and abduction. Significantly, under these provisions parents and guardians are exempt but there is evidence of family collusion in trafficking.

Asia

In Asia, sub-regional hubs for trafficking have been identified and include India, Japan, Korea and Thailand. These hubs serve as a source, transit and destination for trafficking (Senta, 2003). In South-East Asia, IOM (2001) traces the trafficking of Vietnamese women and children to Cambodia, China, Singapore, Taiwan and Thailand. In 2000, IOM noted that women from Eastern Europe and Latin America were being trafficked into Asia. Many of the countries do not have specific legislation on trafficking offences so official statistics are rare. The UN and its agencies, including UNIFEM, the ILO and the Economic and Social Commission for Asia and the Pacific (ESCAP), are co-ordinating an anti-trafficking initiative in the Mekong region. At the ASEAN[1] level, Australia, Indonesia, Malaysia, New Zealand, Thailand and the Indochinese countries have initiated a regional level research and training programme.

In South Asia, the Middle East and Gulf countries are destinations to which women are trafficked for both sex work and domestic work. India is a major hub for trafficked Bangladeshi and Nepali women. Bangladeshi women are trafficked through India to Pakistan, while Sri Lankan women are trafficked to the Gulf States and Singapore. Nepal and India have anti-trafficking legislation. The 2002 SAARC[2] Convention on trafficking provides a framework for sub-regional co-operation and action.

Europe

Lehti and Aromaa (2003) assert that member countries of the European Union are destination countries, while Eastern Europe, the Balkans and the Commonwealth of Independent States (CIS) countries are source or transit countries. IOM (2001) information indicates that trafficked Nigerian women can be found in Belgium, Italy, the Netherlands and Spain. Belgium is often a destination country for trafficked Filipina, Nigerian, Thai and Ukrainian women. Brazilian, Chinese and Thai women have been trafficked to the UK and Ukrainian women to the Balkans and Germany. According to data obtained by STV,[3] of the 205 women known to have been trafficked into the Netherlands in 1998, 131 were from Central and Eastern Europe, 35 from Africa, 24 from Latin America and 15 from Asia. EUROPOL and governments of Europe are working on the issue. In 1988 the Dutch government began granting temporary resident permits for trafficked women who choose to testify against traffickers or who would like some time to determine whether to proceed with criminal action against their traffickers.

The Americas and the Caribbean

According to Woodbridge (2003), geographic and economic factors facilitate the sex trafficking of women from Latin American countries. Colombia has been identified as a hub for trafficking in the region and, as pointed out earlier, Latin American women are increasingly being trafficked to different Asian countries.

In the case of North America, particularly the US and Canada, Albanese and Donnelly (2003) suggest that there are no reliable national estimates for the extent of trafficking, although it is known that trafficking occurs for sex work and sweatshop and domestic labour. The available evidence suggests that Canada is both a destination and transit country for the US. According to Albanese and Donnelly, emerging studies have found links across different ethnic groups to improve efficiency and profits from trafficking.

From the above, it can be said that not many countries of the Commonwealth remain untouched by trafficking in women and girls. Governments and NGOs are attempting to address the issue at policy, programmatic and advocacy levels. However, gaps in policy exist and there have been increased calls to consider the rights of trafficked women during policy planning and implementation.

... not many countries of the Commonwealth remain untouched by trafficking in women and girls. Governments and NGOs are attempting to address the issue at policy, programmatic and advocacy levels. However, gaps in policy exist and there have been increased calls to consider the rights of trafficked women during policy planning and implementation.

Reviewing International Instruments

Let us now consider the concept of trafficked person's rights – as expounded by CEDAW, the Optional Protocol to Prevent, Suppress and Punish Trafficking in Persons especially Women and Children and the Beijing Platform for Action (PFA) – in

Identified practices that put women at special risk of violence and abuse include sex tourism, the recruitment of female domestic labour from developing countries to work in developed countries and organised marriages between women from developing countries and foreign nationals.

order to examine how trafficked women's rights could be protected in the international arena.

Two international instruments, particularly article 6 of the CEDAW Convention and the 1949 UN Convention on Traffic in Persons and Exploitation of the Prostitution of Others, address trafficking mainly in the context of forced sex work. It is only the Optional Protocol that provides the first internationally accepted definition of trafficking and broadens the scope of human trafficking to include exploitative sex work, forced labour or services and the removal of organs.

CEDAW

Article 6 of CEDAW reads: "States Parties shall take all appropriate measures, including legislation, to suppress all forms of traffic in women and exploitation of prostitution of women". The general recommendations to article 6 state clearly that certain practices are incompatible with the equal enjoyment of rights by women and do not respect their rights and dignity. Identified practices that put women at special risk of violence and abuse include sex tourism, the recruitment of female domestic labour from developing countries to work in developed countries and organised marriages between women from developing countries and foreign nationals. Poverty and unemployment are noted as factors that increase opportunities for trafficking in women. In addition, specific protective and punitive measures are recommended for wars, armed conflicts and the occupation of territories as they are seen to increase prostitution, trafficking in women and sexual assault of women.

The main mechanism for getting States to comply with CEDAW's recommendations on trafficking is through the CEDAW Committee's assessments of national reports. While the Committee can urge governments to enact appropriate legislation, there is no means through which governments can be forced to make legislative changes. However, the Concluding Comments released by the Committee for each reporting country often serve to bring to the public domain certain key concerns that may not have been addressed by governments. For example, in the case of Singapore's initial and second periodic report presented in 2001, the Committee noted with some concern that trafficking of women had not been addressed and therefore urged the Government to include trafficking in its next report. Women's groups in Singapore could use the Concluding Comments of the CEDAW Committee as the basis for their advocacy work. In addition, trafficked women who have been unsuccessful in claiming justice could use the Optional Protocol to CEDAW if their countries have signed it. However, given the cross-border nature of trafficking, the use of this Protocol may become complicated.

Optional Protocol on Trafficking

The 1949 UN Convention on Traffic in Persons and Exploitation of the Prostitution of Others classified all cases of recruitment into prostitution as "traffic in persons" and thereby ignored other kinds of trafficking in related areas such as entertainment (Dottridge, 1999). It also criminalised even cases where consent for sex work exists (Wijers and Lap-Chew, 1997). However, the Optional Protocol to Prevent, Suppress and Punish Trafficking in Persons especially Women and Children (2000) attempts to go beyond the 1949 Convention to outline the definition of trafficking as:

> ... the recruitment, transportation, transfer, harbouring or receipt of persons, by means of the threat or use of force or other forms of coercion, of abduction, of fraud, of deception, of abuse of power or of a position of vulnerability or of the giving or receiving of payments or benefits to achieve the consent of a person having control over another person for the purpose of exploitation. Exploitation shall include, at a minimum, the exploitation of the prostitution of others or other forms of sexual exploitation, forced labour or services, slavery, servitude or the removal of organs.

Doezema (2002) has shown that differences at the Vienna deliberation that finalised the Protocol about the notion of 'consent' to define trafficking in women posed problems for activists as they also lobbied for the inclusion of protective human rights mechanisms for migrant sex workers. Jordan (2002) asserts that an opportunity for including a human rights approach was lost as governments perceived the Protocol as only a law enforcement instrument and not an outline of pro-

... trafficked women often lose their rights to justice because of entrenched gender and moral biases in laws and policies and the discriminatory perceptions and attitudes of state agents in institutions such as the judiciary and the police force.

tective human rights measures. They held that national legislation served that purpose. Jordan, however, maintains that activists and international institutions still have an opportunity to influence national efforts to create anti-trafficking laws as many governments have signed the new Protocol and are obliged to adopt domestic laws that are in keeping with its provisions.

Other instruments

The 1995 Beijing PFA, Strategic Objective D.3, calls on governments to protect the rights of trafficked women and girls through strengthening existing legislation. Further, the Protocol against the Smuggling of Migrants by Land, Air and Sea, supplementary to the UN Convention against Transnational Organised Crime, entered into force on 28 January 2004 and offers the scope to lobby for changes in laws. Under this Protocol, governments have agreed to make migrant smuggling a criminal offence under national laws, adopt special measures to crack down on migrant smuggling by sea, boost international co-operation to prevent migrant smuggling and seek out and prosecute offenders. States parties to the Protocol have also agreed to adopt domestic laws to prevent and suppress activities related to the smuggling of migrants. Commonwealth governments that have signed the Protocol include Botswana, Canada, The Gambia, Jamaica, Namibia, New Zealand and Nigeria.

Despite assurances and commitments by governments, it is acknowledged that trafficked women often lose their rights to justice because of entrenched gender and moral biases in laws and policies and the discriminatory perceptions and attitudes of state agents in institutions such as the judiciary and the police force. There is also often a tendency towards criminalisation of all categories of trafficked workers. Rehabilitation and reintegration mechanisms seeking to improve trafficked women's situations are often inadequate and seem to draw attention to women's social stigma if they have been engaged in sex work.

Discussing Policy Gaps

The critical element about trafficked women's rights is not the process through which they were trafficked or the work sector they ended up in but that they are in positions of 'no-return' or without recourse to securing their rights. Policy approaches should therefore focus on this area of 'protection'. The two other levels of intervention are 'prevention' and 'reintegration'. Jana et al (2002) assert that not many attempts have been made by governments and NGOs engaged in addressing trafficking to either plan and implement standard human rights codes of practices or involve trafficked women in devising strategies for prevention and reintegration.

Protection

Given the global and transborder nature of trafficking, international instruments and bilateral and regional agreements represent policy response at the different levels. Therefore CEDAW, the Beijing PFA, the various Conventions and regional agreements, such as the SAARC Convention on trafficking and bilateral arrangements like the 1994 accord between Belgium and the Philippines, convey governments' recognition of the problem and their intentions to protect trafficked women's rights. However, Toepfer and Wells (1997) assert that international instruments on trafficking in women often lack legal force as they are qualified by reservations that limit their binding effects.

At the regional level, limitations to an agreement can be demonstrated through examining the SAARC Convention on trafficking. This has been criticised for restricting the scope of trafficking to sex work when women in the region are also trafficked, for example, for domestic work and the circus industry and boys and men are trafficked for other types of work (ILO, 2003). Sanghera and Kapur (2000) argue that the notion of 'consent' is not acknowledged and is considered irrelevant to the issue of sex trafficking; more importantly, State parties are directed to use criminal law, which may not heed women's rights. For example, the Convention requires 'victims' to be repatriated to their country of origin irrespective of individual choices made to remain in sex work in a foreign country (ADB, 2002). IOM (2002) points out that the Convention

Current mechanisms/ strategies for the protection of trafficked women in sex work are mainly about 'rescue' and not focused on protecting the women from pimps, traffickers or brothel owners who violate their rights.

does not have provisions to secure the rights of trafficked women when they are detained or imprisoned.

In addition, activists working on trafficking in countries of origin (Bangladesh, Nepal and Sri Lanka) have pointed out that the Convention does not address the accountability and responsibilities of destination countries (India and Pakistan). Trafficked women's testimonies are also not considered in the investigation procedures set out in the Convention. Given that state agents in the different countries would be mainly interested in the mechanisms of working out procedures for repatriation, they are not likely to consider individual trafficked women's needs to stay on in a foreign country due to fears about reintegration and social stigma. Activists assert that because of such flaws in addressing accountability, the legal framework of the Convention is also flawed and therefore would not provide trafficked persons with sufficient social and legal redress (Mo, 2001).

Current mechanisms/strategies for the protection of trafficked women in sex work are mainly about 'rescue' and not focused on protecting the women from pimps, traffickers or brothel owners who violate their rights. In other words, trafficked women are taken out of exploitative environments, but the dominant and oppressive structures and persons remain largely unaddressed. A Kvinnoforum study (2003) of European good practice on trafficking approaches found that there were no good practices for witness protection in destination countries and no protection whatsoever in countries of origin.

Prevention

Other examples of gaps in policy arise when the fines or penalties for trafficking are not enough of a deterrent to override the substantial profits that can be made through trafficking (Bertone, 2000). Some countries have addressed this issue. Canada, for example, increased fines for convicted traffickers from Can$10,000.00 to Can$100,000.00 in 1993, and passed a law in 1997 stipulating that women who seek entry into the country as 'entertainers' have to show proof of their profession in order to prevent them from being trafficked. However, businesses in Canada have criticised this law as it restricts their procedures and business plans (ibid).

In Nigeria, the July 2003 law that imposes a life sentence on anyone caught trafficking in humans, and which also prescribes a fine of 100,000 Naira (about US$1,000) for any Nigerian convicted of human trafficking, has been welcomed by activists. Until recently, laws on human trafficking and sex work in Nigeria had been found in various criminal codes, and punishments for offenders were largely not enforced.

However, an example of a well-intentioned law to address prevention of trafficking that has had negative consequences for women's rights to movement and livelihoods is found in Bangladesh, where single women are prevented from travelling across borders (Jana et al, 2002). CARE[4] (2001) has noted that the State, in collaboration with certain NGOs, has set up booths in border areas where women are questioned about their identity and intentions before being allowed to proceed or not.

Reintegration

At the level of reintegration, rescued trafficked women are usually kept under police custody and/or under the supervision of social services or welfare departments in remand homes or shelters. D'Cunha (1991) and Shivdas (2003) have suggested that government remand homes in Mumbai, India, are not without problems and that police officials – particularly beat constables in red light areas – have informal financial arrangements with brothel keepers to ignore the presence of trafficked women in brothels. Repatriation measures are complex and often take time to be worked out as investigations and lengthy court procedures get underway in destination countries, and NGOs and governments in countries of origin grapple with preparing families and communities to accept trafficked women returnees. A crucial aspect of repatriation is the shame and stigma that surround returnee women's lives when they attempt to reintegrate. If the women are HIV positive their return is further complicated and they may not find appropriate health services in the country of origin.

The transborder nature of trafficking necessitates co-operation between governments of countries of origin and countries of destination so that laws in different countries work in tandem to not only prosecute traffickers but also protect trafficked women victims.

Best Practices

Given all of the above, and other gaps in policy highlighted by analysts and academics (Sanghera and Kapur, 2000; Makkai, 2003; Skrobanek et al, 1997), this section outlines some innovative practices that consider trafficked women's rights and needs during interventions.

The transborder nature of trafficking necessitates co-operation between governments of countries of origin and countries of destination so that laws in different countries work in tandem not only to prosecute traffickers but also to protect trafficked women victims. An example of such co-operation can be found in the collaboration between US, EU and Eastern European officials and represents a policy approach that brings together countries of origin and countries of destination to determine appropriate common and compatible measures that are in keeping with national laws.

To accord trafficked women their rights to protection at the time of prosecution of their traffickers, the governments of Belgium, Italy and the Netherlands issue temporary resident permits to trafficked women victims to enable them to give evidence against traffickers. The US government is to issue T visas for victims of trafficking who assist authorities with the investigation of trafficking cases, and the EU is considering the introduction of short-term residence permits for trafficked victims (ILO, 2002). While the policy of granting temporary resident permits to trafficked victims is gaining ground, the crucial area of witness protection still remains unexplored.

At the level of international organisations, agencies and NGOs, there are a number of examples of appropriate interventions. The ILO initiative on trafficking, called the Special Action Programme to Combat Forced Labour, works in different regions and collaborates with other UN agencies and NGOs to conduct research, devise programmes and work with governments to address the causes and consequences of trafficked labour.

Because trafficking often involves the movement of women from different cultures and ethnicity to richer countries, an NGO like TAMPEP (Transnational AIDS/STD Prevention among Migrant Prostitutes in Europe) works towards empowering migrant and trafficked sex workers in Europe by using information that is culturally appropriate (Brussa, 1999).

SAGE, a human rights NGO based in the US, works to raise awareness about the impact of sex trafficking and exploitation on the lives of women and girls through its programmes for male clients (Commonwealth Secretariat, 2003). The Durbar Mahila Samanwaya Committee in Sonagachi, Kolkata, India also works with clients to raise awareness about HIV/AIDS issues and violations of trafficked women's rights. In addition, this committee has instituted self-regulatory boards that address trafficked female sex workers' rights in the context of the exploitation and oppression prevalent in brothels. The boards comprise sex workers, locally elected officials, legal experts, state representatives and medical doctors. Board members counsel the women and devise supportive and informal repatriation for them in collaboration with sex workers' groups and NGOs in their countries of origin. Jana et al (2002) argue that collectivisation of sex workers and the establishment of self-regulatory boards may be a way forward. These boards are well placed not only to monitor the exploitation and oppression in the trade but also to address the issues of trafficked minors in brothels. They build on trafficked women's agency, both individual and collective, and attest to their capacity to know about their rights and act on them.

... there is a tendency to conflate the situation of girls and women in the literature on sex trafficking that may lead to some confusion about rights. In some cases the rights of children could be subsumed under the rights of adults, with the result that particular rights of trafficked children are not given special attention and treatment.

Significant Points for Consideration

A number of conceptual points on trafficking and sex trafficking that have a bearing on the planning and implementation of interventions need to be considered. First, there is a tendency to conflate the situation of girls and women in the literature on sex trafficking that may lead to some confusion about rights. In some cases the rights of children could be subsumed under the rights of adults, with the result that particular rights of trafficked children are not given special attention and treatment. For example, during the 1996 brothel raids by police in Mumbai, India, trafficked children engaged in sex work were not treated any differently from adults (Fernandes et al, 2002). At another level, the agency of adults tends to get ignored, resulting in the infantilisation of women in both policy approaches and treatment of trafficked women. A case in point is the construction and policy treatment of trafficked women outlined in Nepal's anti-trafficking laws (Sanghera and Kapur, 2000; Shivdas, 2003).

Second, it is known that men and boys are also trafficked and engage in sex work. For example, the work of Ebron (1997) and Brown (1992) highlight the case of Gambian men. Third, Wijers and Lap-Chew (1997) found from their study of responses of organisations working with trafficked victims that a majority of the cases of trafficking involved women who knew they were going to work in the sex industry but were duped about the conditions of their work. In a related issue, my research findings in Nepal and Mumbai, India, revealed that family collusion in trafficking of women and girls is often ignored in both state and NGO discourses, with the result that policy interventions at the community and household levels may be ineffective (Shivdas, 2003).

Truong (2003) has shown that as trafficked women often rely on information put out by networks of their ethnic affiliations, they are subjected to informal control by traffickers. For example, it has been reported that trafficked Nigerian women are often subjected to voodoo to silence them into oaths of secrecy (EUROPOL, 2000). Through fear instilled in them about destruction of their families, they are effectively prevented from informing the authorities. Further, the lack of legislative mechanisms to ensure the safety of victims also deters these women from coming forward with complaints. In addition, as Truong (2003) asserts in the European context, there is the crucial fact that programmes tend to strengthen institutional capacities to deal with monitoring and control of trafficking rather than empowering trafficked women.

Turning to trafficking statistics, Wijers and Lap-Chew (1997) noted, after their one and a half years of investigations into the extent of international trafficking for the UN Special Rapporteur on violence against women, that it was impossible to get reliable statistics. They contend that when statistics on trafficked women are available, they usually refer to the number of migrant or domestic sex workers rather than cases of trafficking. Makkai (2003) has also suggested that statistics on trafficking tend to be imprecise, with significant disparities between estimates and actual cases. Makkai contends that statistics are often culled from media reports and case studies without any explanation about how estimates were made. The IOM, however, attempted in 2001 to put together some figures on a global scale by gathering statistics from 120 of its field offices.

The Human Rights Framework and What it Means for Policy Intervention

Divisions in the perceptions and political positions of organisations that attempt to intervene in trafficked women's lives have been discussed extensively by activists and academics (Bertone, 2000; D'Cunha, 1998 and 1997; Pickup, 1998). On the one hand, the main lines of schism concern the two interrelated issues of migration and trafficking and the consequent notion of 'voluntary'/'forced' sex work. These distinctions become ambiguous and complicate the protection of trafficked women's rights to movement and livelihoods given that interventions are often about prosecution and repatriation. On the other hand, the concept of human rights is enshrined in various international instruments and commitments. But these instruments are also problematic as the concepts on which they are premised are often limiting and flawed and their implementation is reportedly weak.

Elaborating a gender-responsive human rights framework to trafficking

What is a human rights-based response to trafficking? Human rights standards for the treatment of trafficked persons has been outlined by GAATW (1999). Eight obligations are set out for States and include:

1 Principle of non-discrimination evident in procedural law, policy and practice;

2 Protection of trafficked persons and their rights, any irregular immigration status notwithstanding;

3 Access to justice assured to trafficked persons;

4 Enable trafficked persons to seek reparations from traffickers;

5 Provision of temporary residence visas, including the right to work during the time of legal actions;

6 Health and social services for trafficked persons during temporary residence;

7 Appropriate repatriation and reintegration of trafficked persons;

8 Co-operation to ensure full implementation of the above standards.

GAATW (1999) also asserts that empowering strategies adopted by governments and NGOs should necessarily be gender sensitive and should recognise and protect trafficked women's rights to control their bodies and lives, to be free from violence and abuse, to migrate and to engage in work including sex work.

Jordan (2002) argues that adopting a human rights framework would shift the focus from seeing trafficked persons as objects to understanding their situations and according them human rights. She further maintains that a human rights approach overcomes anti-immigrant bias, misogyny and moral condemnation of trafficked women who choose to be sex workers. The human rights approach may mitigate the current trafficking scenario which, according to Morrison (2000), is facilitated by xenophobic, tightly controlled immigration laws in destination countries. More importantly, a human rights policy approach to trafficking could ensure that women are perceived as adults and therefore treated appropriately. The Commonwealth Secretariat (2003) stresses the need for strategies to combat trafficking that are gender sensitive and enhance women's rights, particularly given the restrictive and controlling tenor of current protective measures.

Conclusion

In the light of the discussion on the current trends and patterns in trafficking, differences in concepts, gaps in policy consideration and statistics and the outline of a gender-responsive human rights approach to trafficking offered here, it is useful to conclude with thoughts for policy consideration. Makkai's (2003) summation of key areas that require immediate policy attention includes:

- The lack of victim protection from deportation and witness protection in their country of origin, which make it difficult for both trafficked women and governments to prosecute traffickers;
- The need for increased international co-operation to address a global problem, particularly to track the profits of trafficking;
- The need to address factors on the demand side of trafficking as well as the supply side.

To these I would add one more specific area for policy consideration: the need to bring in an integrated approach to trafficking along the lines of the Commonwealth Secretariat's approach to combating gender-based violence. An integrated policy approach to the trafficking of women and girls would consider a systematic evaluation of the policy environment, including assessing the capacities and capabilities of organisations and institutions, before working with stakeholders to come up with solutions. In conclusion, this paper calls for a gender-responsive human rights approach that also involves trafficked women in the planning and implementation of anti-trafficking strategies because, more than anyone else, women who have been trafficked and survived know what is best for them.

[There is a] *need to bring in an integrated approach to trafficking along the lines of the Commonwealth Secretariat's approach to combating gender-based violence ...* [that] *would consider a systematic evaluation of the policy environment, including assessing the capacities and capabilities of organisations and institutions, before working with stakeholders to come up with solutions.*

Notes

1 Association of South-East Asian Nations.
2 South Asian Association for Regional Co-operation.
3 Stichting tegen Vrouwenhandel (Foundation Against Trafficking), the Netherlands.
4 An international NGO engaged in anti-trafficking initiatives.

References

ADB (2002). 'Nepal country report on combating trafficking of women and children in South Asia'. Manila: Asian Development Bank.

Albanese, Jay and Jennifer Donnelly (2003). 'Trafficking in Human Beings in North America', Paper presented at the PNI Workshop on trafficking in human beings, especially women and children, 12th Session of the Commission on Crime Prevention and Criminal Justice, Vienna, 15 May.

Barry, K (1995). *The Prostitution of Sexuality*. New York: New York University Press.

Bertone, AM (2000). 'Sexual trafficking in women: international political economy and the politics of sex', *Gender Issues* 18(1), Winter.

Brown, N (1992). 'Beach boys as cultural brokers in Bakau Town, The Gambia', *Community Development Journal*, 27(4).

Bruggeman, W (2002). 'Illegal immigration and trafficking in human beings seen as a security problem for Europe', Statement to the ILO/STOP Conference on Trafficking, Brussels, September.

Brussa, L (1999). 'Migrant sex workers in Europe', *Research for Sex Work* 2.

CARE (2001). 'Proceedings of workshop on "cross-border trafficking prevention"', CARE Bangladesh, Dhaka, October 17–18.

Commonwealth Secretariat (2003). *Report of the Expert Group on Strategies for Combating the Trafficking of Women and Children*. London: Commonwealth Secretariat.

D'Cunha, J (1991). *The Legalisation of Prostitution Laws: A sociological enquiry into the laws in relation to prostitution in India and the West*. Bangalore: Wordmakers.

—— (1997). 'Prostitution: The contemporary feminist discourse'. In Thapan, M (ed.), *Embodiment: Essays on Gender and Identity*. New Delhi: Oxford University Press.

—— (1998). 'Feminist perspectives on prostitution and trafficking for prostitution'. In Kuchedkar and Al-Issa (eds), *Violence Against Women, Women Against Violence*. New Delhi: Pencraft International.

Doezema, J (2000). 'Loose Women or Lost Women? The reemergence of the myth of white slavery in contemporary discourses of trafficking in women', *Gender Issues* 18(1), Winter.

—— (2002). 'Who Gets to Choose? Coercion, consent and the UN Trafficking Protocol', *Gender and Development* 10(1), March.

Dottridge, M (1999). 'International Instruments against Traffic in

Persons: When the "excellent" is the enemy of the "good"', Paper presented at the meeting on 'Trafficking and the global sex industry: need for human rights framework', 21–22 June, Geneva.

Ebron, P (1997). 'Traffic in Men'. In Grosz-Ngate, M and Omari, HK (eds), *Gendered Encounters: Challenging Cultural Boundaries and Social Hierarchies in Africa*. London: Routledge.

EUROPOL (2000). 'Report on Trafficking in Human Beings'. The Hague, the Netherlands: EUROPOL.

Fernandes, G and CR Stewart (2002). 'Raids, Rescue, Rehabilitation: The story of the Mumbai brothel raids'. Mumbai: College of Social Work.

GAATW (1999). *Human Rights in Practice: A guide to assist trafficked women and children*. Bangkok: the Global Alliance against Traffic in Women (GAATW).

International Centre for Migration Development Policy (ICMDP) (1999). 'The relationship between Organised Crime and Trafficking in Aliens', Study prepared by the Secretariat of the Budapest Group, June, Vienna, Austria.

International Labour Organization (2002). *Trafficking in Migrants*, 25, Spring.

—— (2003). 'Trafficking in Human Beings: New approaches to combating the problem'. Geneva: ILO.

International Organisation for Migration (2001). 'New IOM Figures on the Global Scale of Trafficking', *Trafficking in Migrants* 23, April.

—— (2002). Trafficking in Migrants, *Quarterly Bulletin* 25, Spring.

Jana, S et al (2002). 'A Tale of Two Cities: Shifting the paradigm of anti-trafficking programmes', *Gender and Development* 10(1), March.

Jordan, A (2002). 'Human Rights or Wrongs? The struggle for a rights-based response to trafficking in human beings', *Gender and Development* 10(1), March.

Kvinnoforum (2003). 'Report on European Good Practice on Recovery, Return and Integration of Trafficked Persons'. Stockholm: Stiftelsen Kvinnoforum.

Lehti, M and K Aromaa (2003). 'Trafficking in women and children in Europe', Paper presented at the PNI Workshop on trafficking in human beings, especially women and children, 12th Session of the Commission on Crime Prevention and Criminal Justice, Vienna, 15 May.

Makkai, T (2003). 'Thematic Discussion on Trafficking in Human Beings', from PNI workshop on trafficking in human beings, especially women and children, 12th Session of the Commission on Crime Prevention and Criminal Justice, Vienna, 15 May.

Mo, C (2001). 'The SAARC Convention to Prevent and Combat Trafficking: A blessing or a threat to the women and girl children of Nepal?', unpublished paper, Kathmandu.

Morrison, J (2000). 'The Trafficking and Smuggling of Refugees: The end game in European asylum policy'. On *http://www.unhcr.ch/refworld/pub/wpapers/wpno39.pdf*

Pickup, F (1998). 'More Words but No Action? Forced migration and trafficking of women', *Gender and Development* 6(1).

Sanghera, J and R Kapur (2000). 'An Assessment of Laws and Policies for the Prevention and Control of Trafficking in Nepal'. New Delhi: Asia Foundation, Nepal and Population Council.

Senta, Keisuke (2003). 'Trafficking in Human Beings in the Asia-Pacific Region', Paper presented at the PNI Workshop on trafficking in human beings, especially women and children, 12th Session of the Commission on Crime Prevention and Criminal Justice, Vienna, 15 May.

Sita, Masamba (2003). 'Trafficking in Women and children: Situation and some trends in African Countries', Paper presented at the PNI Workshop on trafficking in human beings, especially women and children, 12th Session of the Commission on Crime Prevention and Criminal Justice, Vienna, 15 May.

Shivdas, M (2003). 'Resisting Stigma and Interventions: Situating trafficked Nepali women's struggles for self-respect, safety and security in Mumbai and Nepal', unpublished PhD thesis, University of Sussex, Brighton.

Skrobanek, S, N Boonpakdee and C Jantateero (1997). *The Traffic in Women: Human Realities of the International Sex Trade*. London: Zed Books.

Toepfer, SF and BS Wells (1994). 'The Worldwide Market for Sex: A review of international and regional legal prohibitions regarding trafficking in women', *Michigan Journal of Gender and the Law* 2:83–128.

Truong, TD (2003). 'Gender, Exploitative Migration and the Sex Industry: A European perspective', *Gender, Technology and Development* 7(1), January–April.

Wijers, M and L Lap-Chew (1997). *Trafficking in Women, Forced Labour and Slavery-like Practices in Domestic Labour and Prostitution*. Utrecht: Foundation against Trafficking in Women (STV) and Bangkok: Global Alliance against Traffic in Women (GAATW).

Williams, S and R Masika (2002). 'Editorial', *Gender and Development* 10(1), March.

Woodbridge, Ronald (2003). 'Trafficking in Human Beings in Latin America and the Caribbean', Paper presented at the PNI Workshop on trafficking in human beings, especially women and children, 12th Session of the Commission on Crime Prevention and Criminal Justice, Vienna, 15 May.

Using CEDAW to Address Trafficking in Women[1]

Shanthi Dairiam

... the strength of CEDAW lies in its framework of discrimination. Taken holistically, the Convention provides many answers through different articles when the problem [of trafficking in women] is framed as discrimination.

Introduction

The Convention on the Elimination of All Forms of Discrimination against Women (CEDAW), the sole international legal instrument specifically designed to protect women from continuing discrimination and human rights violations, has been ratified by 177 countries. Consisting of a total of 30 articles, CEDAW identifies specific areas of life where women do not yet enjoy full equality with men and requires State parties to eliminate such discrimination *de facto* as well as *de jure*.[2] Hence, the question arises: How can CEDAW be used to address the problem of trafficking in women?

From a glance at the individual provisions of CEDAW, the answer may seem obvious. Recognising the specific vulnerability of women to exploitation, article 6 of the Convention requires State parties to suppress trafficking in and exploitation of prostitution of women. However, the strength of CEDAW lies in its framework of discrimination. Taken holistically, the Convention provides many answers through different articles when the problem is framed as discrimination. The CEDAW Committee, through its jurisprudence, has clarified the links between CEDAW and trafficking against women in General Recommendation 19 and in its review of State party reports. The individual complaint mechanisms recently introduced through the adoption of the Optional Protocol to CEDAW also present survivors and advocates with an effective tool to address the wider issue of discrimination.

A Closer Look at the Convention

Objectives

CEDAW aims at guaranteeing full protection of women's human rights. It is the starting point for eliminating discrimination against women in all spheres of life: in the family, in the community and in the workplace. It ensures equal participation in political and public life and aims at lifting the cultural and traditional burdens placed on women. By emphasising the position of women both in public and private life, the Convention reflects the recognition that women encounter discrimination in law and in fact in all aspects of life. As such, it is the first human rights treaty to go beyond imposing state obligation in the field of public life to require State parties to undertake a series of measures to ensure equality in private life. CEDAW thus provides State parties with an agenda for action at the national level, making it more than simply an international bill of rights for women. Rather, CEDAW is a unique tool to ensure full and equal participation and enjoyment of rights of women in all spheres of life, thus reducing their vulnerability to abuse and exploitation.

Key provisions

The Convention highlights measures to be undertaken by State parties to end discrimination in 16 substantive articles covering civil and political rights and the legal status of women, reproductive rights and non-discrimination on the basis of culture and tradition. A substantial amount of these are relevant to combating trafficking if this struggle is placed within the framework of discrimination.

First of all, the Convention explains the concept of discrimination as "any distinction, exclusion or restriction made on the basis of sex which has the effect or purpose of impairing or nullifying the recognition, enjoyment or exercise by women, irrespective of their marital status, on a basis of equality of men and women, of human rights and fundamental freedoms in the political, economic, social, cultural, civil or any other field (article 1)

Any act of restriction, exclusion or distinction, whether intentional or unintentional, that impedes the recognition of women's human rights or denies women the exercise of any such right is discrimination. This definition is applicable to all provisions of CEDAW.

Article 6 states that "States Parties shall take all appropriate measures, including legislation, to suppress all forms of traf-

Breaking down the trafficking cycle into separate human rights violations reveals, for example, which rights are infringed when women are deceived or lured into leaving their home out of economic despair or because they simply have no other option, or when their passports are seized and they are forced to perform a job they never wanted or which is subject to conditions they never agreed to.

fic in women and exploitation of prostitution of women". State obligation also extends to other areas such as law enforcement, as well as underlying issues, such as social and economic factors, that render women vulnerable to exploitation.

Using the framework of non-discrimination

To guarantee a multi-faceted approach to combating trafficking, however, it is recommended not to make use of one particular CEDAW provision alone, but to use CEDAW as a whole, and to place the problem of trafficking in women within the wider context of discrimination against women.

As a first step, this requires showing that trafficking against women is indeed a form of discrimination. Consequently, we have to establish which rights of women are denied or infringed when they are trafficked. Breaking down the trafficking cycle into separate human rights violations reveals, for example, which rights are infringed when women are deceived or lured into leaving their home out of economic despair or because they simply have no other option, or when their passports are seized and they are forced to perform a job they never wanted or which is subject to conditions they never agreed to. This, in turn, allows us to seek a wide range of remedies. The comprehensiveness of CEDAW becomes an appropriate instrument to address the wide-ranging issues that need to be tackled when dealing with trafficking.

General Recommendation 19

In establishing which rights are violated during the course of the trafficking process, it is useful to turn to General Recommendation 19, adopted by the CEDAW Committee in 1992. This covers the issue of gender-based violence – a human rights violation not explicitly included in the Convention. Paragraphs 6 and 7 clarify, however, that all forms of gender-based violence are discrimination and spell out the rights denied to women when they experience gender-based violence:

> 6 The Convention in article 1 defines discrimination against women. The definition of discrimination includes gender-based violence, that is, violence that is directed against a woman because she is a woman or that affects women disproportion-

ately. It includes acts that inflict physical, mental or sexual harm or suffering, threats of such acts, coercion and other deprivations of liberty. Gender-based violence may breach specific provisions of the Convention, regardless of whether those provisions expressly mention violence.

7. Gender-based violence, which impairs or nullifies the enjoyment by women of human rights and fundamental freedoms under general international law or under human rights conventions, is discrimination within the meaning of article 1 of the Convention. These rights and freedoms include:
(a) The right to life;
(b) The right not to be subject to torture or to cruel, inhuman or degrading treatment or punishment;
(c) The right to equal protection according to humanitarian norms in time of international or internal armed conflict;
(d) The right to liberty and security of the person;
(e) The right to equal protection under the law;
(f) The right to equality in the family;
(g) The right to the highest standard attainable of physical and mental health;
(h) The right to just and favourable conditions of work.

During the process of trafficking women, most, if not all of the above rights are violated. As a result, the definition of gender-based violence applies to trafficking in women. As such, trafficking constitutes discrimination against women. Consequently, many articles of the Convention are applicable in relation to the rights violated.

A denial-of-rights approach

In order to identify which articles are relevant, it is mandatory to look at the different levels of discrimination that constitute trafficking and closely analyse the circumstances surrounding and contributing to it. For this we have to distinguish three stages (before, during and after) in the trafficking cycle during which women experience discrimination:

1 Immediate as well as deep-rooted causes of trafficking (before);

2 Manifestations of abuse that women face while they are trafficked (during);

3 Inadequate remedies for victims and survivors (after).

The denial-of-rights approach compels us to not only provide services for the relief and rehabilitation of trafficked women, but also to take additional punitive action against those responsible for the denial of rights ...

Discrimination is evident in all these aspects and they have to be addressed in a comprehensive manner. This approach prevents us from reducing the actions to combat trafficking to the immediate issues of rescue, repatriation and rehabilitation, and helps us look at the social context that facilitates trafficking. It helps us further to look at the long-term issues of discrimination, resulting in the denial of life chances to women, that perpetuates the vulnerability of women to trafficking.

The denial-of-rights approach compels us to not only provide services for the relief and rehabilitation of trafficked women, but also to take additional punitive action against those responsible for the denial of rights and draw on the accountability of those obligated to be duty holders to prevent trafficking, to punish traffickers and to provide other forms of remedies for survivors of trafficking. This approach is crucial for the deterrence of trafficking. If programmes to combat trafficking stop at rescue and rehabilitation initiatives, then nothing is being done about the nexus of collusion between law enforcers, traffickers, state officials and receivers of trafficked persons acting with impunity. The fact that nothing is done about them gives them the power to continue their criminal activity. Secondly, as a long-term measure, it is also imperative to engage in advocacy that will focus on the larger issue of the disadvantaged position of women, such as their unmet needs for economic independence and their devaluation that puts them at risk of being trafficked.

Hence not only do we have to view trafficking in itself as discrimination but we also have to consider the discrimination that women face because they are women which intensifies their vulnerability to trafficking. CEDAW has great relevance when this approach is taken.

Obligations for State Parties Arising under CEDAW

As noted above, article 1 of CEDAW and the definition of discrimination is central to the analysis of trafficking in women. More importantly, the prohibition of discrimination under CEDAW is not restricted to action by or on behalf of the State. Rather, the State has to ensure there is no discrimination by any person, organisation or enterprise – thereby extending state obligation into the private sphere of life. Furthermore, State parties are also responsible for modifying or abolishing existing customs or practices that constitute discrimination against women (article 2e and f). Consequently, the responsibility to take action against all acts of abuse perpetrated by recruiting agents and unscrupulous employers falls on the State.

Secondly, articles 3 and 4 require State parties to CEDAW to take all appropriate measure including changes in law and policy to ensure the full advancement of women, as well as temporary special measures to accelerate women's *de facto* equality.

In the context of combating trafficking, such measures cover public information campaigns on the risks of trafficking and other preventive measures and extend to providing adequate support services for rehabilitation of victims and survivors of trafficking, halfway houses and other refuges.

Thirdly, article 5 obligates State parties to strive to eliminate traditional attitudes that see women as inferior to men. This reflects the recognition that even if women's legal status is equal to that of men's, there is another level of discrimination that has to be eliminated: discrimination in the private sphere through adherence to cultural stereotypes and social patterns of behaviour.

Finally, several other substantive articles apply. These are the obligation to ensure equality of women in the field of employment (article 11), the right to equality in access to health facilities (article 12), the responsibility of State parties to ensure equal development for rural women (article 14), and the right to equality before the law (article 15) and equality in the family (article 16).

In addition, sections of General Recommendation 19 have great relevance and applicability in establishing measures to be taken in combating trafficking. Reference to the General Recommendation is important because it identifies a range of specific actions that need to be taken by the State to fulfil its obligation to respect, protect and fulfil women's rights. Its provisions complement the statement of rights and obligations contained in CEDAW. For example:

1 The definition of discrimination, and the importance of CEDAW articles 2 e–f, 3, 4 and 5 is reinforced in paragraphs 7, 9, 10 and 11.

2 Poverty and unemployment are identified as contributing factors to trafficking.

3 The prevalence of new forms of exploitation, recruitment for domestic labour and sex tourism is emphasised as incompatible with the concept of equal rights.

4 Factors leading to trafficking, such as armed conflict and living in occupied territories, are identified in paragraph 16 as warranting specific protection and punitive measures.

5 Duties of the State have been identified as the adoption of appropriate legislation – both preventive and punitive; provision of protection and support services for victims; and gender sensitive training of judicial and law enforcement officers and other public officials (para. 24).

6 Paragraph 24 also requires the compilation of data and research on the extent, causes and effects of violence and on the effectiveness of measures to prevent and deal with the problem, as well as public education and information campaigns to overcome prejudices against women.

7 Finally, State parties are obligated to monitor their actions (para. 24).

Implementing and Monitoring CEDAW

In line with monitoring systems of other international human rights treaties, article 17 of CEDAW establishes the Committee on the Elimination of Discrimination against Women (CEDAW Committee), which monitors the progress individual State parties have made in implementing their obligations arising under the Convention. This takes place primarily by examining reports that these States have submitted to the Committee.

The CEDAW Committee meets for a period of two weeks each year to discuss reports submitted by State parties, based on which it will suggest and recommend further action to be taken. In addition to state reports, the Committee may also consider reports by UN specialised agencies, as well as information from NGOs. Through the Economic and Social Council, the Committee reports once a year to the UN General

Assembly as well as the Commission on the Status of Women.

Officially, the parties in the review process are the State party concerned and the CEDAW Committee. However, NGOs participate unofficially and provide valuable information to the Committee, which helps to evaluate States' performance in fulfilling their obligations under the Convention. By stating problems and issues addressed by the State in question in direct relation to the article concerned, NGO reports, called shadow reports, can be extremely useful in assessing the factual situation of women in a particular country.[3]

All State parties to CEDAW are obligated to submit a report to the CEDAW Committee one year after ratification of or accession to the treaty. Thereafter, they are required to report on measures taken to implement the Convention every four years.

All State parties to CEDAW are obliged to submit a report to the CEDAW Committee one year after ratification of or accession to the treaty. Thereafter, they are required to report on measures taken to implement the Convention every four years. Resource and time constraints, however, as well as lack of capacity present difficult challenges for States' compliance with this obligation. To overcome these challenges, State parties can ensure effortless collection of information from various ministries and government agencies by designating a reporting agency and ensuring effective collaboration of all agencies involved. It is further suggested that NGOs should be included in this process, as they may be able to share a wide range of resources.

To improve the timeliness and adequacy of reports submitted by State parties, the UN Division for the Advancement of Women organises training courses for government officials.[4] In addition, the UN Centre for Human Rights conducts training on reporting obligations under all major international human rights treaties, one of which is CEDAW.

In order to review periodic reports in a timely manner, the Committee established a pre-session working group, which drafts questions based on the first reading of the State party's written report. These questions are sent to the reporting state six months in advance. At the face-to-face review, the State party concerned is expected to present an oral report based on its written report combined with the answers to the questions of the pre-session working group. The review process is similar to an exchange of information and ideas resulting in a set of written conclusions and recommendations to the State Party concerned. These are called Concluding Comments.

Identifying elements of the problem of trafficking and relating them to a particular article of the Convention is essential in combating trafficking in women through the use of CEDAW.

Two Country Examples

This section looks briefly at the reviews of two countries' periodic reports – China as a country of origin of trafficked women and the Netherlands as a receiving country.[5] These countries have been chosen as examples because it is vital to look at issues to be addressed at both ends and to hold both sets of States accountable in addressing the problem of trafficking in women.

China

During the Committee session in January 1999, the CEDAW Committee reviewed the third and fourth periodic reports of China. In addition to the steps taken to implement CEDAW set out in the state reports, NGOs raised several issues with regard to trafficking in women in their shadow report.[6]

In its review of progress in China, the Committee expressed concern regarding the levels of poverty experienced by women, unemployment among women and the adverse effect of economic reform on women. The Committee was also concerned regarding the effect of economic reform on social services. Further concerns were illiteracy among women, the education of girls and the lack of women in leadership positions. In particular, the Committee raised issues around the adequacy of legal remedies to protect the personal rights of women and in particular the rights of rural women, as well as to protect women in the context of crime committed against them including trafficking and prostitution.

In its Concluding Comments, the Committee suggested that social services for survivors of trafficking be provided by the Government. It urged decriminalisation of prostitution and measures for the rehabilitation and reintegration of prostitutes, including provision of health services. It also urged the Government to take action in connection with allegations of officials colluding in trafficking in women.

Applicable articles

Identifying elements of the problem of trafficking and relating them to a particular article of the Convention is essential in combating trafficking in women through the use of CEDAW.

When specific issues have been established as areas mandating action, it becomes clear which articles are applicable in this context. For example, where collusion between traffickers and state officials exists, article 2(d) must be used to challenge this collusion. This article reads: "[States parties undertake] to refrain from engaging in any act or practice of discrimination against women and to ensure that public authorities and institutions shall act in conformity with this obligation".

The Netherlands

In July 2001, the CEDAW Committee reviewed the second and third periodic report submitted by the Kingdom of the Netherlands. Like the reports submitted by China, NGO shadow reports[7] provided useful information in addition to the measures presented by the government representatives.

They also illuminated several incongruities. Whereas national law allows for the prosecution of traffickers, victims of trafficking are not enabled to report in practice; or whereas in theory it is possible to seek asylum, women end up in hopeless asylum-seeking situations because legal and other organisations are ill-informed about the protection available. The fact that they are survivors of trafficking is ignored or not recognised, and consequently they do not receive full protection. In addition, although temporary residence permits may be granted to survivors, no assistance to build a future through providing skills training, housing or work permits is given.

Applicable articles

These examples elucidate the importance of the review process in identifying areas in the field of anti-trafficking measures that require improvement. Here, the broad provisions of article 3, which require State parties to take appropriate measures in all fields to ensure women's full development and enjoyment of human rights[8] and article 4, which provides for temporary special measures, need to be used to challenge the gaps in state action.

Summing up

Engaging different actors in the process of providing information on the implementation of CEDAW in the field of elimi-

... the issues to be addressed in sending countries differ greatly from those in receiving countries.

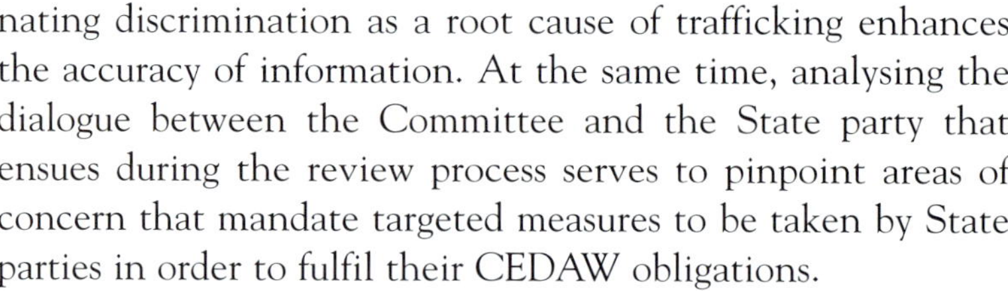

nating discrimination as a root cause of trafficking enhances the accuracy of information. At the same time, analysing the dialogue between the Committee and the State party that ensues during the review process serves to pinpoint areas of concern that mandate targeted measures to be taken by State parties in order to fulfil their CEDAW obligations.

On a different note, an analysis of the state reports review of China and the Netherlands reveals that the issues to be addressed in sending countries differ greatly from those in receiving countries. In the former, it is not only matters directly related to trafficking against women that need to be addressed. It is also issues that refer to the broader concern of discrimination against women, matters pertaining to the empowerment of women and those aspects of culture that differentiate between women and men in stereotypical ways that lead to the subordination of women. These aspects make women vulnerable to trafficking. In receiving countries, however, the issues to be tackled revolve around laws and programmes relating to the criminalisation of trafficking and slave-like conditions of work, cross-border crime control, the sensitivity of authorities to legal and illegal immigrant women and their problems, issues of asylum law and issues concerning the provision of security measures for women seeking to free themselves from traffickers.

The Optional Protocol to CEDAW

In October 1999, the UN General Assembly adopted the Optional Protocol to CEDAW.[9] A year later, ten States had ratified the Optional Protocol, allowing it to enter into force on 22 December 2000 in accordance with article 15.

Objectives

The Optional Protocol provides a course of action to prevent or remedy violations of women's full enjoyment of human rights and fundamental freedoms. It is closely modelled on other UN human rights complaints procedures and incorporates a range of practices of other treaty bodies. Mainly, it establishes a communication procedure that allows individuals and groups of women to complain about violations of CEDAW provisions, as well as an inquiry procedure that permits the Committee to conduct inquiries into grave or systematic abuses of women's human rights in countries that are State parties.

Key provisions

Article 1 establishes the competence of the CEDAW Committee to receive and consider communications under the protocol. Article 2 sets up the communications procedure, followed by articles 3 to 7, which lay out the rules governing this procedure. In detail, these provisions stipulate that individuals or groups of individuals are enabled to submit a complaint to the Committee once all available domestic remedies have been exhausted. This admissibility criterion may be waived if these remedies are unlikely to be effective in the pursuit of relief of a violation of the Convention. A complaint may also be submitted on behalf of an individual if the person concerned has consented or if it is explained why that consent was not received.

If the facts of the complaint brought before the Committee mandate interim measures to avoid irreparable damage to the victim of the alleged violation, article 5 permits the Committee to present such measures for urgent consideration to the State party concerned. Unless the complainant consents to the disclosure of their identity to the State party in question, article 6 stipulates that the Committee shall bring the communication to the attention of the State party in a confidential manner. A timeframe of six months is provided for the State party to submit written explanations or statements regarding the alleged violation of the Convention and/or remedies taken.

As an additional procedure, article 8 establishes the inquiry procedure, which allows the Committee to embark on a confidential investigation into grave or systematic violations of the Convention – if necessary and consented to by the State party concerned – even by way of a visit to its territory. For those States wishing to ratify the Optional Protocol but unable to recognise the competence of the Committee to conduct inquiries, article 10 provides an opt-out clause. However, no other modifications are possible as article 17 prohibits all reservations to this protocol. Thus, States that ratify the Optional Protocol are bound by the entirety of its provisions.

The communications procedure ... allows women who are nationals of a State party to the Optional Protocol and have been rescued from being trafficked to lodge a complaint at the international level if the national judicial system has failed to provide relief.

Relationship with the Convention

The Optional Protocol serves as a supplement to CEDAW and provides a new avenue for implementation and enforcement of the CEDAW provisions. As such, only State parties to CEDAW are eligible to ratify it. Similarly, only those complaints concerning alleged violations of CEDAW by a State party to both CEDAW and the Optional Protocol may be brought before the Committee.

Using the Optional Protocol

The Optional Protocol provides the framework for effective enforcement of CEDAW provisions by endowing an independent body of international experts with the competence of receiving complaints about individual violations and investigating systematic violations.

The communications procedure, as an individual complaints procedure, may prove useful in remedying violations of those CEDAW provisions that have occurred during the process of trafficking. It allows women who are nationals of a State party to the Optional Protocol and have been rescued from being trafficked to lodge a complaint at the international level if the national judicial system has failed to provide relief, thereby expanding the avenues of redress significantly. This route guarantees individual remedies for specific violations and places the survivor at the centre of the proceedings, providing her with full ownership of judicial redress.

In a similar vein, the inquiry procedure provides a useful tool to investigate systematic violations of women's human rights, which may lie at the heart of women's vulnerability to trafficking. These systematic violations may relate, for example, to economic rights, property rights, the right to education or systematic discrimination in connection with women's social status.

The Optional Protocol offers an effective remedy and can prove vital in combating trafficking. It is hoped that the current level of global interest in combating trafficking and awareness of the problem will create the momentum for wider ratification.

Conclusion

This paper has pointed out the relevance of CEDAW to combating trafficking in women and has attempted to provide a methodology for its application. By using the definition of discrimination in article 1 of CEDAW, it is possible to identify a wide range of women's rights violated during the process of trafficking. To remedy these violations, it is suggested that not only article 6 of the Convention, which expressly requires State parties to suppress trafficking in women, should be invoked, but also that use various relevant articles of the Convention as well as General Recommendation 19.

As a first step, it is of utmost importance to analyse the circumstances surrounding the problem of trafficking and, as a second step, to work out the applicability of CEDAW. Advocates and stakeholders in search of identifying factors that contribute to trafficking in a particular country are advised to turn to the periodic reports submitted to the CEDAW Committee by the State party in question. An analysis of the information presented both by the government and, if applicable, by NGO shadow reports, can offer valuable insights into areas of the *de jure* and *de facto* situation of women. Thus, violations of the Convention and issues deserving of improvement may be easily identified.

Advocates and stakeholders in search of identifying factors that contribute to trafficking in a particular country are advised to turn to the periodic reports submitted to the CEDAW Committee by the State party in question.

The CEDAW review is a very useful process that provides guidance to State Parties on how to implement their obligations under the Convention, as the constructive dialogue with the Committee facilitates a more rigorous approach to the implementation of the Concluding Comments. State Parties are encouraged to report regularly to the CEDAW Committee to benefit from this guidance. What is also needed is a monitoring and follow-up of the CEDAW review in which all parties concerned, State representatives as well as NGOs, come together.

Notes

1 Adapted from a paper written for ESCAP, 2002.
2 *De jure* refers to the situation in law, whereas *de facto* describes the situation in fact.
3 NGOs wishing to submit a shadow report may write to the CEDAW Committee, care of the Division for the Advancement of Women, Room CD2-1220, P.O. Box 20, United Nations, New York, NY 10017, USA. Representatives of accredited NGOs may attend the Committee Sessions as observers.
4 United Nations Division for the Advancement of Women, 2 UN Plaza, DC2-12th Floor, New York, New York 10017, U.S.A., Fax:(1 212) 963 3463, *www.un.org/womenwatch/daw*
5 It is not intended to establish that women are trafficked from China to the Netherlands. These countries have been selected merely as examples of the possible issues arising in both sending and receiving countries.
6 Prepared by Human Rights in China, December 1998.
7 Prepared by a consortium of 23 NGOs.
8 The provisions of article 3 is interpreted by the CEDAW Committee to include enabling conditions or further programmatic measures that need to be taken to enable women to benefit from law, policy or existing programmes.
9 Resolution A/54/4, 6 October, 1999, opened for signature on 10 December 1999.

Trafficking as a Human Rights Issue: Thoughts on How to Address it in the Commonwealth

Lin Lean Lim

Because of the very nature of trafficking, there are no precise data available. However, available evidence, though piecemeal, reveals an alarming increase in its incidence, severity and global reach, the highly systematic and sophisticated mechanisms involved, the links with organised crime and official corruption, the varied purposes for which people are trafficked and the exploitative and abusive effects of trafficking.

Trafficking is but one component in the complex and shifting continuum of population mobility and migration. It is critical to distinguish between regular and irregular migration, people smuggling and trafficking. Trafficking is defined by the coercive, non-consensual and exploitative or servile nature of the purpose of movement and involves a number of serious human rights violations.

It is critical to distinguish between regular and irregular migration, people smuggling and trafficking. Trafficking is defined by the coercive, non-consensual and exploitative or servile nature of the purpose of movement and involves a number of serious human rights violations.

This distinction is made in the trafficking and smuggling protocols to the UN Convention on Transnational Organised Crime, 2000. This states that while smuggling is consensual, trafficking is distinguishable by the presence of force, coercion and/or deception throughout or at some stage of the process, such coercion being for the purpose of exploitation.

It is crucial not to conflate trafficking with various manifestations of migration and mobility on the one hand, and with prostitution and sex work on the other. The dangers are:

1 Equating trafficking with migration can lead to simplistic and unrealistic solutions. In order to prevent trafficking, there are both conscious and inadvertent moves to stop those who are deemed vulnerable to migrating. This results in reinforcing the gender bias that women and girls need

constant male or state protection from harm and therefore must not be allowed to exercise their right to movement or right to earn a living in a manner they choose.

2 Curbing migration through, for example, restrictive migration policies and tighter border controls – especially if they are biased against women – does not stop trafficking, it only drives it further underground. In the face of strong push and pull factors such curbs may, on the one hand, make irregular channels the only alternative for migrants and, on the other hand, present lucrative opportunities for unscrupulous traffickers who make a profitable business (estimated to be the fastest growing aspect of organised crime and third in terms of profits only after drugs and guns) out of circumventing these restrictions.

3 Conflating trafficking with sex work leads to anti-trafficking measures being invariably anti-prostitution measures. Trafficking is not only about prostitution and sexual exploitation but involves many other forms of forced labour, debt bondage, peonage in domestic service, agriculture, sweat shop manufacturing, etc, as well as sale of organs, etc.

If there is one thing the Commonwealth Secretariat can help to do in terms of raising awareness, it should be to place trafficking in the appropriate perspective vis-à-vis migration: "Over-emphasising trafficking and taking it out of context in relation to migration is strategically counter-productive in the fight for human rights because: (a) trafficking puts migration in a crime control, crime prevention context, rather than talking about migrants' human rights; and (b) trafficking is being used by governments as a vehicle to develop more restrictive approaches to migration in general" (Asian Migration Centre, 2000:18).

What are the Human Rights Dimensions of the Problem?

Violations of human rights are both a cause and a consequence of trafficking in persons. Accordingly, it is essential to place the protection of all human rights at the centre of any measures taken to prevent and end trafficking. Anti-trafficking measures should not adversely affect the human rights and dignity of persons.

Traffickers use threats, intimidation, deception and violence to subject victims to involuntary servitude, peonage, debt bondage and forced or phoney marriages, to engage in forced prostitution or to labour under conditions comparable to slavery for the trafficker's financial gain. The ILO Forced Labour Convention, 1930 (No. 29) defines forced or compulsory labour as "All work or service which is exacted from any person under the menace of any penalty and for which said person has not offered himself voluntarily".

A rights-based concern is necessarily also a gender-inclusive concern. Gender is a determining factor in trafficking, both on the supply and demand sides. Women and girls are much more likely than men and boys to be the victims of trafficking.

A rights-based concern is necessarily also a gender-inclusive concern. Gender is a determining factor in trafficking, both on the supply and demand sides. Women and girls are much more likely than men and boys to be the victims of trafficking. Trafficking is a serious manifestation of the feminisation of poverty and the broader challenges facing women and girls – in a world still characterised by gender discrimination both within and outside the labour market.

It is important to emphasise that although trafficking is now high on national and international agendas, legal provisions and policy interventions are inadequate, failing to reflect the gravity of the offences involved. According to the ILO:

1 "Most countries do not have legislation that would allow the perpetrators to be prosecuted directly for the crime of trafficking. This leads to a situation whereby even the most obvious cases of trafficking are prosecuted under laws that apply to lesser offences – such as laws on prostitution or on pimping. The limited scope of these laws allows traffickers to receive a relatively light penalty that does not reflect the serious and brutal nature of trafficking;

2 Even when trafficking is defined as a crime in law, it is sometimes confined to trafficking for the purpose of sexual exploitation and does not cover other forms of forced labour, slavery or servitude. Such an approach of conflating trafficking with prostitution not only means that traffickers often escape deserved punishment; it can also lead to further discrimination against female victims of trafficking because of prejudicial attitudes of law enforcers and society at large towards prostitutes;

3 On the other hand, the victims of trafficking are often punished more harshly than the traffickers themselves; they are prosecuted and deported, rather than protected. The authorities tend to treat trafficked persons as criminals rather than as victims, because of their irregular residence and employment status in the destination country, or because they work in prostitution. These actions lead victims to mistrust authorities and to refuse to co-operate with investigations, thereby decreasing the chance that traffickers will be successfully prosecuted;

4 The government approach is to combat 'illegal migration', organised crime and (illegal) prostitution, whereas the need for prevention programmes and victims' rights protection does not receive adequate attention. This narrow approach deprives trafficked persons of their basic human rights, and may create or exacerbate existing situations that cause or contribute to trafficking;

5 Law enforcement agencies may simply move trafficked persons from one system of control to another – from being controlled by traffickers to being controlled by law enforcement officials. They tend to prioritise the needs of law enforcement over the rights of trafficked persons, who are seen primarily as witnesses, as tools of law enforcement. The right of victims to have access to justice is often denied, and prosecutions tend to fail because trafficked persons will not be willing to testify;

6 Law enforcement is often hampered by official indifference, corruption, collusion with traffickers, lax or under-funded regulatory mechanisms, such as the police, border guards, labour inspection services and the judiciary, and the failure of governments to prosecute public officials involved in trafficking" (ILO, 2003).

How Can We Address the Trafficking Problem?

1 Recognising multifaceted causes, manifestations and consequences, the response framework must be comprehensive, multi-pronged and multi-level.

2 The framework should be guided by the UN Protocol to Prevent, Suppress and Punish Trafficking in Persons, Especially Women and Children 2000 and the UN Recommended Principles and Guidelines on Human Rights and Human Trafficking 2002. Other international instruments are also important, including CEDAW, the new UN Convention on Migrant Workers that has just come into force, the ILO Migration for Employment Convention (Revised), 1949 (No. 97); the ILO Declaration on Fundamental Principles and Rights at Work and its Follow-Up, and related core Conventions.

3 Policies must cover the three 'Ps': prevention, protection and prosecution. Prevention of trafficking means addressing the root causes of the supply and demand for trafficked persons (with implications for action by both sending and receiving countries and also transit countries). The protection of trafficked persons involves gender-sensitive assistance and support to victims both in the destination country (including temporary residence permits to allow victims to take up cases against traffickers) and repatriation and reintegration to their home countries and local communities. Prosecution of traffickers should be directly for the crime of trafficking and not for lesser crimes.

4 In addressing the root causes of trafficking, it is extremely important that attention be given to poverty, particularly the feminisation of poverty, and all forms of discrimination. It cannot be over-emphasised that unless gender inequality in all spheres – such as education, access to information and other resources (land and credit) and occupation segregation in the labour market – is effectively addressed, women and girls will always be vulnerable to being trafficked. But it is not just gender discrimination that must be dealt with. Women from indigenous groups and ethnic minorities are more vulnerable, and race also determines the treatment trafficked women receive in countries of destination.

5 It is important to avoid what is known as the 'push-down, pop-up' phenomenon. One lesson learned from the Asia Pacific region is that while successful interventions to stop trafficking may be made in one community or country, the

It cannot be over-emphasised that unless gender inequality in all spheres – such as education, access to information and other resources (land, credit) and occupation segregation in the labour market – is effectively addressed, women and girls will always be vulnerable to being trafficked.

What is needed is to address labour market and employment policies in both origin and destination countries .... The aim should be to work towards regulated, orderly and humane labour migration systems.

lack of reduction on the supply side merely results in a shift of the supply pool to the next vulnerable community or country. Attention needs to be paid to regional co-operation involving sending, transit and receiving countries.

6 Migration in abusive conditions, exploitation and trafficking occur in contexts of serious deficits related to decent work – in terms of the absence of rights at work, lack of freely-chosen, productive and remunerative jobs, inadequate social protection and lack of representation and voice. However, in most countries, migration policy is the purview of the ministries/agencies responsible for national security and law enforcement and does not involve the ministries of labour, sectoral ministries or the national machineries for women. But trafficking cannot be effectively tackled without addressing the reasons behind labour market failures. Rising unemployment and underemployment and poor working conditions, persistent occupational segregation and the disadvantaged position of women relative to men in the labour market, and flexibilisation and casualisation of productions and employment relationships are increasing the demand for undocumented migration workers. What is needed is to address labour market and employment policies in both origin and destination countries, and enhance measures for extending labour regulations to cover domestic service (which in many countries absorbs the bulk of female migrant workers but is not covered by labour legislation), strengthen labour market institutions, including inspection and also employment services, to better inform job-seekers of their options. The aim should be to work towards regulated, orderly and humane labour migration systems.

One last word about the protection of trafficking victims. One of the main problems in identifying trafficked persons and treating them as such is that often they do not see themselves as victims. Wrong expectations of how a victim should behave often leads to misinterpretations by both the authorities and service providers, which may often shift blame on to the trafficked persons. Many trafficked persons do not feel that they have been 'rescued' from their situation, but that they have been 'captured' by the authorities. However, this should not affect their ability to exercise their basic rights. And gender-sensitive assistance and support should be provided to trafficked persons, e.g. to take up cases against traffickers.

In both countries of destination and origin, trafficked women are often treated as criminals rather than as victims. Unfortunately, neither the UN Trafficking Protocol nor the Crime Convention place an explicit obligation of the State to refrain from criminalising trafficked persons.

References

Asian Migrant Centre and Migrant Forum in Asia (2000). *Asian Migrant Yearbook 2000: Migration Facts, Analysis and Issues in 1999*. Hong Kong: Asian Migrant Centre.

ILO (2003). 'Booklet 6: Trafficking of Women and Girls'. In *Preventing Discrimination, Exploitation and Abuse of Women Migrant Workers: An Information Guide*. Geneva: ILO.

Response Framework for Trafficking of Women and Girls[1]

From ILO Booklet 6: Trafficking of Women and Girls

Response mechanisms to address the multifaceted causes, manifestations and consequences of the discrimination, exploitation and abuse of trafficked women and girls should be comprehensive, multi-pronged and multi-level. They should:

1 Treat trafficking as a distinct crime and address all stages of the trafficking cycle and all victims;

2 Address the root causes of both the supply of and demand for trafficked persons;

3 Promote human rights, including labour rights and migrant rights;

4 Promote a standards-based approach to combat trafficking, together with protecting the basic rights of all migrants;

5 Promote decent work for all workers;

6 Work towards informed and transparent labour migration systems;

7 Take action at all levels: community, national, regional and global;

8 Establish institutional mechanisms to involve all social actors;

9 Gather and share information;

10 Ensure adequate and harmonised legal frameworks and effective law enforcement;

11 Ensure that legislation, policies and programmes are gender-sensitive; and

12 Promote the principle of non-discrimination and fight racism and xenophobia.

1 Treat Trafficking as a Distinct Crime and Address All Stages of the Trafficking Cycle and All Victims

A response framework will be co-ordinated and effective only if all parties – government officials, law enforcers, workers' and employers' organisations and NGOs – are focusing on the same crime and identifying the same set of victims and the same set of perpetrators. Trafficking should be treated as a distinct crime and should not be conflated with smuggling or prostitution. Trafficking is not just for sexual exploitation; it encompasses all forms of forced labour, slavery and servitude in any sector of the economy. Trafficking also does not just affect women and girls. Men and boys are also victims, in some areas even more so than females.

A response framework will be co-ordinated and effective only if all parties – government officials, law enforcers, workers' and employers' organisations and NGOs – are focusing on the same crime and identifying the same set of victims and the same set of perpetrators.

Since trafficking is a multi-phased problem, all countries of origin, transit and destination in the trafficking cycle should be involved in a comprehensive response that aims to:

1 ***Prevent trafficking*** – not only by effective legal frameworks, strong law enforcement mechanisms and co-operation between States, but also by addressing both the supply and demand factors and tackling the underlying root causes of trafficking, including poverty, unemployment, inequality and all forms of discrimination and prejudice;

2 ***Extend appropriate protection and support to all trafficked persons*** without discrimination, and respect the rights and needs of those who have been trafficked;

3 ***Investigate, prosecute and adequately penalise traffickers and their collaborators***, paying full attention to due process rights and without compromising the rights of the victims;

4 ***Provide trafficked persons, as victims of human rights violations, with access to adequate and appropriate remedies***, including access to justice, the right to be free from reprisals, rights to recovery, rights to legal redress, and ability to sustain themselves and their families.

It is ... necessary to address the root causes on both the supply and demand sides – with implications for action by both source and destination countries.

2 Address the Root Causes of Both the Supply of and Demand for Trafficked Persons

The United Nations Recommended Principles on Human Rights and Human Trafficking emphasise that strategies aimed at preventing trafficking should address demand as a root cause of trafficking; and States and inter-governmental organisations should ensure that their interventions address the factors that increase vulnerability to trafficking, including inequality, poverty and all forms of discrimination. It is thus necessary to address the root causes on both the supply and demand sides – with implications for action by both source and destination countries.

Supply-side causes include:

1 Feminisation of poverty;
2 Chronic unemployment and lack of economic opportunities;
3 Growing materialism and desire for a better life;
4 Dysfunctional family situations;
5 Gender inequality in access to education and training;
6 Lack of access to information;
7 Discrimination on the basis of gender and/or ethnicity;
8 Cultural contexts and community attitudes and practices that tolerate violence against women;
9 Sex-selective migration policies;
10 Ineffective legal and regulatory frameworks;
11 Displacement and disruption due to natural and human-created catastrophes.

Demand-side causes include:

1 Employer demand for cheap and exploitable labour;
2 Consumer demand for services sometimes provided by trafficked persons;
3 Gender discrimination;
4 Increasing casualisation and informalisation in the labour market;
5 Growth of sex and entertainment industries;
6 Low-risk, high-profit nature of trafficking;
7 Absence of effective regulatory framework and lack of enforcement;
8 Lack of organisation and bargaining power of workers;
9 Discriminatory socio-cultural practices relating, for example, to marriage;

10 Lack of respect for/violations of human rights.

Although admittedly not easy, and although measures would need to be over the long term, these root causes must be dealt with if efforts to address trafficking are to be effective and sustainable.

On both supply and demand sides, there is one uniting and pervasive factor: "the multi-layered discrimination and inequality which serve to prevent women and girls from exercising power over their lives" (UN Economic and Social Council, 1999:7). In the context of globalisation, while trade and capital flows have been liberalised, deregulated and integrated globally, people flows have not. Restrictive immigration laws and policies are obstacles to the demand for cheap, unskilled labour in destination countries and a large supply of human resources from source countries. This generates a lucrative market for traffickers.

It is necessary to avoid what has been described as the 'push down–pop up' phenomenon. The lesson learned from the Asia Pacific region is: While successful interventions may be made in one community or country, the lack of reduction on the demand side results in a shift of the supply pool to the next vulnerable community or country. Successful community-based protection strategies will have limited impact and only result in transferring the problem until more attention is paid to regional co-operation and tackling the demand side.

Trafficking is a grave human rights abuse and, in responding to this problem, States should prioritise the protection of the human rights of trafficked persons ...

3 Promote Human Rights, Including Labour Rights and Migrant Rights

Trafficking is a grave human rights abuse and, in responding to this problem, States should prioritise the protection of the human rights of trafficked persons, taking the steps necessary to prevent abuses and provide remedies where abuses occur. "Trafficking in human beings must not be seen primarily or exclusively from the perspective of national security; it must not be viewed merely from the point of view of national protective interests; it must not be seen only as a fight against organised crime and illegal migration. Human trafficking is first and foremost a violation of human rights" (UNICEF, UNOHCHR and OSCE-ODIHR, 2002:xiii).

The following principles are key in applying a human rights framework. Human rights are:

1 Universal: they apply everywhere;

2 Indivisible: political and civil rights cannot be separated from social and cultural rights;

3 Inalienable: they cannot be denied to any human being;

4 Interdependent: all rights are equally important.

The ILO Declaration on Fundamental Principles and Rights at Work and its Follow-Up, which was unanimously adopted by the member States in 1998, reaffirms the right to freedom of association and the effective recognition of the right to collective bargaining; the elimination of all forms of forced or compulsory labour; the effective abolition of child labour; and the elimination of discrimination in respect of employment and occupation for all workers, nationals and non-nationals. The Preamble of the Declaration makes specific reference to the protection of migrant workers:

4 Promote a Standards-based Approach to Combat Trafficking, Together with Protecting the Basic Rights of All Migrants

A response framework must have its foundation in the rule of law. It is critical to establish legal rights and policy standards so as to ensure social legitimacy and accountability. Therefore, the aim should be to promote the adoption and implementation of the key UN and ILO Conventions:

1 United Nations Convention Against Transnational Organised Crime, 2000;

2 Protocol to Prevent, Suppress and Punish Trafficking in Persons, Especially Women and Children, 2000;

3 Protocol Against the Smuggling of Migrants by Land, Sea and Air, 2000;

4 International Convention for the Protection of the Rights of All Migrant Workers and Members of their Families, 1990;

5 ILO Migration for Employment Convention (Revised), 1949 (No. 97);

6 ILO Migrant Workers (Supplementary Provisions) Convention, 1975, (No. 143); and

7 ILO Declaration on Fundamental Principles and Rights at Work and its Follow-Up, and the related core Conventions.

... a comprehensive response to the problem of trafficking must be based on the promotion of decent work.

5 Promote Decent Work for All Workers

Migration today is about work. Addressing migration means promoting opportunities for women and men, national and migrant, to obtain decent and productive work in conditions of freedom, equity, security and human dignity. Migration in abusive conditions and the exploitation and trafficking of migrant workers occur in contexts of serious decent work deficits – in terms of the absence of rights at work, lack of productive and remunerative jobs, inadequate social protection and lack of representation and voice – in source, transit and destination countries.

Therefore, a comprehensive response to the problem of trafficking must be based on the promotion of decent work. The ILO views decent work as comprising four main pillars: the promotion of fundamental principles and rights at work for all workers, national and non-national; the creation of productive and remunerative employment; the extension of social protection, especially to marginalised and vulnerable groups; and the organisation and representation of workers and employers in social dialogue institutions and processes.

It is crucial to address the labour market and employment situation, labour standards and working conditions in origin and destination countries. Trafficking cannot be effectively tackled without addressing the reasons behind labour market failures (rising unemployment and under-employment and poor working conditions); persistent occupational segregation and the disadvantaged position of women relative to men in the labour market; and why and how informalisation, flexibilisation and casualisation of production and employment relationships is increasing the demand for unregulated migrant workers. The aim is to focus not only on migration policies or on crime control but also, and very importantly, to include: labour market and employment policies in both origin and destination countries; measures for strengthening labour institutions, including labour inspection and monitoring; and employment services to inform job seekers of their options.

It is also necessary to enforce national minimum standards for the employment and working conditions of all workers, national and migrant. ILO Conventions provide international norms and guidelines for such national legislation. The aim should also be to establish monitoring and inspection systems to cover unregulated work in the informal economy – in particular domestic work, the sex industry and sweatshop subcontracting work – to detect and stop exploitation and forced labour and to uphold minimum decent work conditions.

6 Work Towards Informed and Transparent Labour Migration Systems

Informed and transparent labour migration systems would be a most effective way to fight trafficking. Countries of origin should adopt clear migration policies that reconcile inherent conflicts among policy goals, so that, for instance, the goal of the State to protect women migrant workers from exploitation and abuse does not lead to restrictive emigration policies that infringe on women's basic human rights to free movement and in fact make them more vulnerable to traffickers.

However, measures to protect vulnerable migrant workers and prevent trafficking cannot focus only on the supply of such workers and the factors in the source countries. The aim should be to 'manage' or promote orderly migration by admitting labour migrants into a destination country based on a systematic and realistic assessment of the labour market situation and "respond to measured, legitimate needs, taking into account domestic labour concerns as well. Such a system must be based in labour ministries, and rely on regular labour market assessments conducted in consultation with social partners to identify and respond to current and emerging needs for workers, high and low skilled" (Taran and Geronimi, 2002). The aim should be to establish legal labour migration channels that will contribute to reducing exploitation, trafficking and smuggling of migrant workers.

7 Take Action at All Levels: Community, National, Regional and Global

It is important to work at the grassroots, community level so as to reach vulnerable women and girls directly. In source communities, programmes and practical interventions have focused mainly on raising the awareness of vulnerable women and girls and their families to the dangers of trafficking and on the provision of livelihood alternatives, since unemployment and poverty are major root causes. In transit and destination communities, efforts have focused on shelter, health and counselling services for the victims of trafficking.

All such micro-level efforts are important, but inadequate unless combined with a range of complementary interventions and supported by socio-economic development policies at the macro level that address the root causes of the supply of and demand for trafficked women and girls. Alternative livelihood schemes in communities where women and girls are vulnerable to being trafficked should be supplemented by employment-intensive development policies and social protection schemes at national level. There should also be a review of policies at regional and international/global levels: including regional or bilateral agreements for the temporary or permanent movement of persons across borders; and trade policies to cover the temporary movement of service providers (highly skilled, semi-skilled and unskilled). Regional action programmes and global initiatives have also been developed to combat trafficking.[2]

Socio-economic development policies should also be complemented by law reform and law enforcement, so as to eliminate deep-rooted gender discrimination and to ensure proper working conditions and labour standards in all sectors of the economy and for all workers. Trafficking is still not widely recognised as related to the global macroeconomic environment and to specific macro policies in both countries of origin and destination.

Socio-economic development policies should also be complemented by law reform and law enforcement, so as to eliminate deep-rooted gender discrimination and to ensure proper working conditions and labour standards in all sectors of the economy and for all workers.

8 Establish Institutional Mechanisms to Involve All Social Actors

Since the current approach to trafficking is very much from a criminal law enforcement and crime prevention perspective, the responsible government agencies are normally the Ministries of Interior, Immigration, Police and Judiciary. Hardly ever are Ministries of Labour involved. Yet, as emphasised above, migration today is about work and if the aim is to achieve informed and transparent orderly labour migration systems based on realistic assessments of labour market needs, Ministries of Labour and the social partners – workers' and employers' organisations – need to be closely involved. The role of the Ministries of Labour in countries of origin and destination is also in providing employment services and labour inspection.

The role of NGOs in the fight against trafficking is important and normally highlighted – the majority of them are concerned with trafficking for sexual exploitation. But, unfortunately, the (potential) role of employers' organisations and trade unions is often forgotten or ignored. Yet they are best placed to help realistically determine the labour market needs for migrant labour and to promote the use of proper contracts and observance of basic labour standards for migrant labour. Employers' organisations are often an important lobby group in destination countries for the orderly admission of migrant workers. The protection of migrant workers is part of the larger trade union fight against racism, racial discrimination, xenophobia and related intolerance. The International Confederation of Free Trade Unions (ICFTU) *No to Racism and Xenophobia! Plan of Action for Trade Unions* has a section specifically devoted to migrant workers.[3] In the United States, the American Federation of Labour-Congress of Industrial Organizations (AFL-CIO) announced: "All workers – immigrant, native-born, documented or undocumented – should have the full protection of our system of workplace rights and freedoms".[4]

The role of the media is also very important, especially in terms of responsible, ethical reporting and raising public awareness of the pros and cons of labour migration and the dangers of trafficking. Rescued victims of trafficking could also voluntarily play an important role in advocacy. The role of religious institutions in responding to the needs of the most vulnerable at community level should also be recognised, encouraged and supported. In several countries, religious groups have long played a role in assisting trafficking victims.

Various networks of organisations and co-operation frameworks at local, national or regional levels have been established to combat trafficking.[5] A major challenge is to find mechanisms that ensure that the many and diverse networks that have developed to combat trafficking do not work as 'closed circles', but that they come together in as many ways as possible to share information and exchange experiences. Where networks have different experiences, they can be potentially important points at which evaluation of impacts, drawing together of lessons and realistic assessment of progress can be made and then shared.

Where networks have different experiences, they can be potentially important points at which evaluation of impacts, drawing together of lessons and realistic assessment of progress can be made and then shared.

An important lesson learned by a working group looking at effective models of co-operation was the importance of not 'over-co-operating', but decide what levels of co-operation are necessary in order to maximise relative strengths but not waste scarce resources on co-operation mechanisms that add nothing to the impact or efficiency of programming. Sometimes co-operation needs to be no more than just sharing information with others working in the same area, whereas in other circumstances, it might need regular meetings and consultation (often having budgetary implications) and also closely co-ordinated planning and policy formulation.[6]

9 Gather and Share Information

Realistic, relevant and effective anti-trafficking strategies must be based on current and reliable information. However, the nature of the phenomenon means that it is very difficult to conduct research or gather quantitative or qualitative information; for example, respondents may be too scared or ashamed to speak out. The quality of information presently available makes it extremely difficult to determine the real dimensions of the trafficking phenomenon and to prepare appropriately targeted responses at either national or community level.

At community level, many women and children in difficult circumstances remain invisible or highly mobile and engaged in occupations and activities that are not regularly monitored by any government body or NGO. Methodologies for obtaining more reliable information on such women and children need improvement, particularly a community-based mecha-

Realistic, relevant and effective anti-trafficking strategies must be based on current and reliable information.

nism where data and information are collected, analysed and acted upon by people at that level. For example, communities could use a Table of Risks to assess and monitor departure from the community.

The Trafficking Protocol also calls for information exchange between countries, so as to more effectively co-ordinate efforts to address trafficking.

10 Ensure Adequate and Harmonised Legal Frameworks and Effective Law Enforcement

The importance of good laws, strong enforcement and co-operation among States cannot be over-emphasised in the fight against trafficking. Legislation must protect, promote and give practical effect to the rights of trafficked persons. The United Nations has, therefore, developed specific principles and guidelines. It is worth re-emphasising that, to be effective, there should be specific legislation setting out a criminal offence that covers trafficking for all purposes – not just sexual exploitation but all forms of forced labour. Examples of laws that adopt a comprehensive coverage of the crime of trafficking are:

1 United States Victims of Trafficking and Violence Protection Act of 2000;

2 Canadian Immigration and Refugee Protection Act of 2002.

The need for legislative harmonisation should also be highlighted. The lack of legislative harmonisation has been identified as a major obstacle towards effective prosecution and protection efforts, impeding any efforts of trans-border co-operation between the respective national authorities in the States of origin, transit and destination. Such harmonisation should, however, not be restricted to the sole approximation of existing laws, but should take place in the light of international and regional human rights standards.

In addition, legal literacy should be promoted, especially among vulnerable women and girls and their families so that they understand the law and are able to claim and defend their rights under the law. Access to affordable legal assistance in a language victims of trafficking can understand is also important. Setting up telephone hotlines and effective information networking systems could encourage trafficking victims to seek legal advice and redress. Effective law enforcement would also require sensitisation of all officials, so that they are able to identify if someone might have been trafficked and can inform that person of her/his rights. Enforcement would also require clean and transparent authorities. Often enforcement is hindered by official indifference, corruption and collusion with traffickers, and lax or under-funded regulatory mechanisms.

To be effective, there should be specific legislation setting out a criminal offence that covers trafficking for all purposes – not just sexual exploitation but all forms of forced labour.

There should be measures to address direct and indirect discrimination – based on nationality, sex, racial or ethnic origin, religion or belief, disability, age, sexual orientation or other status – both within and outside the workplace.

11 Ensure that Legislation, Policies and Programmes are Gender-sensitive

To realise human rights equitably for women and men, it is essential to mainstream gender concerns in the formulation, implementation, monitoring and evaluation of legislation, policies and programmes. Adopting a gender perspective means addressing the similarities and differences in the trafficking experience of women and men (girls and boys) in relation to vulnerabilities, violations and consequences; addressing the different impacts of policies on women and men; and – importantly – tackling trafficking by tackling the social constructs that stereotype, marginalise and disadvantage women relative to men. The focus should be not only on providing equal treatment but also on ensuring equal outcomes for women and men.

12 Promote the Principle of Non-discrimination and Fight Racism and Xenophobia

There should be measures to address direct and indirect discrimination – based on nationality, sex, racial or ethnic origin, religion or belief, disability, age, sexual orientation or other status – both within and outside the workplace. It is important to deal with the fact that trafficking is not only rooted in gender discrimination but also in ethnic/racial discrimination. Women and girls from socially marginalised ethnic minorities and indigenous groups are much more likely to be trafficked, and therefore require specifically targeted interventions.

There should also be measures to promote social cohesion and fight xenophobia. Xenophobia describes attitudes, prejudices and behaviour that reject, exclude and often vilify persons, based on the perception that they are outsiders or foreigners to the community, society or national identity. Racism generally implies distinction based on difference in physical characteristics, such as skin colour, hair type, facial features, etc. An important reason behind increasingly restrictive immigration policies is the increasing manifestations of hostility and violence against non-nationals – migrant workers, refugees and asylum seekers, immigrants, sometimes even students and tourists. There is increasing vilification of migrants and foreigners in the media, political discourse and public sentiments. Migrants and the migration phenomena are associated – especially through usage of terminology of 'illegal migrants' and 'combating illegal migration' – with criminality and more recently with international terrorism. In this context, the increased occurrence of discrimination and outright violence against migrants reported in a growing number of countries is clearly more than mere coincidence.

The Durban Declaration and Programme of Action adopted at the World Conference Against Racism, Racial Discrimination, Xenophobia and Related Intolerance, 2001 has no less than 40 paragraphs on the treatment of migrant workers. The text specifically urges States to address discrimination and xenophobia and to ensure full equality for all before the law, including labour law.[7]

Notes

1 Adapted from ILO (2003). Booklet 6: Trafficking of Women and Girls. In *Preventing Discrimination, Exploitation and Abuse of Women Migrant Workers: An Information Guide*. Geneva: ILO.

2 See, for example, the summary of regional initiatives given in Table 1 of UNICEF, UNOHCHR and OSCE-ODIHR, 2002:169–81.

3 See *www.icftu.org*

4 See *www.aflcio.org*

5 See, for example, Anti Slavery International website: *www.anti-slavery.org*; the Global Alliance against Traffic in Women (GAATW) website: *www.inet.co.th./org/gaatw*; the La Strada Foundation website: *www.soros.org/women.html/info_trafficking.htm*; and the Asian Migrant Centre website: *asian-migrants.org*. See also description of networks and co-operation frameworks in ILO, 2002:38–44.

6 ILO, 2002:43.

7 See Office of the High Commissioner for Human Rights Commission and Sub-Commission Team and Anti-Discrimination Unit, 'List of Paragraphs in the Durban Declaration and Programme of Action which include provisions relating to Migrants and Refugees', 3 May 2002.

References

International Labour Organization (ILO) (2002). *Unbearable to the human heart: Child trafficking and action to eliminate it*. Geneva: ILO International Programme for the Elimination of Child Labour.

Taran, P and E Geronimi (2002). 'Globalisation, labour and migration: protection is paramount', Paper presented at the Hemispheric Conference on International Migration: Human Rights and the Trafficking in Persons in the Americas, organised by the Economic Commission for Latin America and the Caribbean (ECLAC) and the International Organization for Migration (IOM), Santiago, Chile 20–22 November.

United Nations Economic and Social Council (1999). *Trafficking in women and girls: Note prepared by the Office of the High Commissioner for Human Rights and the Economic Commission for Europe Secretariat*. E/ECE/RW.2/2000/3, 1 December 1999.

UNICEF, UNOHCHR and OSCE-ODIHR (2002). *Trafficking in Human Beings in South-eastern Europe*. Belgrade: UNICEF.

6 Gender and Land Rights

Land, Property and Housing Rights

Lucia Kiwala

Introduction

Land is a useful natural and economic resource, which is central to sustainable livelihoods for both urban and rural populations. Land, property, housing and inheritance rights are inextricably linked (Kothari, 2003: 11). Many times a discussion on any of these issues brings forth a focus on another. It is essential that the Commonwealth Secretariat pays attention to land and property rights at this critical time as countries prepare the next ten-year plans of action for women.

It is essential that the Commonwealth Secretariat pays attention to land and property rights at this critical time as countries prepare the next ten-year plans of action for women.

This paper provides a conceptual framework for looking at the issue and then focuses on the reality of women's rights to land, property and housing. It then examines some of the standards and norms on land, property and housing at the international and regional level before looking at how these translate to the national level in terms of constitutional guarantees and legal frameworks. It then looks briefly at the work of NGOs in the area.

Conceptual Framework

Land is a productive resource, just like capital and technologies. It is also sometimes a measure of status, as distinctions are made between landlords and tenants. It is a symbol of wealth and power, as the more land people acquire in their own right, the more powerful they become. Land can be used as a form of security to access loans and credit from financial institutions. It is a key ingredient in the bid for secure tenure and improved living environments. Land ownership signifies economic, social and political power (Nicol, 2002: 66).

Property can mean land and possessions, which can be distinguished respectively as immovable and movable property. Land denotes home, house, estate or acreage on the one hand, while possessions represents belongings, goods, assets, material goods and chattels, on the other. So land and property are indeed unified, and since one cannot be discussed without implicitly touching on the other, this paper also looks at housing rights. Housing rights refer to the right of every woman, man, youth and child to gain and sustain a secure home and community in which to live in peace and dignity (Kothari, 2001: para. 8). Inheritance is the acquisition of property, that is, land or movable property upon the death of a person. It is done according to the wishes of the deceased expressed in writing or orally before his/her death, known as testate succession, or by operation of laws or customs relevant to the deceased (Nicol, 2002).

Women, Land, Property and Housing Rights: The Reality

Women's equal rights to land, housing and property are not recognised in many countries. This is for a variety of reasons. Women's rights are largely linked to marital property and inheritance laws, and are limited by customs, traditions, religious practices and other cultural factors. This is expressed in the registration of land and housing in the husband's name, and the customary handing down of land to male heirs in many societies. Under African customary law, property belongs to the man or is entrusted to a male, who could be a father, brother or husband. Women and daughters very often have only a life interest. Moreover, upon divorce and when settling out of court, women take nothing other than their personal effects and the rest remains in the family.

Lack of access to credit and housing finance, which can enable poor women in rural areas and poor women and men in urban areas to purchase their own property and land, aggravates the problem. This is coupled with lack of awareness of women's human and legal rights, and the low representation of women in decision-making bodies, including the legislative and other bodies responsible for the administration and management of land and property. Women encounter numerous problems regarding land administration at the administrator-general offices and district/national land tribunals, as well as from court clerks, magistrates and judges, because the majority are men who are biased against women's access to, control and ownership of land.

The legal and regulatory frameworks relating to land markets and land acquisition, including land registry, land valuation and legal instruments to facilitate land acquisition, are ineffective in many developing countries (UN-HABITAT, 2003). There is a dire need for significant improvement in the legal, regulatory and financial systems to enable poor women and men to access land and acquire property in their own right.

There is a dire need for significant improvement in the legal, regulatory and financial systems to enable poor women and men to access land and acquire property in their own right.

When addressing land, property and housing issues, it is imperative to recognise that women are not a homogeneous group and that their needs may vary over time. Much depends on whether they are single, married, widowed, separated or divorced; victims of domestic violence or the HIV/AIDS pandemic; indigenous and tribal women; victims of forced evictions; or women in conflict or post-conflict situations. There are also differences between rural and urban poor women. While rural women are discriminated against by agrarian reforms undertaken by various governments, urban poor women and men in slums and informal settlements lack secure tenure and are constrained by inadequate and subjective policies with respect to land, which condemn them to depend on informal land systems for survival.

It is projected that in the next 30 years, the urban population in the developing world will double to about 4 billion people, at a rate of about 70 million per year (UN-HABITAT, 2003). The rural population will barely increase and will begin to decline after 2020 (ibid). The majority of these people will settle in slums and informal settlements. It is also estimated that 72 per cent of the urban population in Africa are residing in slums. A discussion on land, property and housing rights for women should recognise women's rights and issues pertaining to rural and urban settings.

Women, land, property and housing rights in international and national law

Women's rights to land, property and housing are enshrined in a number of international and regional conventions, as well as in UN resolutions and declarations from inter-governmental meetings. In addition, at the national level, many countries have constitutional guarantees of this right, though this is not always translated into national law. The following section looks at these aspects of the issue.

International and regional standards and norms

The Convention on the Elimination of All Forms of Discrimination against Women focuses on women's rights to land, property and housing, especially in articles 1, 2(f), 3 and 5(a). Article 14 paragraph 2(h) addresses the rights of women in rural areas to enjoy adequate living conditions, especially in relation to housing. Article 15 focuses on women's equal rights to conclude contracts and administer property, and their right to equal treatment in court procedures. Article 16, paragraph 1(c) stresses that States parties shall take all appropriate measures to ensure the same rights and responsibilities to women and men during marriage and at its dissolution. Article 16 paragraph 1(h) emphasises the same rights for spouses in relation to the ownership, acquisition, management, administration, enjoyment and disposition of property, whether free of charge or for a valuable consideration.

The Universal Declaration of Human Rights, particularly in articles 2, 16, 17 and 27, contains provisions for equality and non-discrimination and recognises that women should enjoy on equal terms with men rights to property, housing, security of person and equality before, during and upon dissolution of marriage. The Convention on the Elimination of All Forms of Racial Discrimination (articles 5d and 5e(iii)), the International Covenant on Civil and Political Rights (articles 2, 16, 17, 23, paras 4 and 26), the International Convention on Economic, Social and Cultural Rights (article 2, para. 2, 3 and article 11, para. 1) and the Convention on the Rights of the Child (article 16, para. 1 and article 27) also provide for non-discrimination and women's rights to land and property.

At the regional level, the African Charter on Human and People's Rights (article 2 and article 18, paras 2 and 3) and its Protocol on Women's Rights makes provision for non-discrimination and women's rights to property, land and housing, as do the European Convention on Human Rights (articles 5, 8 and 14) and its protocol No. 1 (article 1) and No. 8 (article 3), the revised European Social Charter and the Inter-American Convention on Human Rights (articles 1, 17, 21 and 2(4) and its Additional Protocol.

There are a number of normative provisions which, though not legally binding, contain clauses supporting women's rights to land, property and housing. These include the Beijing Platform for Action (para. 58(m)) in which governments committed themselves to remove all obstacles for women in obtaining affordable housing and access to land. Furthermore, governments are requested to undertake legal and administrative reforms so that woman can have equal access to economic resources and gain the right to own and inherit property. The Istanbul Declaration and the Habitat Agenda (CA/CONF 147/18) adopted by governments at the Human Settlement Second World Conference in 1996, urges governments to provide legal security of tenure and equal access to land to all people, including women and those living in poverty (para. 40(b)). Governments are called upon to undertake legislative and administrative reforms to provide women with full and equal access to economic resources, including the right to inheritance and to ownership of land and other property, credit, natural resources and the right to security of tenure and to enter into contractual agreements.

[In] the Beijing Platform for Action … governments committed themselves to remove all obstacles for women in obtaining affordable housing and access to land.

The Johannesburg Plan of Implementation, endorsed by the World Summit on Sustainable Development (A/CONF. 199/20, Annex para. 67(b)), recognises the importance of women's rights to land, including the right to inheritance, in order to achieve sustainable development in Africa and the realisation of relevant Millennium Development Goals.

UN resolutions on women's rights to land, property and housing include resolutions 1997/19, 1998/15 and 1999/13 adopted by the Sub-Commission on Protection and Promotion of Human Rights; resolution 42/1 adopted by the Commission on the Status of Women; resolutions 2000/13, 2001/34, 2002/49 and 2003/22 on 'Women's equal ownership of access to and control over land and equal rights to own property and to adequate housing' adopted by the Commission on Human Rights; and Resolution on 'Women's role and rights in human settlement development and slum-upgrading' adopted by UN-HABITAT Governing Council, 9 May 2003 (HSP/19c/19/16) (Benschop, 2003).

Constitutional guarantees and national laws

In Bangladesh, the Constitution states that "all citizens are equal before the law and are entitled to equal protection before the law" but, in practice, laws relating to eliminating discrimination are never strongly enforced. The laws relating to property and inheritance are still discriminatory on the basis of gender. Personal law (both Muslim and Hindu) guides the laws of Muslims and Hindus, while common law guides the laws of Christians. Under Muslim family laws, female heirs inherit less than male relatives do, while daughters inherit half of what sons inherit of their father's and mother's property. A wife receives one-eighth of deceased husbands property, whereas the husband receives one-quarter of the deceased wife's property (USAID, 2002a).

According to the statutory law of Kenya, anyone who is above the age of 18 may own property, irrespective of marital status. However, the rights of a married woman to access to, use of, control over and ownership of matrimonial property is dependent on the marriage system and the ethnic group in which she is married. Property rights in civil marriages are based on the English Married Women's Property Act of 1882, which states that a married women can acquire, hold and dispose of property in the same manner as if she is unmarried. She can keep this property separately from her husband's after marriage (USAID, 2002b). Under Hindu law, family property is for use on a communal basis, and individual interests are not defined, whereas under Muslim law, property rights of women are those provided under the Koran. A woman can acquire no interest in her husband's property by reason of marriage, but she has access to the property during marriage (ibid). Although the Registered Land Act of Kenya aimed at providing titles to individuals, many people believed that registration was intended to confirm the entitlement of a male head of household to the family land. The Law of Succession Act 1981 aimed at unifying all inheritance laws. However, it was weakened by the exemption which allows Muslims to follow the Koran, and by the provision that inheritance of livestock and agricultural lands outside the municipality was to be governed by customary law (ibid). However, the Community in Voi has come up with the innovation of a Community Land Trust, which promises to provide women's right to access and control land in the long run. Although the community owns the land, there is no discrimination between men and women.

Under the Constitution of Malawi women have the right to full and equal protection by law and may not be discriminated against on the basis of sex or marital status. In customary marriage, however, women do not own property beyond utensils, with the rest belonging to the family of the husband.

In Sri Lanka, women have equal rights under the country's Constitution and in civil and criminal law. For property rights, the laws of Sri Lanka recognise the equal distribution of property except for inheritance principles under Muslim laws, and, in certain circumstances, under Kandyan law. Furthermore, the devolution of titles under the Land Ordinance Act passed by the British in 1935 introduced the practice of inheritance by one heir to be identified and registered under the statutory provisions (USAID, 2002c).

According to the Tanzanian Constitution, anyone has a right to own property. In 1999, the mainland government passed the Land Act and the Village Land Act, which established women's equal rights with men in the ownership of land. The Land Act provides for spouses to hold land as occupiers in common and to hold the right to occupancy by contributing to the upkeep and improvement of the land. The Act promotes gender balance on the National Land Advisory Council established to advise the Minister of National Lands Policy.

The Constitution of Namibia prohibits discrimination on the grounds of sex, race, colour and ethnic origin and states that men and women have equal rights in all aspects of marriage. The new Married Persons Act allows joint ownership of the estate for the husband and wife married in a 'community of property'. If they are married out of property, they will each keep separate assets including property, control their own belongings and can take out separate loans. Customary land is allocated to the husband, and upon death without a will the widow might lose out to the husband's male relatives. However, the Communal Land Reform intends to give widows and widowers equal rights to stay on communal land that was allocated to the deceased spouse.

In Sierra Leone, two systems of land law apply – the General Law and Customary Law – which operate in urban and rural areas respectively. The Law of Property/Adoption Act 1960 does not prohibit women's title to property. But in practice some women are discriminated against, especially single women, to whom landlords are reluctant to rent premises (Nicol, 2002: 70).

An East African study on women's rights to land, property and housing carried out in 2000/2001 revealed the following (Benschop, 2002):

Women's Rights to Land, Property and Housing in East Africa

Women's Rights	Uganda	Tanzania	Kenya
Gender-based discrimination prohibited	Yes	Yes	Partly
Customary laws prohibited if discriminating against women	Yes	Partly	No
Women's equal right to land/ housing recognised	Yes (implicitly)	Yes (explicitly)	Yes (implicitly)
Spousal co-ownership occupancy rights presumed	No	Yes	No
Equal inheritance rights	For widows: No For daughters: Partly	Partly	For widows: No For daughters: Yes
Equal rights before, during and upon dissolution of marriage	No	No	No

Other findings of the study include:

1 The tradition of 'dowry' contributes to the view of women as 'property' who cannot own property in their own right;

2 Without marriage registration, women are more vulnerable upon divorce from or death of their husband;

3 Alliances/task forces of NGOs play an important role in lobbying for law reform;

4 Non-governmental and community-based organisations greatly contribute to the implementation of laws on the ground;

5 Paralegals play an important role in raising awareness on women's rights and in challenging discriminating customs.

In some countries, laws relating to land, property and housing rights are progressive and in other countries they are retrogressive. While in Uganda the laws require the consent of the spouse before transfer of property, in Tanzania the law provides for joint ownership. However, in Lesotho and Swaziland, for example, some laws discriminate against women. This is illustrated by Section 16 of the Deeds Registration Act of Swaziland, which particularly prohibits registration of title to land in the name of women married in community of property. In Lesotho married women are still regarded as legal minors under the protection of their husbands; therefore they cannot make contractual arrangements without assistance. This means that women's access to land, irrespective of their education, is severely affected (Kothari, 2001).

There is no such a thing as gender-neutral laws in practice, because laws do discriminate against women in the name of culture and tradition even where this contradicts the constitution.

There is no such thing as gender-neutral laws in practice, because laws do discriminate against women in the name of culture and tradition, even where this contradicts the constitution. There is a real need to recognise the specific circumstances of women. Problems arise in the application and interpretation of the law and land administration. The result of any case involving women's rights to land and property in many respects depends on the jurisprudence and good will of the magistrate and/or judges on the bench. Influenced by their beliefs, customs and values, at times judicial officers ignore the written law when passing judgements. The Magaya case in Zimbabwe perhaps illustrates this point.[1]

Positive Responses to Addressing Women's Rights to Land, Property and Housing

There are various non-governmental and women's organisations engaged in promoting and protecting the rights of women to land, property and housing. Initiatives include Land Alliance in Uganda and Kenya, Federation of Women Lawyers Associations, Women in Law in Southern Africa, Women in Law in East Africa, Women in Law and Development in Africa, Asia and Pacific, etc. The Gender Land Task Force in Tanzania raises awareness among parliamentarians, government officials and the public with respect to addressing women's rights issues in the country's new land law.

A number of regional and international organisations have carried out research on women's land and property rights .... What remains to be done is to co-ordinate, share experience and exchange information for the improvement of women's rights.

In Kenya, the Federation of Women Lawyers undertakes advocacy work at all levels, working with policy-makers, bureaucrats, parliamentarians and administrative chiefs at the community level. Through awareness creation and capacity-building, chiefs in some locations in Kenya are able to decide positively on cases based on their knowledge of the law and human rights of women instead of their traditional beliefs and customs. "Instead of supporting a brother who would want to stop and evict his sister from developing the land allocated to her by her father, although, she is married elsewhere, the chief nowadays can allow the sister to build a house because it is her entitlement" (FIDA Kenya Chairperson, personal communication).

Other NGOs facilitate women's access to ownership of land, for example, the Deacon Development Society (DDS) in Andhra Pradesh, India, works with poor women's collectives in 75 villages, helping women from landless families establish claims on land through purchase (Kothari, 2003).

The International Human Rights Law Group assists women's rights organisations in Africa to promote and protect women's equal rights to inheritance. A number of regional and international organisations have carried out research on women's land and property rights. For example, FAO/IFAD/World Bank Network for Negotiated Land Reform (NELAREM) partnerships between landless groups and civil society in South Africa promote gender equality. What remains to be done is to co-ordinate, share experience and exchange information for the improvement of women's rights.

Conclusion

In conclusion, I would argue that strategies for addressing women's rights to land, property and housing should attempt to understand the land tenure systems that exist in different countries and identify opportunities and constraints. Land tenure refers to the rights of individuals or groups in relation to land. Tenure often involves a complex set of rules, frequently referred to as a 'bundle of rights'. Men have access to the entire bundle of rights, with full use and transfer rights, while women may be limited in their use of the resources (UN-HABITAT,

1995:168). This issue should be addressed in addition to legal reform and other practical and administrative measures that have been adopted in a number of countries. Market reforms with respect to the sale and lease of land and property and the administration of loans can increase women's rights and access. Land tenure reform focusing on more equitable and efficient institutions through good legal support, land information systems and a decrease in transaction costs, and creating unambiguous rights, can improve tenure security. Other strategies could include involving women in development and application of tools (title, registries and land surveys), including women as right holders in registries and designing affordable and equitable dispute resolution mechanisms (Crowley, 1999).

Note

1 Discussed in Catherine Muyeka Mumma's paper on 'Reconciling Competing Rights', pp. 62–80.

References

Benschop, Marjolein (2002). 'Rights and Reality: Are women's rights to land, housing and property implemented in East Africa?'

—— (2003). 'Land and Property Rights', Presentation at the Expert Group Meeting on Gender and Women's Issues in Human Settlements, 18 February, UN-HABITAT, Nairobi Kenya.

Crowley, Eve (1999). 'Women's Rights to Land and Natural Resources: Some implications for a human rights-based approach", Sustainable Development Department (SD), Food and Agricultural Organisation, *www.fao.org/sd/Ltdirect/Ltan0025htm*

Kothari, Miloon (2001). 'Adequate housing as a component of the right to an adequate standard of living', Study by the Special Rapporteur on adequate housing, E/CN.4/2001/51. Geneva: Commission on Human Rights.

—— (2003). 'Women and Adequate Housing', Study by the Special Rapporteur on adequate housing, E/CN.4/2003/55. Geneva: Commission on Human Rights.

Nicol, Valerie (2002). 'Promoting Gender Equality through Legal Form'. In *Women and Men in Partnership for Post-Conflict Reconstruction*. London: Commonwealth Secretariat

UN-HABITAT (2003). *The Challenge of Slums: Global Report on Human Settlements 2003*. London: Earthscan UK.

USAID Office of Women in Development NGO Small Grants Program (2002a). 'Bangladesh Country Profile', Conference on Women's Property and Inheritance Rights, 18–21 June.

—— (2002b). 'Kenya Country Profile', Conference on Women's Property and Inheritance Rights, 18–21 June.

—— (2002c). 'Sri Lanka Country Profile', Conference on Women's Property and Inheritance Rights, 18–21 June.

Land Rights and Women's Claims[1]

Bina Agarwal

Introduction

A neglected issue

In largely agrarian economies, arable land is the most valued form of property and productive resource. It is a wealth-creating and livelihood-sustaining asset. For a significant majority of rural households it is the single most important source of security against poverty. Traditionally, it has been the basis of political power and social status. For many, it provides a sense of identity and rootedness. It is an asset that has a permanence that few other assets possess. In some communities, ancestral land also symbolically stands for continuity of kinship and citizenship.

While many of these links are well recognised at the household level, their importance specifically for women has received little attention. Indeed, the issue of women's rights to land (and more generally to property) has been, until recently, largely neglected in both research and policy. In almost all developing countries, large-scale surveys and agricultural censuses collect property-related information only by household, without disaggregating by gender. Thus we still have to depend on small-scale surveys and village studies to assess women's access to land. These sources reveal that typically few women own arable land and even fewer effectively control any.

... the issue of women's rights to land (and more generally to property) has been, until recently, largely neglected in both research and policy.

The social and economic implications of this are wide-ranging. Millions of women in Asia, Africa and Latin America depend on land for their livelihood. In India, for instance, 58 per cent of all male workers, but 78 per cent of all female workers, and 86 per cent of all rural female workers, are in agriculture. Women's domestic work burden, lower mobility, lesser education and fewer investable assets limit their entry into areas other than agriculture and also their range of non-farm options. Moreover, women's agricultural work is, to a greater extent than for men, casual in nature. Relative to men, women also continue to have lower real wage rates and lower average real wage earnings in both agriculture and non-agriculture.

As more men shift to urban or rural non-farm livelihoods, a growing number of households will become dependent on women managing farms and bearing the major burden of family subsistence. The percentage of *de facto* female-headed households is already large and growing. Estimates for India range from 20 to 35 per cent. These include not just widows and deserted and separated women, but also women in households where the men have migrated out and women are effectively farming the land. These women shoulder growing responsibilities in agricultural production but are seriously constrained by their lack of title to land.

The male biases in land ownership and transfers that have been noted in many developing countries are in danger of being replicated in new land reform initiatives and property rights formulations. For instance, agrarian reform is a major policy issue in post-apartheid South Africa, and new private property rights in land and other assets are now being constituted in Eastern Europe and the former USSR. Here new gender inequalities are already being created (Meer, 1997; Verdery, 1996). It is therefore timely and essential to examine in more detail why it is important for women to have effective and independent land rights, what obstructs their realising their claims and what could be done to improve the situation.

While these issues are discussed here largely in the Indian and South Asian context, many of them are also relevant to other developing regions and to transition economies. And although the focus here is on arable land, since that is such a crucial form of property and means of livelihood in South Asia, many of the arguments and concerns could be extended to cover women's rights in a dwelling house or in other forms of property.

Defining land rights

Rights (in any form of property) are defined here as claims that are legally and socially recognised and enforceable by an external legitimised authority, be it a village-level institution or some higher level body of the State. Land rights can stem from inheritance, transfers from the State, tenancy arrangements, land purchase and so on. They can be in the form of ownership or usufruct (rights of use) and can encompass differing degrees of freedom to lease out, mortgage, bequeath or sell.

Three additional distinctions are relevant here:

1 There is a difference between the legal recognition of a claim and its social recognition, and between recognition and enforcement. A woman may have a legal right to inherit property, but this may remain merely on paper if the claim is not recognised as socially legitimate or if the law is not enforced.

2 There is a distinction between ownership and effective control. It is sometimes assumed incorrectly that legal ownership carries with it the right of control in all its senses. In fact, legal ownership may be accompanied by restrictions on disposal (e.g where a married woman needs her husband's consent to alienate the land she legally owns).

3 We need to distinguish between rights vested in individuals and those vested in groups. Our concern here is with women having effective and independent rights in land, effective rights being rights not just in law but also in practice, and independent rights being rights that women enjoy in their own capacity and independent of those enjoyed by men.

Effective and independent land rights for women are important on at least four counts: welfare, efficiency, equality and empowerment.

Why Land is Important for Women

Effective and independent land rights for women are important on at least four counts: welfare, efficiency, equality and empowerment.

Welfare

It is generally accepted that access to land can reduce a household's risk of poverty, but for several reasons land solely in men's hands need not guarantee female welfare. First, there are persistent gender inequalities and a bias favouring males in the distribution of resources within households, including allocations for basic necessities such as health care, education and, in some regions, even food. Biases in food and health care are revealed especially in anthropometric measures (e.g. weight and height for age, weight for height, etc.), morbidity rates and, most starkly, in female-adverse sex ratios. In contrast, direct land transfers to women are likely to benefit not just women but also children. Evidence from many parts of the world shows that women, especially in poor households, spend most of the earnings they control on basic household needs, while men spend a significant part of theirs on personal goods, such as alcohol, tobacco, etc. (Dwyer and Bruce, 1988). Apart from differences in spending patterns, women with assets such as land have greater bargaining power, which can lead to more gender-equal allocations of benefits even from male incomes.

Second, women without independent resources are highly vulnerable to poverty and destitution in case of desertion, divorce or widowhood. In parts of western and north-western India, it is not uncommon for rural women, even from rich parental and marital families, deprived of their property shares when widowed, to be found working as agricultural labourers on the farms of their well-off brothers or brothers-in-law. The fate of deserted and divorced women is worse. Relatives, including sons and brothers, often do not provide the expected economic security to women who are widowed or whose marriages break down. Many of these women end up living on their own. In fact, mortality risks among widows tend to be higher among those living as dependents of male relatives compared with those who are heads of households and who presumably have some independent means of subsistence (Rahman and Menken, 1990). For widows and the elderly, entitlement to family care can depend critically on whether they have property to bequeath.

Land can provide women with both direct and indirect benefits. Direct advantages can stem from growing not just crops but trees, a vegetable garden or grass for cattle. Indirectly, owned land can serve as collateral for credit or as a mortgageable or saleable asset during a crisis; it increases the probability of women finding supplementary wage employment and serves as an important asset base for rural non-farm enterprises. Women's access to even a small piece of land can be a critical element in a diversified livelihood system, and can significantly improve women's and the family's welfare, even if the plot is not large enough to provide full family subsistence. And independent access to land will become increasingly important for women as marital and kin support erodes and female-headed households multiply.

Women's access to even a small piece of land can be a critical element in a diversified livelihood system, and can significantly improve women's and the family's welfare ...

Efficiency

In addition to welfare gains, more gender-equal land rights could also enhance productive efficiency. First there is an incentive effect. Although it is widely recognised that security of tenure can be critical in motivating farmers to make productivity-enhancing investments in their fields, the need for similar incentives within the family has been largely ignored. Some recent studies suggest that incentives could be as important within families. In Kenya, for example, where men and women often cultivate separate plots, the introduction of weeding technology in maize production raised yields on women's plots by 56 per cent where women controlled the output, and by only 15 per cent on their husbands' plots, where women also weeded but men got the proceeds (Elson, 1995).

Second, where land access is in the form of titles (which serve as collateral in many regions), secure rights for women would help increase output by improving women's access to credit. This can prove especially crucial in situations where women are the principal farmers, as where male out-migration is high or where widows (or wives) are cultivating separate plots still formally owned by kin.

Third, research from some other parts of the world suggests that women might use land more efficiently than men in certain contexts. In Burkina Faso, for instance, due to their choice of cropping patterns, women achieved much higher values of output per hectare on their own plots than their husbands did on theirs (Udry et al, 1995). Although women's yields for given crops were lower than men's, this was due to their lesser access to inputs such as fertilisers that were concentrated on the men's plots. The study estimated that output could be increased by as much as 10–20 per cent if such inputs were reallocated from plots controlled by men to those controlled by women in the same household. A literature review of the effect of gender on agricultural productivity in several countries of Africa and Asia also concludes that output could be notably

Endowing women with land would empower them economically as well as strengthen their ability to challenge social and political gender inequities.

increased if women farmers had the same access to inputs and education as male farmers (Quisumbing, 1996).

Fourth, women in many parts of South Asia are often better informed than men about traditional seed varieties and the attributes of trees and grasses. If they had greater control over land and farming, this knowledge could be put to better use.

Fifth, tenure security and especially titles can empower women to assert themselves better with agencies that provide inputs and extension services. While some argue that land transfers to women will have a negative efficiency effect, in that such transfers will reduce output by reducing farm size and increasing fragmentation, there is no noteworthy evidence of this. In India and other parts of South Asia, small farms are found to have a higher value of output per cultivated unit than large farms (Banerjee, 2000); fragmentation can arise equally with male inheritance.

Equality and empowerment

The equality argument is an important one in and of itself, since gender equality is a measure of a just and progressive society. But in addition, equality in land rights is a critical element in women's economic empowerment. 'Empowerment' is defined here as "a process that enhances the ability of disadvantaged ('powerless') individuals or groups to challenge and change (in their favour) existing power relationships that place them in subordinate economic, social and political positions" (Agarwal, 1994:39). Endowing women with land would empower them economically as well as strengthen their ability to challenge social and political gender inequities.

Land rights can thus serve multiple functions in rural women's lives that are not easy to replicate through other means. This is important to keep in mind since the present thrust of most national and international agencies is not on land rights but on micro-credit programmes that are being promoted as a panacea, especially (but not only) for poor rural women. Although credit is clearly an important need for poor women, many individual women not only face problems in retaining control over such loans, but the privileging of this one form of support over all other livelihood sources can prove problematic and diversionary. A number of evaluations show that such credit programmes do not reach the poorest households, let alone change the gender balance in property ownership and control. In fact, a recent study for Bangladesh (cited in IFAD, 2001) identified a lack of access to land and homesteads as major factors in the exclusion of the poorest from credit NGOs.

An alternative to the existing approach of promoting micro-credit for non-land-related micro-enterprises is to link land and micro-credit by providing rural women who depend on land-based livelihoods with credit for leasing in or purchasing land in groups. Here micro-credit would complement rather than substitute for efforts to enhance women's land rights. This would require a significant shift from the existing focus of most micro-credit programmes.

Women's Land Access in Practice

There are three major ways by which women can gain land: inheritance, state transfers and the market.

Inheritance

In most countries arable land is largely privatised. In India, 86 per cent of arable land is privately held. It is not easy to determine how many women inherit land in practice, given the noted absence of gender-disaggregated land ownership data at the all-India level. Small-scale studies can nevertheless be revealing, such as a 1991 sample survey of rural widows by Martha Chen (2000) covering seven States. Chen found that of the 470 women with landowning fathers, only 13 per cent inherited any land as daughters.

Women as widows fared somewhat better. Of the 280 widows whose deceased husbands owned land, 51 per cent inherited some. But this still means that half the widows with legal claims did not inherit anything. And of those that did, typically their shares were not recorded formally in the village land records. Other studies have shown that where the land is so recorded, invariably the widow's name is entered jointly with adult sons, who effectively control the land. The popular perception is that the widow's share is for her maintenance and

Land purchase through the market ... cannot compensate for gender inequalities in inheritance or government transfers.

not for her direct control or use. Widows without sons rarely inherit. Moreover, widows in India constitute only about 11 per cent of rural women, and 76 per cent of them are over 50 years old, many of them too old to effectively work the land. Hence, inheritance as widows does not compensate women for their being disinherited as daughters.

Government transfers

A second potential source of land for women is state transfers. These transfers can be part of land reform programmes, resettlement schemes for those displaced by large dams and other projects, or anti-poverty programmes. Irrespective of the programme under which the transfers occur, typically the land is allotted almost exclusively to males, even in communities that traditionally practiced matrilineal inheritance (i.e. ancestral property passed through the female line). This male bias has a long history and even in peasant movements in which women were significant participants, they were not recognised as independent claimants to land.

In the more recent period, a few of India's Five Year Plans have given some recognition to women's land claims. The crunch, however, lies in whether state governments are willing to implement these recommendations. In addition, the ceiling surplus land available for distribution is extremely limited: it was only 0.56 per cent of India's arable land at the time of the Eighth Plan and today it is less than 0.2 per cent of the country's arable land.

Through the market

The third source of land for women is through lease or purchase. The importance of this option will depend on financial, institutional and infrastructural support to women. In itself, this is a limited option since individual rural women seldom have access to adequate financial resources for this purpose. Also, in terms of purchase, rural land markets are often constrained and land is not always available for sale. Land purchase through the market thus cannot compensate for gender inequalities in inheritance or government transfers. There is somewhat greater potential for obtaining land on lease, since this is more readily available.

For both lease and purchase, however, external support to women would improve access. For instance, in parts of South Asia, groups of landless women have been using subsidised credit provided by the State for leasing or purchasing land in groups, and cultivating it jointly. Such collective endeavours could well prove an important supplementary means by which women can acquire land, even if not the primary means.

Obstacles to Women's Land Access

What stops women from gaining greater land access? While the difficulties that individual women face in getting land through the market were indicated above, those relating to private and government land are more complex.

Privatised land: legal, social and administrative biases

Inheritance laws

In most of India, inheritance was traditionally patrilineal (that is, ancestral property passed through the male line), with some limited matrilineal pockets in the south and north-east (Agarwal, 1994; 1995). Among the majority Hindu community, for instance, the common pattern was for women to inherit only in the absence of male heirs, typically in the absence of four generations of men in the male line of descent. Widows had the first claim and daughters followed. What women received, however, was only a limited interest, that is, they enjoyed the property during their lifetime after which it reverted to the original source. Women's rights of disposal were also restricted: they could not mortgage, give or sell the land, except in exceptional circumstances. In most cases, the rights of Muslim women in customary practice were very similar to those of Hindu women in their regions of location.

During the 20th century, however, through the concerted efforts of women's organisations, liberal lawyers and social reformers, inheritance laws shifted significantly toward gender equality. For instance, the Hindu Succession Act (HSA) of 1956 made sons, daughters and widows equal claimants in a man's separate property and in his share in the joint family property. It also gave women full control over what they inherited, to use and dispose of as they wished. Similarly, the Muslim Personal Law Shariat (Application) Act of 1937 substantially enhanced Muslim women's property rights compared with those prevailing under custom.

Yet, in both communities some notable inequalities remain. Both Hindu and Muslim inheritance laws, for instance, treat agricultural land differently from other property. The HSA exempted tenancy rights in agricultural land from its purview. Likewise, the Shariat Act excluded all agricultural land (both tenanted and owned). Subsequently, some of the southern states extended the provisions of this Act to also cover agricultural land. In all other regions, however, agricultural land, unlike other property, continues to devolve according to customs, tenurial laws or other pre-existing laws. In most of northwest India, such laws and customs give women's property rights very low priority.

A second source of inequality lies in the differential inheritance shares for men and women. In the HSA, for instance, although sons and daughters have equal shares in a man's separate property, there is also the continued recognition of joint family property in which sons but not daughters have rights by birth. The situation remains highly unequal in most States. In the case of Muslim law, differential shares arise because daughters are allowed only half the share of sons in any property.

Social bias

In addition, there is a gap between legal rights and actual ownership. In most communities that were traditionally patrilineal there is strong male resistance to endowing daughters with land. Apart from a reluctance to admit more claimants to the most valuable form of rural property, resistance also stems from social practices that determine marriage choices and post-marital residence. Traditionally among matrilineal communities where daughters had strong claims in land, post-marital residence was in or near the natal home. This kept the land under the overall purview of the natal family, as did close-kin marriage. In contrast, in traditionally patrilineal communities, post-marital residence was patrilocal (the woman joined her husband in his natal home) and often in another village. In addition, in northern India close-kin marriage was forbidden among most communities, and there were social taboos against parents asking married daughters for help during economic crises.

Many of these customs continue today and obstruct women's claims, especially among upper-caste Hindus of the north-west who are the strictest in forbidding in-village and close-kin marriages and in socially restricting parents from seeking help from married daughters. Here, endowing a daughter with land is seen as bringing virtually no reciprocal benefit, and any land inherited by her is seen as lost to the family. Daughters face the greatest opposition to their inheritance claims among such communities. Opposition is less in south and north-east India where in-village and close-kin marriages are allowed and parents can, if they need to, seek support from married daughters.

Many women also forgo their shares in parental land in favour of brothers. In the absence of an effective state social security system, women see brothers as an important source of security, especially in case of marital break-up, even if in practice brothers are seldom willing to support sisters for extended periods. Cultural constructions of gender, such as how a 'good sister' would behave, and practices such as female seclusion in some areas also discourage women from asserting their rights. Where women do not 'voluntarily' forego their inheritance claims, male relatives have been known to file court cases, forge wills or resort to threats and even physical violence.

The gender gap between the ownership and effective control of land is as striking as that between law and practice. Here too social practices and notions of male entitlements play an important role. For instance, marriages in distant villages make direct cultivation by women difficult. In many areas this is compounded by illiteracy, high fertility and social restrictions on women's mobility and public interaction. While the practice of veiling is geographically restricted, the ideology of female seclusion is more widespread and operates in complex ways. Effectively, it restricts women's contact with men by gendering forms of behaviour, and gendering public and private space. This reduces a woman's mobility and participation in activities outside the home, especially market interaction; limits her knowledge of the physical environment; and disad-

The gender gap between the ownership and effective control of land is as striking as that between law and practice.

vantages her in seeking information on new agricultural technologies and practices, in purchasing inputs and in selling the product.

Other difficulties facing women farmers include their limited control over cash and credit for purchasing inputs, gender biases in extension services, ritual taboos against women ploughing and demands of advance cash payments by tractor or bullock owners for ploughing women's fields. Taboos against ploughing increase women's dependence on male help and reduce yields if ploughing is not done in time.

Administrative bias

Community- and family-related social constraints are compounded by the unhelpful approach of many government functionaries who typically share the prevailing social biases and often obstruct the implementation of laws favouring women. The bias is especially prevalent in the recording of daughters' inheritance shares by village officials. In the north-western state of Rajasthan, for instance, a number of village officials told the author that although they encouraged widows to claim their shares, they discouraged daughters from doing so. Village councils also tend to favour men on this count.

At one level, all these constraints – legal, social, and administrative – appear formidable. Yet, the striking regional variability in the strength of the constraints provides entry points for change. South India, which has the fewest obstacles, could provide an important starting point for furthering the goal of gender equality in effective property rights. Demonstrated achievements in one region could help subsequent attempts in other regions.

Government transfers

While male bias within families can to some extent be explained in terms of conflicting interests and social attitudes in relation to private land, why do governments also transfer public land mostly to men? There appear to be several reasons for this bias.

To begin with, there is the common assumption that men are the primary cultivators and breadwinners and women are the helpers and dependents. There is also a widespread social perception regarding women's appropriate roles and capabilities. More generally, land-related policy continues to be formulated largely on the assumption of a unitary household within which resources transferred to men are seen as benefiting the whole family. However, the substantial evidence of unequal intrafamily resource allocations, noted earlier, indicates otherwise. Interestingly, those who most vociferously oppose such resource transfers to women often implicitly recognise that families are far from harmonious or altruistic institutions. Rather they fear that women will leave the family if they have the fallback option that property ownership would provide.

A concern with family unity also limits the nature of transfers to women in the rare cases when such transfers do take place. For instance, there is a long-standing assumption in public policy that farms will be cultivated on a family basis. As a result, the emphasis has been mostly on giving women joint titles with husbands, and allotting titles to widows only in the absence of adult men in the family. In fact, it is fallacious to assume that improving women's economic situation will lead to family break-up. The likelihood is that greater economic equality between men and women within the Indian family will help improve intrahousehold resource allocation and gender relations and strengthen family relationships. For instance, husbands will be less likely to desert or divorce wives who own property or have other means of access to assets such as land or homesteads.

To enhance gender equality in land and livelihoods, changes appear necessary on at least five counts: conceptual, legal, social, institutional and infrastructural.

What Should Be Done?

To enhance gender equality in land and livelihoods, changes appear necessary on at least five counts: conceptual, legal, social, institutional and infrastructural.

Conceptual and empirical

For a start, it appears necessary to challenge the conventional model of a harmonious male-headed family in analysis as well as policy, and to recognise the family for what it is: a unit of both co-operation and conflict, of both sharing and selfishness, where women and men can have different interests, preferences and motivations, where self-interest also enters and where allocations are often unequal and affected by differential bargaining power. Indeed, there is an emerging consensus among gender-aware economists about the validity of the bargaining approach to understanding intrahousehold dynamics.

It is important to gather systematic gender-disaggregated information on land ownership and use, both for better understanding of the existing situation and for effective monitoring. Researchers collecting land-related data in other projects could also be encouraged to collect gender-disaggregated information on land ownership and use.

Legal

The legal aspects should include at least three elements.

1 Amending the inheritance laws

These would include a number of changes, such as placing agricultural land on a par with other forms of property in the laws applicable to Hindus as well as those applicable to Muslims and abolishing the joint family property provision in the HSA, as has been done in Kerala. Even though legal changes are not a sufficient condition for ensuring women's ownership and control over property, legal equality provides an essential tool in the hands of gender-progressive groups, who could then work for *de facto* equality. Progressive legislation also underlines the State's commitment to the idea of gender equality.

2 Legal literacy

This is essential to make laws effective and needs to reach both adults and near-adults. For the latter, legal literacy could be made part of the curriculum in the senior years of school.

3 Recording women's shares

Village women need support to ensure that their land shares are correctly recorded by the relevant village official, and need legal advice and help if they wish to contest their claims with either the family or the administration.

In all these efforts, gender-progressive groups could play a significant role.

Social

Unless and until women's claims begin to be seen as socially legitimate, parents who have a male bias are likely to use the right of making wills to disinherit daughters, even if the laws are made fully gender equal. Similarly, efforts are needed to change conservative or negative perceptions about women's appropriate roles and abilities and to challenge social norms that restrict women's public mobility and interaction.

... efforts are needed to change conservative or negative perceptions about women's appropriate roles and abilities and to challenge social norms that restrict women's public mobility and interaction.

Although social attitudes, norms and perceptions are not easy to alter, certain types of interventions could further the process. For instance, government initiatives to transfer land titles and infrastructural support to women farmers would have a notable demonstration effect. Interventions to strengthen extra-family economic support for women, including through a government social security scheme, would help reduce women's dependence on relatives and especially on brothers in whose favour women often forgo their claims. Overall, economic support would also enhance women's ability to challenge inequalities in the family and community. In so far as the popular media is one of the arenas where gender roles and relations are both projected and constructed, media interventions in a gender-progressive direction would also help transform social attitudes.

Institutional

Reforms in this area need to be holistic and innovative. For instance, policy-makers generally assume that farms will be cultivated on a family basis. Hence to the extent that the government is beginning to recognise that women farmers too have legitimate claims in land, joint titles (titles held jointly by husbands and wives) are mostly favoured. Such titles have both positive and negative implications. On the positive side, clearly getting some land is better for women than having none. But on the negative side, joint titles also present women with several potential problems. Women often find it difficult to gain control over the produce, to bequeath the land as they want or to claim their shares in case of marital conflict. Also with joint titles wives cannot easily exercise their priorities in land use if these priorities happen to differ from those of their husbands. Most importantly, joint titles constrain women from exploring alternative institutional arrangements for cultivation and management.

Individual titles, by contrast, give women greater flexibility and control over the land. At the same time, individual women often lack funds for equipment or inputs, and where holdings are very small individual investment in equipment can prove uneconomical. Individual women also face considerable pressure from male relatives who want to acquire or control the land.

Solutions might include the following:

1 Women who own individual holdings invest in capital inputs jointly with other women, while managing production individually. Male farmers have done this in several regions, by jointly investing, say, in a tubewell where they have contiguous plots. This reduces the individual cost of major investments.

2 Women purchase land jointly while owning it individually and farming it collectively.

3 Women lease land as a group and cultivate it jointly.

4 Women's groups manage and oversee cultivation on land owned by men.

5 Women hold group rights over land distributed by the government, or otherwise acquired by women (Agarwal, 1994). Effectively, the women would be stakeholders in a kind of land trust. Each woman in the group would have use rights but not the right to alienate the land. The daughters-in-law and daughters of such households who are resident in the village would share these use rights. Daughters leaving the village on marriage would lose such rights but could re-establish them by rejoining the production efforts, should they return, say on divorce or widowhood. In other words, land access would be linked formally with residence and working on the land, as was the case under some traditional systems when land was held collectively by a clan.

In these various institutional alternatives, women are not just adjunct workers on family farms; they have direct control over production and distribution. Co-operation is between women with common interests and not between households. The arrangements enable women to gain access to land through the market or through the community – access that women rarely have as individuals. Where linked with land pooling, joint investment and collective management, these arrangements can also help overcome any problems of small size and fragmentation.

Moreover, a collective approach to land management helps women to mobilise funds for capital investment on the farm, take advantage of economies of scale and co-operate in labour-sharing and product marketing. In addition, if the land is held under a system of group rights (as in the fifth alternative) it would strengthen women's ability to withstand pressure from relatives and retain control over the land, and it would circumvent the problem of inheritance since the women would not have rights of alienation. It would also circumvent the issue of outside-village marriages, since women's rights would be based on residence.

... a collective approach to land management helps women mobilise funds for capital investment on the farm, take advantage of economies of scale and co-operate in labour-sharing and product marketing.

Some policy-makers and scholars argue against co-operative farming by pointing to India's failed efforts of the 1950s and early 1960s. However, the focus then was on households, and on male heads as representatives of households. Not only did gender receive no mention, but inadequate attention was paid also to socio-economic inequalities between households, with the result that co-operatives were often large-farmer dominated. A crucial difference in the approaches outlined here is that the institutional forms discussed shift the focus of co-operative efforts from disparate village households to disadvantaged individuals with common interests. Focusing on the effects on poor women could open an important window of opportunity to revive land reform, community co-operation and joint farming in a radically new form.

Infrastructural

The success of women's farming efforts, whether as individuals or groups, can depend crucially on their access to infrastructure. As noted earlier, there are significant gender (in addition to class) inequalities in access to credit, labour, other production inputs (including hired equipment) and information on new agricultural technologies. Poor women cultivating very small plots have the most difficult time in this regard.

The experiences of many NGOs working with poor women, using a group approach, suggest that some restrictive social norms could be challenged successfully as a by-product of forming groups for the more effective delivery of economic programmes.

Prevailing gender biases in the delivery of government infrastructure thus need to be removed. To some degree, this could be done by employing more women in agricultural input and information delivery systems (women extension agents are often recommended for this purpose), but such systems also need a reorientation of male functionaries so that they too contact and assist women farmers. Also, dependence on the State alone may not be enough, or have the same potential for success in reaching women, as non-governmental initiatives. For instance, in credit delivery to poor women, NGOs in India have been more successful than government agencies. The role of NGOs could similarly be important in providing technical information, production inputs and marketing facilities to groups of women farmers.

Collective action

For initiating and sustaining the complexity of changes required to strengthen women's land claims, the committed involvement of a range of actors, and especially of a wide spectrum of women, will be necessary. It will require various forms of collective action by women, both in relation to State policy and its implementation, and in relation to land access via the market, the community and the family. Such collective action should also seek to bring into its fold gender-progressive elements (men and women) within the State, political parties and civil society groups.

The local bureaucracy would be more likely to register individual women's claims in family land if there were collective pressure from gender-progressive groups. Such organisations could also provide women with vital information about the laws and legal support if necessary. They could also strengthen women's bargaining position through economic and social support structures that reduce women's dependence on male relatives, especially their brothers. Such organisations could also help women demand that the government put in place a well-structured social security system.

The experiences of many NGOs working with poor women, using a group approach, suggest that some restrictive social norms could be challenged successfully as a by-product of forming groups for the more effective delivery of economic programmes. Group support for village women can be provided both by separately constituted groups that give women specialised help and by organisations comprised of village women themselves. The presence of more women in the village panchayats, as a result of the one-third reservation for women provided by the 73rd Constitutional Amendment in India in 1992, can also strengthen rural women's hands. Although simply having more women in such bodies cannot guarantee gender-progressive programmes, the record leaves room for optimism: women in these bodies were found to be more sensitive to women's concerns and to give priority to their needs in ways that male panchayat members typically did not (Gandhi and Shah, 1991). Women's presence in positions of authority also has a favourable demonstration effect and can change social attitudes and perceptions about women's roles. Moreover, village women are more likely to take their grievances to women representatives than to all-male bodies.

However, support for women's land claims on a large scale will need much more broad-based collective action by women. Although economic and social differences between women might prove to be obstacles on certain counts, there are still significant areas of mutual benefit that cut across class/caste lines, around which successful co-operation would be possible, which could serve as starting points. One is legal reform. Women of both rich and poor peasant households with a stake in family land stand to gain from gender-equal inheritance laws. Equally, challenging restrictive social norms will bring benefits for women of both well-off and poor households. The experience of the women's movement in India also indicates that women of different socio-economic backgrounds can co-operate strategically for legal reform, as they did in campaigns to amend dowry and rape laws, despite differences in ideologies, agendas and social composition.

Moreover, many urban middle class women activists have played and continue to play important roles in promoting poor rural women's economic and social concerns, such as supporting their campaigns for higher wages and their programmes for wasteland management, credit and small-enterprise development. In more recent years, there have been also some significant cases of middle class activists promoting poor women's land claims.

... there needs to be a shift away from the overwhelming preoccupation of most rural NGOs, donor agencies and governments with micro-credit delivery toward the creation of productive assets, especially landed assets, in women's own hands, and toward enhancing women's capacities as farmers.

All said, there now appears to be a favourable climate for raising the question of women's independent claims to land and livelihood; it is imperative to do so, given the importance of land in women's lives. Some NGOs that earlier concentrated on other issues are now beginning to focus on women's property issues, including agricultural land and homestead plots in rural areas and dwelling houses in urban areas. A number of South Asian women's groups also have been arguing for gender equality in inheritance laws by emphasising that their constitutions promise equal treatment of women and men. Moreover, women's groups that have not raised the issue of women's land and property claims directly have still, over the years, spread an awareness of gender concerns. This has created an environment within which women's claims to land can be placed more centrally in the arena of public concerns – something that was not easy to do 20 years ago.

A window of opportunity is also provided by the growing attention being given to watershed development and localised irrigation schemes by a number of NGOs and some government agencies in several parts of South Asia. But once land becomes more valuable with the availability of irrigation, women's land claims are unlikely to be recognised. The opportune time to establish women's claims is during the process of developing the watershed or irrigation facility, not afterwards.

Moreover, there needs to be a shift away from the overwhelming preoccupation of most rural NGOs, donor agencies and governments with micro-credit delivery toward the creation of productive assets, especially landed assets, in women's own hands, and toward enhancing women's capacities as farmers. In this context, women's rights in arable land and homesteads need to become a central part of the development discourse. Here development agencies that fund research or grassroots action could also play a significant positive role.

Finally, given that this issue is significant and relevant for women in many countries, there is scope here for sharing experiences and strategies for change; for building horizontal linkages between groups with similar goals; and for international coalitions both between South Asian countries and between South Asia and other parts of the globe. This would be facilitated by emerging international support for women's claims in property. CEDAW has focused on equality in property as one of its important directives. The UN Conference on Human Settlements, at its Istanbul meeting in 1996, also focused on women and land. Since then the Huairou Commission – in conjunction with the UNDP, UN-HABITAT, the Women's Environment and Development Organization (WEDO) and the Women's Caucus of the UN Commission on Sustainable Development – has held several discussions with women's groups worldwide to examine regional progress in enhancing women's access to land and property. The Huairou Commission is also requesting support for a global campaign to promote women's claims in land and property and housing rights for the urban poor under the auspices of UN-HABITAT.

All these national, regional and international efforts which are beginning to emerge suggest that today the climate is certainly more favourable than it was two decades ago for responding positively to the concerns raised by poor women in West Bengal: "Why don't we get a title? Are we not peasants?"

References

Agarwal, B (1994). *A Field of One's Own: Gender and Land Rights in South Asia*. Cambridge: Cambridge University Press.

—— (1995). 'Women's Legal Rights in Agricultural Land'. In *Economic and Political Weekly*, Bombay, Review of Agriculture, March.

Banerjee, A (2000). 'Land Reform: Prospects and Strategies', mimeo, Department of Economics, Massachussetts Institute of Technology, Cambridge, MA.

Chen, M (2000). *Perpetual Mourning: Widowhood in Rural India*. Philadelphia, PA: University of Pennsylvania Press.

Dwyer, D and J Bruce (eds) (1988). *A Home Divided: Women and Income in the Third World*. Stanford, CT: Stanford University Press.

Elson, D (1995). 'Gender Awareness in Modelling Structural Adjustment', *World Development* 23(11):1851–68.

Gandhi, N and N Shah (1991). *The Issues at Stake: Theory and Practice in the Contemporary Women's Movement in India*. Delhi: Kali for Women.

IFAD (2001). *Assessment of Rural Poverty in Asia and the Pacific Region: Draft Final Report*. International Fund for Agricultural Development (IFAD), Asia and the Pacific Division.

Meer, S (ed.) (1997). *Women, Land and Authority: Perspectives from South Africa*. Cape Town: David Philip and Oxford: Oxfam UK and Ireland.

Quisumbing, A (1996). 'Male-Female Differences in Agricultural Productivity: Methodological Issues and Empirical Evidence', *World Development* 24(10):1579–95.

Rahman, OM and J Menken (1990). 'The Impact of Marital Status and Living Arrangements on Old Age Female Mortality in Rural Bangladesh', Paper No. 1, Department of Epidemiology, Harvard School of Public Health, and Population Studies Center, University of Pennsylvania.

Udry, C, J Hoddinott, H Alderman and L Haddad (1995). 'Gender Differentials in Farm Productivity: Implications for Household Efficiency and Agricultural Policy, *Food Policy* 20(5): 407–23.

Verdery, K (1996). *What Was Socialism, and What Comes Next?* Princeton, NJ: Princeton University Press.

7 Indigenous Peoples' Rights

Indigenous Peoples' Rights in the Commonwealth, with a Focus on Indigenous Women

Helena Whall

Introduction

Current estimates put the number of indigenous people worldwide at more than 300 million people (approximately 7,000 indigenous societies or cultures) – 5 per cent of the global population (CWIS, 1999). In the absence of reliable censuses, however, hard figures are difficult to come by. Half of the world's indigenous people, approximately 150 million, are living in the Commonwealth (Whall, 2003a). It can be estimated that half of these, i.e. some 75 million, are indigenous women.

The greatest concentration of indigenous people in the Commonwealth is found in the following countries: Bangladesh, India, Pakistan and Sri Lanka (South Asia); Botswana, Cameroon, Kenya, Namibia, Nigeria, South Africa, Tanzania and Uganda (Africa); Australia, Fiji, Malaysia, New Zealand and Papua New Guinea (Pacific and South-East Asia); and Belize, Canada, Dominica and Guyana (Caribbean and Americas).[1]

Commonwealth Policy Studies Unit

Research conducted by the Commonwealth Policy Studies Unit's (CPSU) Indigenous Rights in the Commonwealth Project during 2001–2004 reveals the extraordinary similarity of experiences of indigenous peoples across the Commonwealth.[2] Wherever they may live – in an industrialised country or a developing one, in a rural or urban area, from the Aborigines and Torres Strait Islanders in Australia to the Twa in Uganda – indigenous peoples routinely suffer from social,

... research on the situation of indigenous peoples in 20 Commonwealth countries reveals a disturbing picture of serious socio-economic disparities between majority communities and indigenous peoples ...

economic and political marginalisation, discrimination and poverty (Whall, 2003b; Whall, 2003c).

CPSU research on the situation of indigenous peoples in 20 Commonwealth countries reveals a disturbing picture of serious socio-economic disparities between majority communities and indigenous peoples, including high levels of poverty; poor access to education, health services and employment opportunities; limited political participation and representation; racial discrimination; social and cultural assimilation; rapid loss of languages; environmental destruction and alienation of indigenous lands and resources; and abrogation of treaty rights and extinguishment of native title.

The CPSU urged Commonwealth Heads of Government to make a commitment to the promotion and protection of the rights of indigenous peoples by including a statement of support in the 2003 Commonwealth Abuja Declaration, taking note of recent developments at the United Nations and at other international and regional forums.

Commonwealth Expert Group on Development and Democracy

That indigenous peoples in the Commonwealth suffer discrimination, intolerance and prejudice was clearly recognised in the report of the Commonwealth Expert Group on Development and Democracy, 'Making Democracy Work for Pro-Poor Development', endorsed by Commonwealth Heads of Government at their summit in Abuja, 2003. The Expert Group notes:

> Around half of the world's 300 million indigenous peoples live in the Commonwealth, and frequently suffer discrimination, intolerance and prejudice, and violation of their land rights. (Commonwealth Secretariat, 2003: para. 88)

The report also recognises that indigenous peoples in the Commonwealth frequently suffer "comparatively low life expectancy" (para. 89), and that there are "limits on the rights of indigenous peoples to own, develop, control and use their lands and territories" (para. 114). Significantly, the report acknowledges the importance of group rights (paras 25 and 64).

The report goes on to recognise the right of indigenous peoples "to establish and control their education systems and institutions in a manner appropriate to their cultural methods of teaching and learning" (para. 188). It stresses that parliaments "should take account of the interests" of indigenous peoples (para. 64) and recommends that member States adopt social and economic policies "directed at challenging discrimination against ... indigenous peoples even in developed Commonwealth countries" (para. 115).

The report made it clear that the realisation of the economic, social and cultural rights of indigenous peoples must be a particular concern to Commonwealth member States if the Millennium Development Goals are to be achieved. As a 2003 CPSU report revealed, indigenous peoples in the Commonwealth are among the poorest of the poor, and few countries will meet the MDGs if an improvement in their situation is not made an urgent priority (Bourne, 2003).

... a cursory examination of [the situation of indigenous women in the Commonwealth] *reveals that they suffer from multiple discrimination, "as indigenous peoples, as citizens of colonised and neo-colonial countries, as women and as members of the poorer classes of society" and as members of a minority group.*

Indigenous women in the Commonwealth

As for indigenous peoples in general, there are very little statistical data on the status of indigenous women in the Commonwealth. However, a cursory examination of their situation reveals that they suffer from multiple discrimination, "as indigenous peoples, as citizens of colonised and neo-colonial countries, as women and as members of the poorer classes of society"[3] and as members of a minority group.

Over the past two decades, the international community has increasingly recognised the discrimination faced by indigenous peoples, the need to promote and protect their distinct identities and their unique contribution to sustainable development (Vienna Declaration and Programme of Action, UN World Conference on Human Rights, 1993, para. 20;[4] Durban Declaration and Plan of Action, UN World Conference against Racism, Racial Discrimination, Xenophobia and Related Intolerance (UNWCAR), Durban, 2001, para. 39; and Declaration on Sustainable Development, UN World Summit on Sustainable Development (WSSD), 2002, para. 25).

Moreover, the UN has acknowledged the distinct interests and concerns of indigenous women. At the 23rd special session of the UN General Assembly in June 2000 on 'Women 2000:

gender equality, development and peace for the twenty-first century' (Beijing +5), the Political Declaration and Outcome Document, entitled 'Further actions and initiatives to implement the Beijing Declaration and Platform for Action', identified indigenous women as one of the nine specific groups of women that the UN should target during 2000–2005.

Paragraph 27 of the Outcome Document, 'Human Rights of Women – Obstacles', states: "Some women and girls continue to encounter barriers to justice and the enjoyment of their human rights because of such factors as their race, language, ethnicity, culture, religion, disability or socio-economic class or because they are indigenous people …".

Since 2000, however, there has been very little evidence to suggest that Commonwealth governments have risen to the challenges set by the UN at Beijing +5 to improve the lives of indigenous women. This is not surprising, given the fact that the Commonwealth has not yet formally recognised the rights of its indigenous peoples. The decision by the Commonwealth Secretariat to include indigenous women as one of the key issues to be addressed in its ten-year Plan of Action on Gender and Development is therefore to be welcomed.

Conceptual Framework

Who are indigenous peoples?

Indigenous peoples are generally referred to in the plural, because there are many different groups that make up the entire global tapestry of indigenous peoples. The use of the plural 'peoples' indicates the diversity of people within the group as a whole (Hughes, 2003).

There is no agreed definition of who is indigenous. Indigenous peoples claim the right to define who they are themselves. They argue that self-identification as indigenous is one of the basic rights. Nevertheless the term 'indigenous peoples' is generally used to describe a non-dominant group in a particular territory, with a more or less acknowledged claim to be 'aboriginal' – or the original inhabitants.

While the Aboriginal peoples of Australia and the Mäori of New Zealand were undoubtedly there first, in some places the issue is not always so clear cut. For example, in Africa, nomadic migrants from the north of the continent displaced other early peoples from territories further south that the incomers later claimed as their ancestral lands. Moreover, some would say all groups in Africa are indigenous. The Botswana Government, for instance, considers all Batswana as indigenous and does not see any need to make special arrangements for the San 'Bushmen'. In Asia, where successive waves of people moved here and there, displacing other populations, similar problems with the term 'first' also apply. The Indian Government refuses to recognise the Adivasis or Scheduled Tribes as indigenous, claiming that that the whole population of India is indigenous. It may be safer to say, therefore, that indigenous peoples are those who arrived in a territory before single nation States (as we know them today) were formed.

Indigenous peoples tend to be socially, economically and politically marginalised and to suffer from oppression/ discrimination and poverty.

Indigenous peoples are also often defined as 'non-state' and can be distinguished according to their different ways of life – how they survive and produce. While many have now left their traditional rural life behind for urban areas and many others may work for wages, hundreds of thousands of indigenous peoples worldwide continue to be pastoralists, hunters and gatherers, and peasant farmers/shifting cultivators, whether full- or part-time. In most cases, the so-called subsistence economy remains the bedrock of how indigenous peoples make their living. These ways of life are highly sustainable, although this is fast changing as development projects encroach upon indigenous peoples' fragile habitats.

'Tribal peoples' can mean much the same thing. The major difference is that they do not or cannot always claim to be descended from the aboriginal inhabitants of a territory. Many minorities are also indigenous, but not necessarily so.

Indigenous peoples tend to be socially, economically and politically marginalised, and to suffer from oppression/discrimination and poverty.

Official definitions

The UN does not have an official definition of indigenous peoples. However, there are three main working definitions within the UN. The first was provided by the International Labour Organization's Convention No. 169 Concerning Indigenous and Tribal Peoples in Independent Countries (1989).

This came into force in 1991, replacing the earlier 1957 Convention. The ILO distinguishes indigenous from tribal peoples in article 1, saying the Convention applies to:

> Tribal peoples in independent countries whose social, cultural and economic conditions distinguish them from other sections of the national community and whose status is regulated wholly or partially by their own customs or traditions or by special laws or regulations;
>
> Peoples in independent countries who are regarded as indigenous on account of their descent from the populations which inhabited the country, or a geographical region to which the country belongs, at the time of conquest or colonisation or the establishment of present State boundaries and who, irrespective of their legal status, retain some or all of their own social, economic, cultural or political institutions.
>
> Self-identification as indigenous or tribal shall be regarded as a fundamental criterion for determining the grounds to which the provisions of this Convention apply.

The other two widely used definitions were suggested by UN rapporteurs Dr Jose R Martinez Cobo and Mme Erica-Irene Daes. In his 1986 Report for the UN Sub-Commission on the Prevention of Discrimination and Protection of Minorities, Martinez Cobo wrote:

> Indigenous communities, peoples and nations are those which, having a historical continuity with pre-invasion and pre-colonial societies that developed on their territories, consider themselves distinct from other sectors of the societies now prevailing in those territories or parts of them. They form at present non-dominant sectors of society and are determined to preserve, develop and transmit to future generations their ancestral territories, and their ethnic identity, as the basis of their continued existence as peoples, in accordance with their own cultural patterns, social institutions and legal systems.

He cited 'historical continuity' as meaning the continuation, for an extended period reaching into the present, of one or more of the following factors: "occupation of ancestral lands, or at least part of them; common ancestry with the original occupants of these lands; culture in general, or in specific manifestations; language; residence in certain parts of the country, or in certain regions or the world; other relevant factors".

Erica-Irene Daes, Chairperson of the UN Working Group on Indigenous Populations, while concluding in 1995 that "the concept of 'indigenous' is not capable of a precise definition which can be applied in the same manner to all regions of the world", has nevertheless suggested this variation, designating certain peoples as indigenous:

> Because they are descendants of groups which were in the territory of the country at the time when other groups of different cultures or ethnic origins arrived there;
>
> because of their isolation from other segments of the country's population they have preserved almost intact the customs and traditions of their ancestors which are similar to those characterised as indigenous; and
>
> because they are, even if only formally, placed under a State structure which incorporates national, social and cultural characteristics alien to theirs.

Both Martinez Cobo and Daes emphasise self-identification as one of the main variables in any definition of indigenous peoples.

In order to give its staff policy guidance to ensure that indigenous peoples benefit from development projects and are not harmed by projects that affect their territories and communities, the World Bank formulated an Operational Directive in 1991 that provides another definition of indigenous and tribal peoples (World Bank, 1991).[5]

Indigenous Peoples' Rights

Since the early 1980s, the situation of indigenous peoples and the enjoyment of their human rights has become a key issue in the international arena. This development is reflected in the various initiatives taken by inter-governmental and regional associations – such as the UN, the European Union, the African Union, the Caribbean Community (CARICOM) and the Organisation of American States – to address their concerns.

United Nations

In 1982, the UN set up a Working Group on Indigenous Populations (WGIP), whose main task was to set standards by

A milestone was reached in 2000 when the UN created a Permanent Forum on Indigenous Issues, the first permanent mechanism within the UN system to address the problems facing indigenous peoples. ... Many indigenous peoples have high hopes that the Forum will make a real difference to improving their lives.

drawing up a Draft Declaration on the Rights of Indigenous Peoples.[6] The biggest challenge now is to get the Declaration adopted by the end of the UN's International Decade of the World's Indigenous Peoples (1995–2004).[7] If and when the Draft Declaration is eventually adopted by the UN General Assembly, it will be a non-binding statement of aspiration.

A milestone was reached in 2000 when the UN created a Permanent Forum on Indigenous Issues, the first permanent mechanism within the UN system to address the problems facing indigenous peoples.[8] Its first session was held in May 2002. Many indigenous peoples have high hopes that the Forum will make a real difference to improving their lives.

In 2001, the Commission on Human Rights appointed a Special Rapporteur on the situation of the human rights and fundamental freedoms of indigenous people in response to the growing international concern regarding their marginalisation and discrimination against them.

European Union

The European Council passed a resolution on indigenous peoples within the framework of development co-operation of the community and the member States in 1998, and has mainstreamed indigenous peoples' issues in both its development and human rights strategies.

The working document from the European Commission, prepared at the time of the Council resolution, recognises the "economic, social and political marginalisation" of indigenous peoples, their unique contribution to the "sustainable use of resources" and the importance of "the participation and inclusion of indigenous peoples in decision-making processes". It also acknowledged the importance of self-determination to indigenous peoples "in relation to their own development, by which they want to regain control over their land, life and resources, often from a weak political position".

The European Parliament has been getting increasingly involved in the issue of indigenous peoples, passing a resolution in February 1994 calling for effective protection for indigenous peoples and another in January 1995 calling for support for the International Decade.

African Union

At the 34th Ordinary Session of the African Commission on Human and Peoples' Rights (ACHPR), Gambia, November 2003, the 'Report of the African Commission's Working Group on Indigenous Populations/Communities' was adopted. The report contains both an analysis of criteria for identifying indigenous peoples in Africa, an analysis of their human rights situation seen in the light of the provisions of the African Charter on Human and Peoples' Rights (1986), and an analysis of African Charter jurisprudence and its potential for promoting and protecting the human rights of indigenous peoples in Africa.

Caribbean Community (CARICOM)

Article XI of the CARICOM Charter of Civil Society (1997) provides that "[t]he States recognise the contribution of the indigenous peoples to the development process and undertake to continue to protect their historical rights and respect the culture and way of life of these peoples". The Charter was adopted unanimously by the Heads of State of CARICOM and has the status of a regional, inter-governmental human rights declaration.

Organization of American States (OAS)

Apart from the UN Draft Declaration, the OAS Proposed Declaration on the Rights of Indigenous Peoples in the Americas is one of the most important exercises currently underway to address the human rights of indigenous peoples. In some countries, the OAS instrument may accurately be described as a substantial and far-reaching leap forward relative to existing rights found in domestic law.

Indigenous Peoples and the Commonwealth

Inter-governmental Commonwealth

The Commonwealth, by contrast with other regional and inter-governmental associations, has no official position on the

While a number of [Commonwealth] countries have individually developed specific policies to recognise and protect their indigenous people, in the absence of a Commonwealth-wide commitment to indigenous peoples their rights are routinely ignored and violated by many ... member States.

rights of indigenous peoples. The Human Rights Unit (HRU) at the Commonwealth Secretariat has stated informally that the Commonwealth has no consensus or policy on indigenous rights as such, and that it is left up to each government to respond to indigenous people's concerns in the context of their own national policies. It is expected, of course, that such policies would be consistent with the Commonwealth's fundamental political values and international human rights standards. While a number of countries have individually developed specific policies to recognise and protect their indigenous peoples (see below), in the absence of a Commonwealth-wide commitment to indigenous peoples their rights are routinely ignored and violated by many Commonwealth member States.

To date, there is no official Commonwealth publication descriptive of the social, economic, political and cultural status of indigenous peoples in member States (there has been no attempt on the part of any division within the Commonwealth Secretariat to collect and collate data on indigenous peoples), and there is no administrative mechanism within the Secretariat to channel specific enquiries, advocacy or support relating to indigenous peoples.

Commonwealth declarations

The key statement on indigenous issues by Heads of Government was made at the Lusaka Commonwealth Heads of Government Meeting (CHOGM), 1979. In the Declaration of the Commonwealth on Racism and Racial Prejudice, they stated:

> We recognise that the history of the Commonwealth and its diversity require that special attention be paid to the problems of indigenous minorities …
>
> We agree that special measures may in particular circumstances be required to advance the development of disadvantaged groups in society. We recognise that the effects of colonialism or racism in the past may make desirable special provisions for the social and economic enhancement of indigenous populations.

Since 1979, however, Commonwealth Heads have not looked at the issue of indigenous rights at any of their biennial summits. The Harare Commonwealth Declaration, 1991, which saw a commitment by member States to protecting and promoting human rights, made no reference to the rights of indigenous peoples.

While in the 1993 Cyprus CHOGM Communiqué, Commonwealth Heads "expressed their appreciation for the proclamation of 1993 as the International Year of the World's Indigenous People", there was no follow-up on this issue. Moreover, Commonwealth Heads gave no declaratory support to the International Decade at the 1995 Millbrook CHOGM. The Aso Rock Declaration, Abuja CHOGM, 2003, was also silent on the issue of indigenous peoples.

The unofficial Commonwealth or the Peoples' Commonwealth ... has over the past decade increasingly placed the issue of the rights of indigenous peoples on its agenda. This is in part due to the extensive lobbying of Commonwealth civil society organisations by the Commonwealth Association of Indigenous Peoples.

The Peoples' Commonwealth

The unofficial Commonwealth or the Peoples' Commonwealth, by contrast, has over the past decade increasingly placed the issue of the rights of indigenous peoples on its agenda. This is in part due to the extensive lobbying of Commonwealth civil society organisations (CSOs) by the Commonwealth Association of Indigenous Peoples (CAIP).[9]

The Civil Society Meeting Statement issued in Abuja, Nigeria, on 3 December, following the three-day meeting of representatives of CSOs from across the Commonwealth, included a paragraph on 'The rights of Indigenous Peoples and the right to self-determination', as follows:

> In this, the penultimate year of the UN Decade for Indigenous Peoples, we ask the Commonwealth to acknowledge that many Indigenous Peoples in the Commonwealth continue to be significantly disadvantaged and that special measures should be encouraged to overcome the continuing effects of racism, colonialism or globalisation, with their full participation and consent. Further, we urge the establishment of mechanisms to guarantee the rights to self-determination of people in the overseas territories of member countries.

Domestic law

At the country level the position on indigenous rights in the Commonwealth is kaleidoscopic.

Five Commonwealth countries, namely Bangladesh, Ghana, India, Malawi and Pakistan, have signed the ILO Convention

No. 107 on Indigenous and Tribal Populations (1957). However, only Dominica and Fiji Islands among Commonwealth countries have signed the much stronger ILO Convention 169.[10]

A few countries in the Commonwealth have specific ministries or departments responsible for indigenous affairs. These include Australia, Bangladesh, Canada, Dominica, Fiji Islands, Guyana, India, Malaysia and New Zealand. While ministers usually find it useful to meet to share their experiences and to exchange best practices, there is no formal mechanism which enables ministers responsible for indigenous issues to meet. The Commonwealth should consider establishing such ministerial meetings in order to co-ordinate greater understanding of indigenous issues and responsibilities among member States. The Commonwealth should also consider establishing ministries or departments responsible for indigenous affairs in all member States where there is a significant indigenous population.

A few Commonwealth member States provide specific constitutional or legislative guarantees to promote and protect indigenous peoples, notably Australia, Aboriginal and Torres Strait Islanders Commission (ATSIC); Canada (section 35, which provides for Aboriginal Treaty Rights); Guyana, Amerindian Act, 1951; India, articles 15.4 and 46; Malaysia, article 8 and Aboriginal Peoples Act, 1974; and New Zealand, Treaty of Waitangi, 1840 and Waitangi Tribunal, 1975.

A small minority have provisions for land claims agreements with indigenous peoples, notably Australia, Native Title Act, 1993 and Native Title Amendment Act, 1998; Bangladesh, Land Commission, 1997; Canada, constitutional provisions for selective Provincial Aboriginal Title and Land Claims; Dominica, Carib Reserve Act, 1978; Fiji Islands, Native Land Trust Act, 1940; India, Panchayat Act, 1996 (article 244); South Africa, Restitution of Land Rights Act, 1994; and Uganda, Land Act (article 30);

In addition, only limited measures have been taken by Commonwealth member States to provide for indigenous participation and representation in national decision-making processes, notably Australia, Aboriginal and Torres Strait Islanders Commission (ATSIC), where there are currently no indigenous peoples in the House of Representatives and one in the Senate; Bangladesh, Chittagong Hill Tracts Regional Council; Canada, self-government coupled with extinguishment of aboriginal title; Dominica, Carib Council and parliamentary representation in the House of Assembly; Fiji Islands, Council of Chiefs; India, Tribal Legislative Assembly; Namibia, Council of Traditional Leaders; New Zealand, where there are currently 19 Mäori MPs, five of whom are on the Executive, representing 15.8 per cent of Parliament; and South Africa, where the Constitution recognises the status, functions and role of traditional chiefs (sections 211 and 212) and, notably, the right to self-determination (section 235).

While some member States are responding positively to indigenous claims for greater social, economic and political autonomy, other governments are rolling back legislative provisions made for their indigenous communities.

Best practice

On 1 April 1999, a new and unconventional political entity called Nunavut came into being, according the Inuit the right of self-government as part of a land rights settlement between the Inuit and the Canadian government.[11] Canada's newest entity is carved out of the Northwest Territory and has its own government. This expression of indigenous self-government/internal self-determination represents a significant paradigm shift. Nunavut is a case of good practice from which many Commonwealth States could learn.[12]

Under the South African Restitution of Land Rights Act, 1994, the communal lands of the ‡Khomani San were returned to them in 2002. This action was made easier for the Government by the opportunity for wholesale change that came with the end of white majority rule in 1994. Nonetheless it has acted as a beacon for the indigenous movement in Africa and elsewhere, and makes possible a new future with a better socio-economic outlook for at least some of the extremely demoralised San peoples of Southern Africa.

While some member States are responding positively to indigenous claims for greater social, economic and political autonomy, other governments are rolling back legislative provisions made for their indigenous communities. For example, Australia's Native Title Amendment Act, 1998, has been found by the committee monitoring implementation of the Convention on the Elimination of all Forms of Racial Discrimination to be inconsistent with Australia's international legal obligations under the Convention.[13] In the

Secretary-General's report to the UN General Assembly, 2002, 'Measures to combat contemporary forms of racism, racial discrimination, xenophobia and related intolerance', the Special Rapporteur on this issue in his comments on Australia states, "The land question remains crucial and is the key to the Australian problem".[14]

Indigenous Women's Rights

Convention on the Elimination of All Forms of Discrimination against Women

While CEDAW (1979) does not specifically mention indigenous women, it is assumed that indigenous women are nevertheless protected by it. Unfortunately, between 1994 and 2000, indigenous women were mentioned in only 11 of the 97 country reports that were reviewed by the Committee on the Elimination of Discrimination against Women, the body charged with monitoring the Convention. Of these, five were Commonwealth countries, namely Australia, 1994 and 1997; Canada, 1997; Guyana, 1994; India, 2000; and New Zealand, 1994 and 1998 (Kambel, 2004:2). The Committee has traditionally shown little interest in or awareness of the specific concerns of indigenous women, although its 2003 annual report contained several concluding observations and recommendations on indigenous women (ibid:4).

UN Beijing Declaration, Fourth World Conference on Women, 1995

Since 1995, the UN has increasingly recognised the special needs of indigenous women, most notably in the Beijing Declaration, Fourth World Conference on Women, 1995, (para. 32), and in the Beijing Platform for Action, 'Strategic Objectives and Actions' (paras 8, 46, 32 and 34).

Beijing +5

Five years later, at Beijing +5, the UN placed an even greater focus on indigenous women. In the Introduction to the Outcome Document, 'Further actions and initiatives to implement the Beijing Declaration and Plan of Action', para. 5 states: "The Platform for Action recognises that women face barriers to full equality and advancement because of such factors as their race, age, language, ethnicity, culture, religion or disability, because they are indigenous women or of other status".

In the section on 'Actions to be taken' of the Outcome Document, governments were urged to assist indigenous women "in accessing and participating in politics and decision-making" (para. 66(b)); "to address the impact of violence on indigenous women" (para. 69 (h)); "to protect the knowledge, innovations and practices of women in indigenous and local communities" (para. 71 (a)); to "undertake appropriate data collection and research on indigenous women" (para. 93 (d)); "[to], with the full voluntary participation of indigenous women, develop and implement educational and training programmes ... and ensure their access to all levels of formal and non-formal education, including higher education" (para. 95 (e)); and "to give all women, particularly indigenous women, equal access to capacity-building and training programmes to enhance their participation in decision-making" (para. 95 (j)).

In the same section, governments are encouraged to: "Undertake appropriate data collection and research on indigenous women, with their full participation, in order to foster accessible, culturally and linguistically appropriate policies, programmes and services" (para. 93 (d)). This is crucial given the current paucity of statistical data on indigenous women.

However, indigenous women continue to remain largely invisible within the UN human rights system.

UN Working Group on Indigenous Populations

For example, a review of the annual reports of the UN Working Group on Indigenous Populations (WGIP) shows that from its inception in 1983 until 2000, indigenous women were only mentioned in 1991, at its 9th session. Since then "there has been little focused discussion with the WGIP on the human rights problems experienced by indigenous women" (Kambel, 2004).

UN Special Rapporteur on Indigenous Peoples

Furthermore, while the UN Special Rapporteur is explicitly mandated to pay special attention to discrimination against indigenous women and take into account a gender perspective, it is disappointing that in his first thematic report (January 2003), which focused on the impact of large-scale or major development projects on the human rights and fundamental freedoms of indigenous peoples, the Rapporteur only referred to indigenous women once (ibid).

Commonwealth

Despite having signed up to CEDAW, many Commonwealth States continue to ignore the rights of indigenous women. This is not surprising, given that neither the 1995 Commonwealth Plan of Action on Gender and Development nor its update make any reference to indigenous women. In the absence of a Commonwealth-wide policy on indigenous women, member States are left to devise their own policies.

5 Challenges Facing the Commonwealth

So what are the issues facing indigenous women in Commonwealth member States? And what are the challenges that lie ahead for the Commonwealth in addressing these concerns? Before answering these questions, it is important to examine how the thinking of indigenous women/feminists differs from that of Western women/feminists.

The perspective of indigenous women/feminists

While Western women/feminists see male domination as the foundation of women's discrimination and oppression, indigenous women/feminists see colonialism as the cornerstone of discrimination and oppression, with male domination as just one of the values subsequently imposed on and embedded in indigenous communities: their indigenous status, rather than their gender, is seen as the impediment to their enjoyment of human rights (Fox, 2002:1). According to many indigenous women/feminists, racism, national oppression, classism and colonialism are the key targets for activism and change.

Indigenous women/feminists seek the return to cultural traditions that honoured and valued women. Traditionally, indigenous women were placed at the centre of communities and families, and of political and cultural practices, that emphasised the participation of all in achieving balance and consensus. Equality between indigenous men and women and equality between indigenous and non-indigenous communities is at the heart of the indigenous women's struggle.

Equality between indigenous men and women and equality between indigenous and non-indigenous communities is at the heart of the indigenous women's struggle.

This sentiment was clearly expressed in the Beijing Declaration of Indigenous Women, 1995, issued at the Fourth World Conference on Women. The Declaration comprehensively sets out the major global and national causes of the plight of indigenous women from their perspective and offers a critique of the Beijing Draft Platform for Action.[15] It concludes with a section setting out 'Indigenous Women's Proposals and Demands'.

Traditionally, indigenous women and their concerns have been largely invisible to national women's machineries and women's non-governmental organisations (Mulenkei, 2002). Indigenous women have routinely been unrepresented or under-represented at local, national and international gender policy-making forums. While it is a welcome development that the UN and other inter-governmental associations, like the Commonwealth, are now trying to understand the issues facing indigenous women and to develop programmes of action to improve their circumstances, it is imperative that these initiatives are informed by the thinking of indigenous women themselves and that they involve indigenous women at every stage of the policy-making and implementation process.

While indigenous women will benefit from the increasing recognition of the rights of indigenous peoples in the international arena, they have specific needs and concerns which require special programmes of action. This paper considers four areas of concern in detail:

1 **Poverty** – indigenous women suffer from higher levels of poverty, largely due to their unequal opportunities with respect to land (they are often discriminated against by state practice and laws, as well as by customary and traditional practice and laws);

A cursory examination of several Commonwealth countries reveals stark disparities between the poverty levels of indigenous peoples and the dominant society in both developed and developing countries.

2 **Education** – indigenous women have unequal access to social services, such as education, with girls experiencing particularly high drop-out rates;

3 **Health** – indigenous women have unequal access to social services, such as health care, and are particularly vulnerable to domestic and state violence; and

4 **Political participation and representation** – indigenous women have unequal participation and representation in decision-making processes, and are particularly under-represented at the formal/official level.

1 Poverty

It is very difficult to measure the poverty experienced by indigenous peoples, including indigenous women, since the basic US$1 a day marker of extreme poverty does not adequately reflect the way of life of indigenous peoples who live partly outside a cash economy. Moreover, levels of poverty among indigenous peoples may not equate with levels of well-being. There are also not enough statistics on indigenous peoples to give accurate measurements. Nevertheless, it is important to try and compare the levels of poverty between indigenous peoples and the dominant society in order to get an approximate idea of their current poverty levels.

A cursory examination of several Commonwealth countries reveals stark disparities between the poverty levels of indigenous peoples and the dominant society in both developed and developing countries.

In India, the percentage of Scheduled Tribes living below the poverty line in 1991 was 51.9 per cent. This compares with 37.3 per cent of rural Indians living below the poverty line in the same year.[16]

In a study of indigenous peoples in Southern Africa funded by the European Commission, James Suzman (2001) comments: "In both Namibia and Botswana … the vast majority of San are poor or extremely poor". The poverty of the San is related to high degrees of welfare dependency, insecure access to land, low status if not actual discrimination, sedentarisation, unemployment, casual labour, begging or dependence on charity (ibid).

In Guyana, poverty among Amerindians has been recognised as a significant element in overall poverty. The National Development Strategy of 2000 states: "… in 1999, 95 per cent of the population in Regions 8 and 9, who are predominantly Amerindian, was classified as being in a state of absolute poverty" (Government of Guyana, 2000: 278). The Ministry of Amerindian Affairs is trying to redress this situation through its newly created Amerindian Development Fund and Amerindian Skills in Community Development project (Rodrigues, 2003).

According to the Department of Orang Asli Affairs, Malaysia, 80.8 per cent of Orang Asli were living below the poverty line in 1997, compared with only 8.5 per cent of the national population. By 1999, this figure had risen to 81.4 per cent (Nicholas, 2000: 30).

Poverty among indigenous peoples is not restricted to developing countries: for example, serious disparities in socio-economic indicators between the Mäori and non-Mäori continue to exist in New Zealand. Although the median income for Mäori adults in the year ending March 2001 was NZ$14,800, Mäori were still three times more likely to be unemployed than non-Mäori, and the disparity was greater than in 1991.[17] The Government is trying to respond to these disparities with a Reducing Social Inequalities strategy, which aims to build Mäori capacity.

It is clear that indigenous poverty in the Commonwealth is widespread and substantial and is linked to many other factors, including racism, lack of empowerment, invisibility, education, health, levels of employment and access to/control of land.

In the preamble to CEDAW, governments were: "Concerned that in situations of poverty women have the least access to food, health, education, training and opportunities for employment and other needs". This is especially true for indigenous women, who in both developing and developed countries generally suffer from higher levels of poverty than indigenous men and their counterparts in the dominant society. Poverty often reduces an indigenous woman's access to health care and education and other opportunities. Women suffering from ill health, widows and the elderly are particularly vulnerable to poverty and are often the poorest of the poor, since they have far fewer avenues for earning a living.

Landlessness is one of the main causes of poverty amongst indigenous peoples, particularly indigenous women, making land rights critical to the alleviation of indigenous poverty.

Many indigenous women, while playing a significant role in the traditional economies of their communities, are not part of the cash economy. They are therefore dependent on their husbands, sons or male relatives for money. In times of economic hardship, indigenous women are particularly prone to poverty.

The importance of indigenous women's "non-economic activities" to the indigenous community as a whole was stressed in the Beijing Declaration of Indigenous Women, 1995:

> The non-economic activities of indigenous women have been ignored and rendered invisible [by big industries and agribusiness corporations] although these sustain the existence of indigenous peoples. Our dispossession from our territorial land and water base, upon which our existence and identity depends, must be addressed as a key problem. para. 12

Poverty can often lead indigenous women into prostitution, with the attendant risk of being infected with HIV/AIDS.

While there are strong links between poverty among indigenous women and education and health (see below), there is an increasingly important link between poverty among indigenous women and landlessness.

Women and land

Landlessness is one of the main causes of poverty amongst indigenous peoples, particularly indigenous women, making land rights critical to the alleviation of indigenous poverty. Traditionally, many indigenous peoples subsisted on the land. However, with this land increasingly being designated part of conservation or protected areas, or being logged or mined, many indigenous peoples, including women, are becoming reliant on agricultural labour for their livelihoods.

Development projects are not the only cause of landlessness among indigenous peoples. Indigenous peoples have also been displaced from their traditional lands by conflict. For example, due to the conflict in Rwanda in 1994, many Twa now live as internal refugees and have been forced to enter the cash economy. Indigenous women were the most affected by the ethnic conflict in the country. The loss of husbands, sons and uncles to the fighting left many Twa women extremely vulnerable to poverty.

The most vulnerable Jumma women in the Chittagong Hill Tracts (CHT), Bangladesh, are the poorest, and the poorest Jumma women are the landless refugees, i.e. those who were displaced when the Kaptai hydro-electric dam was built, those who were forced off their lands by the military and Bengali settlers who migrated to the CHT between 1978 and 1983 and those hundreds of thousands of Jummas who fled to India for security due to the militarisation of the CHT.

Demilitarisation of the CHT would automatically increase security for Jumma women, and the return of land to the Jumma would reduce the overall poverty in the CHT, not just among the landless women.

Any measures to end discrimination against indigenous women with respect to land rights, such as issuing individual titles to women, must be considered in the light of indigenous strategies to gain recognition of their collective land rights as a necessary condition for the preservation and development of their identity and the social, economic and cultural survival of their communities.[18] Moreover, indigenous peoples, including women, want to be involved in all stages of development projects in their traditional habitats – they want to decide how and when to develop and in the process they do not want to give up their indigenous identity.[19]

Wage labour

Indigenous peoples encounter two kinds of problems upon becoming wage labourers. Firstly, they are discriminated against in terms of wages. Indigenous peoples, including women, generally earn far less than their counterparts in the dominant society. For example, Twa women in Uganda are paid less than 50 cents a day, 50 per cent less than non-Twa women (Jackson, 2003). Similarly, research done among the Ogoni in Nigeria demonstrates that "the incidence of poverty in Ogoni is higher among female adults than among male adults ... women's incomes, on average are about 50 per cent of men's incomes" (Naanen, 2003).

While article 11 of CEDAW states that parties "shall take all appropriate measures to eliminate discrimination against women in the field of employment in order to ensure, on a basis of equality of men and women, the same rights, in

Without land or collateral it is extremely difficult for indigenous peoples to get any kind of credit. Few indigenous people, particularly women, have access to micro credit schemes to assist them in times of difficulty.

particular: (d) The right to equal remuneration", it is equally important that States take measures to eliminate discrimination against indigenous peoples in the field of employment in order to ensure equality of all peoples.

Secondly, where the cash economy and wage employment predominate among indigenous peoples, as in Australia, unemployment makes for poverty. In 2000, the unemployment rate for Aboriginals was 17.6 per cent, more than twice the 7.3 per cent rate for non-indigenous Australians (Jones, 2003). A similar scenario exists in New Zealand, where in 1995 the Mäori unemployment rate was 15 per cent, significantly higher that that of the majority population (Ministry for Mäori Development, 1998).

Credit and savings

Without land or collateral it is extremely difficult for indigenous peoples to get any kind of credit. Few indigenous people, particularly women, have access to micro credit schemes to assist them in times of difficulty.

Article 13 (b) of CEDAW, which urges States to give women equal rights to "bank loans, mortgages and other forms of financial credit", and article 14, which addresses the "particular problems faced by rural women", and which urges States to ensure they have equal access to "agricultural credit and loans", have little meaning for indigenous women who are facing a financial crisis.

Trafficking

With the loss of land, and hence their ability to sustain themselves, some indigenous women are being sold as labourers to other continents. In Sri Lanka, young Wanniyala-Aetto (Veddha) women who have been removed from their traditional forests and who are now living in government rehabilitation villages are sold as contract domestic workers to employers in the Middle East for as little as SL Rupees 7,000 per woman. It goes without saying that once abroad, many of these women face sexual abuse from their employers or end up in brothels (Stegeborn, 2002:11–12).

Traditional knowledge

The loss of land is also often accompanied by a loss of traditional knowledge. This loss has impacted most on women, since indigenous women are the custodians of much of the traditional ecological knowledge (Sen, 2002).

In the section on 'Actions to be taken' of the Outcome Document, paragraph 71(a) urges States to: "Consider adopting, where appropriate, national legislation consistent with the Convention on Biological Diversity to protect the knowledge, innovations and practices of women in indigenous and local communities relating to traditional medicines, biodiversity and indigenous technologies".

It is critical that the traditional ecological knowledge of indigenous women is preserved and utilised in the management of natural resources and the preservation of biodiversity.

It is critical that the traditional ecological knowledge of indigenous women is preserved and utilised in the management of natural resources and the preservation of biodiversity.

Customary law

Article 14 of CEDAW, which addresses the "particular problems faced by rural women", urges States to ensure rural women have "equal treatment in land and agrarian reform as well as in land resettlement schemes".

While not all customary practices are favourable to indigenous women – in many developing countries in the Commonwealth, indigenous women are discriminated against by customary land tenure systems (e.g. the Maasai in Kenya) – on the whole, non-traditional land tenure systems are disadvantageous to indigenous peoples, in particular women, thus further threatening their land security.

In some traditional societies, such as the Twa of Uganda, women have access to resources in their own right and not as a consequence of their relationships with men. However, Twa women are increasingly losing opportunities for access to land, either because they have lost land due to the conflict in Rwanda or because the norms of the majority community (statutory land tenure practices) have influenced customary practice.

... indigenous women are not only routinely less educated than indigenous men, they are also less educated than their female counterparts in the dominant society.

Indigenous consent

It is now generally recognised that no decisions directly relating to indigenous peoples' land rights and interests should be taken without their "informed consent".[20] In 2000, the Committee on the Elimination of Racial Discrimination recognised indigenous peoples' right to "effective participation ... in decisions affecting their land rights, as required under article 5(c) of the Convention and General Recommendation XXIII of the Committee, which stresses the importance of ensuring the 'informed consent' of indigenous peoples".[21] In 2001, the UN Committee on Economic, Social and Cultural Rights recommended that Colombia "ensure the participation of indigenous peoples in decisions affecting their lives. The Committee particularly urges the State party to consult and seek the consent of the indigenous peoples concerned ..."[22]

2 Education

Article 10 of CEDAW states that parties "shall take all appropriate measures to eliminate discrimination against women in order to ensure to them equal rights with men in the field of education ..."

The Outcome Document, Beijing +5, went further and stated in 'Actions to be taken', that governments should: "With the full voluntary participation of indigenous women, develop and implement educational and training programmes that respect their history, culture, spirituality, languages and aspirations and ensure their access to all levels of formal and non-formal education, including higher education" (para. 95 (e)).

There are two issues of concern to indigenous peoples with regard to education: firstly, are their children getting an education? And secondly, if so, is it an education that is culturally sympathetic and empowering, as well as assisting their survival in majority society? Of particular concern is the question: are indigenous girls getting an education and, if so, is it appropriate?

A cursory examination of the levels of education among indigenous women in a selection of Commonwealth member States shows that indigenous women are not only routinely less educated than indigenous men, they are also less educated than their female counterparts in the dominant society.

In India, the enrolment rate for Scheduled Tribal children in 1997–98 was only 66 per cent nationally, and only 53 per cent among girls (Sujatha, 2003). More seriously, there is a high rate of absenteeism (see next section). Despite a strong and quite successful national drive for girls' education in India since then, literacy rates among Adivasi girls over the age of seven remain extremely low. They averaged 18.2 per cent in 1991 and were as low as 4.4 per cent in Rajasthan in that year. In 2001 it was still reckoned that over three quarters of Scheduled Tribeswomen were illiterate (Ministry of Tribal Affairs, India, 2001).

In the Federally Administered Tribal Areas (FATA) of Pakistan, tribal Pushtun women suffer from the highest levels of poverty, illiteracy and poor health not only in Pakistan but in the whole of South Asia, with literacy rates as low as 1 per cent (Bibi, 2002: 1). This is one of the lowest literacy rates in the world. The overall literacy rate for tribals in FATA is 6.38 per cent (ibid: 19). The weight of religious and cultural tradition against women's education is so great in FATA that it will be some time before equity of educational achievement between the sexes is attained.

Drop-out rates

Article 10(f) of CEDAW urges States to ensure "the reduction of female student drop-out rates and the organisation of programmes for girls and women who have left school prematurely".

Traditionally, indigenous children, especially girls, have a high drop-out rate from school. In India, for example, the drop-out rate for Scheduled Tribal children in 1997–98 ranged from 47.7 per cent in Nagaland to 76.8 per cent in Orissa, with nine states seeing rates of over 60 per cent and figures normally worse for girls than boys (Sujatha, 2003: 40–41). There are multiple reasons for absenteeism among indigenous children on the whole (see below), but the main reason why girls so frequently drop out is because they are required to help their parents at home. In many Commonwealth African countries, indigenous parents continue to prefer to spend their limited resources on ensuring that boys get an education at the expense of girls, on the grounds that the girls will marry, have

In most Commonwealth member States, the public education that is being provided for indigenous peoples is unsuitable.

a family and be supported by their husband.

Generally, the proportion of indigenous girls at secondary school falls dramatically. In many Commonwealth African countries, there are very few indigenous girls in tertiary education.

Wider effects of education

As for all women, education is not just about learning, it is about creating opportunities and it is a major tool of empowerment for indigenous women. Moreover, indigenous women play a crucial role in the education of young children, including the transfer of traditional knowledge. Indigenous women are also responsible for educating their children in health issues, both traditional and modern.

As Richard Bourne, in his CPSU report 'Invisible Lives', writes:

> It is impossible to overstate the significance of girls' education not only for their own rights, health and opportunities, but for their children and communities. Improved girls' education is associated with smaller family size, enhanced well being and reduced poverty, although it can be culturally disruptive.
>
> 2003:33

Culturally sensitive education

Going beyond school attendance is a debate about the type of education that is available to indigenous peoples and the degree of participation and empowerment it offers. Most indigenous parents are looking for a type of education that respects their own language, culture and traditions while assisting youngsters and the community to negotiate successfully with the majority society.

In most Commonwealth member States, the public education that is being provided for indigenous peoples is unsuitable. In Guyana, the National Development Strategy, 2000, concludes:

> Despite the best intentions, the result has been that education has a non-traditional focus that may not be applicable to community development. p. 281

It is increasingly being acknowledged that indigenous peoples require an education that is culturally sensitive to their specific needs and worldview, and that the current content of most national curricula poses multiple disadvantages for indigenous children.

For example, research undertaken in Botswana reveals that the failure of the education system to take into account the linguistic, cultural, social and economic barriers to learning for Basarwa (San) children is underpinning low enrolment rates and high drop-out rates. The children are being held back because they do not speak Setswana, the national language and language of the schools. Moreover, what they are being taught bears little relation to their own worldview (Pridmore, 1995).

Research done amongst First Nations in Canada has revealed that the national education system has had the effect of diminishing children's respect for their own cultures and identity and setting up psychological confusion and educational failure. A study in two Innu communities in Labrador shows that most Innu have had almost entirely negative experiences with schools and teachers (Samson, 2001). Many Innu children, of both sexes, have been physically and sexually abused by priests and teachers, and made to feel ashamed of their identity and language.

The very nature of most non-traditional education systems – conducted in school rooms, by designated teachers, at regular hours each day – is anathema to most indigenous traditions, where traditionally education was largely an informal process, undertaken by the parents and grandparents, that provided the young with specific skills, attitudes, knowledge and values required to function in everyday life. Inevitably, where formal education is strange and where indigenous children may find themselves and their traditions disparaged, there will be a huge drop-out rate.

3 Health

Article 12 (2) of CEDAW states: "States parties shall take all appropriate measures to eliminate discrimination against women in the field of health care in order to ensure, on a basis

... the health of indigenous peoples remains far lower than the majority population in both developed and developing countries.

of equality of men and women, access to health care services, including those related to family planning".

In this context, the CEDAW Committee has advised States that "special attention should be given to the health needs and rights of women belonging to vulnerable and disadvantaged groups, [including] ... indigenous women".[23]

However, despite the suggestions of the Committee and the WHO declaration on the health and survival of indigenous peoples in 1999, the health of indigenous peoples remains far lower than the majority population in both developed and developing countries. It was noted in a statement to the UN Commission on Human Rights in April 2001 by Jacqueline Sims, WHO Focal Point on the Health of Indigenous Peoples, that:

> ... Indigenous everywhere have generally higher morbidity and mortality patterns than other population groups; lower life expectancy; and higher infant and child mortality rates. Basic services such as water, sanitation, transport and energy – all strongly linked to health status – tend to be less frequently available to indigenous communities.

In the same statement, WHO noted the "dearth of reliable data and information on indigenous peoples' health", impeding a national and global understanding of the range and extent of health issues affecting them. This information gap is obstructing regional and national efforts to improve the health of indigenous peoples', as called for in WHO Resolution 53.10, May 2000.

The statement goes on to say that the "common denominators linking the types of ill-health experienced by indigenous peoples everywhere are poverty and marginalisation, exacerbated by a lack of access to culturally competent health services".

According to indigenous peoples, however, the causes of poor health are more complex and interrelated. In May 2002, the Permanent Forum was told that the acute health needs of indigenous peoples cut across socio-economic boundaries and that the underlying causes of poor health were multiple, including colonisation, homelessness, poor housing, poverty, lack of reproductive health rights, domestic violence and addiction. The Forum was told that health care must be envisaged from an indigenous perspective, encompassing mental, physical and spiritual health, and that there was a direct relationship between land use and indigenous health. Moreover, it was emphasised that indigenous women and children had special needs, including expanding immunisation and combating domestic abuse and addiction.[24]

A similar conclusion was reached by the Standing Committee on Health and Community Care in the legislative assembly of the Australian Capital Territory, which carried out an inquiry into indigenous health in Canberra in 2000–2001. It concluded that, while health was the focus of its investigations, the committee "could not help but see the extent of Indigenous people's disadvantage; disadvantage which runs through all facets of their lives". The Committee stated:

> Health is tied in to homelessness, poor housing, high rates of incarceration, high rates of alcohol and drug abuse, domestic violence and dependency.[25]

Similar conclusions were expressed in 'The Health of Indigenous Peoples: The Kuching Statement for Action', adopted at the 6th World Rural Health Congress, Spain, 2003.[26]

While it is impossible to disaggregate the causes of ill health for indigenous peoples, it is nevertheless important to try and locate the causes of indigenous women's ill health and their special needs in order to inform regional and national efforts to improve their health. In general, indigenous women suffer from worse health than indigenous men and their female counterparts in the dominant society. There are high levels of maternal mortality, high rates of HIV/AIDS, domestic and state violence, poor access to health care and health risks associated with some traditional cultural practices.

Maternal mortality

Maternal mortality rates among indigenous women in the Commonwealth are far higher than those among the dominant female population, in both developing and developed countries.

In Malaysia, 25 out of the 42 Malaysian mothers who died during delivery in 1994 were Orang Asli. This meant that an

Orang Asli mother was 119 times more likely to die in childbirth than another Malaysian (Nicholas, 2000).

The maternal mortality rate for indigenous women in Australia in 1994–1996 was 35 per 100,000 live births, more than three times higher than the rate of 10 per 100,000 for non-indigenous women. While this rate reflects the higher rate of confinements among indigenous women, according to the modelled estimates of the World Development Indicators the overall maternal mortality ratio in Australia in 1995 was 6 per 100,000 live births, nearly six times lower than the indigenous maternal mortality rate (Jones, 2003:85–86).

HIV/AIDS

In remote areas many indigenous women have little or no education about birth control or sex education, including information about HIV/AIDS. Rape also increases the risk of HIV/AIDS among indigenous women. Perpetrators of the armed conflict in Rwanda are reported to have sexually abused Twa women in Uganda, contributing to an increase in HIV/AIDS infection in the community.

Article 6 of CEDAW states: "States Parties shall take all appropriate measures, including legislation, to suppress all forms of traffic in women and exploitation of prostitution of women". Despite the Convention, prostitution amongst indigenous women is actually growing, increasing the risk of HIV/AIDS infection. Indigenous women are often reduced to prostitution due to poverty.

There is evidence that HIV/AIDS also spreads where development projects, bringing in male workers from elsewhere with cash resources, fuel prostitution among young indigenous women. This has happened on a significant scale in West and Southern Africa; there has been prostitution among Twa women with male workers working on the Chad-Cameroon oil pipeline in Cameroon, and among the Ogoni with oil workers in the Niger Delta, Nigeria. In Nigeria, HIV/AIDS infection rates are reportedly higher in the oil-producing areas than in the rest of the country.[27]

Domestic and state violence

Indigenous women across the Commonwealth experience two forms of sexual violence: domestic and state violence.

Paragraph 69 (h) of the Outcome Document, 'Actions to be taken' urged governments to: "Take concrete steps, as a priority and with their full and voluntary participation, to address the impact of violence on indigenous women …"

Indigenous women across the Commonwealth experience two forms of sexual violence: domestic and state violence. Like their female counterparts in the dominant society, they experience sexual violence from members of their own community. The Toledo Maya women in Belize, for example, are reported to suffer high rates of domestic violence. There is little a Maya woman can do to rectify her situation. As one commentator writes: "Maya women who attempt to leave their abusers may find themselves completely isolated if they try to support a family as a single parent, and are culturally discriminated against by other families" (Teul, 2003).

The high rates of alcoholism among the indigenous male population in many Commonwealth countries (often explained as a response to the cultural collapse of their traditional communities) is partly responsible for the increase in incidents of domestic violence within indigenous communities.

Article 5 of CEDAW reads: "States Parties shall take all appropriate measures: (a) To modify the social and cultural patterns of conduct of men and women, with a view to achieving the elimination of prejudices and customary and all other practices which are based on the idea of the inferiority or the superiority of either of the sexes or on stereotyped roles for men and women".

Despite the Convention, indigenous women continue to suffer from traditional tribal practices that clearly denigrate them. Tribal Pushtun women in FATA, Pakistan, are perhaps the most vulnerable of all indigenous women in the Commonwealth to domestic violence as a result of traditional practices. Indeed, as one commentator writes: "Domestic violence is regarded as the main entertainment of village life, and women routinely display bruises and scars they have received at the hands of their husbands" (Bibi, 2002:22).

Though most tribal peoples in FATA are Muslim, the understanding and application of Islam is often overlaid by

Indigenous women also face sexual violence from members of non-indigenous communities. This is often the case during times of ethnic conflict.

tribal norms and culture. For example, the 'honour' killings, for which FATA is infamous, have nothing to do with Islam. In tribal areas, a woman will be killed to save the family honour if she is suspected of contact with a man outside of her family, or upon refusal to marry a man chosen by her family.

Indigenous women also face sexual violence from members of non-indigenous communities. This is often the case during times of ethnic conflict. For example, as previously mentioned, during the ethnic conflict in Rwanda, Twa women in Uganda suffered sexual violence from the perpetrators of the conflict.

Indigenous women are also the victims of sexual violence by the State. This is the often the case in countries or regions that are highly militarised. The Jumma women in the CHT, Bangladesh, which has been militarised since 1975 (in 1991, the ratio of security personnel to Jumma peoples was 1:10), are particularly vulnerable to sexual violence by the security forces (Chakma, 2002). Jumma women who have been raped by security personnel experience social stigma and are often ostracised by their community as a result, leaving many young women unmarried. This all too often leads to poverty.

It should be noted that both Jumma men and women face continuing human rights violations by the security forces and Bengali settlers in the CHT.[28]

Poor access to health care

Remoteness is a serious factor inhibiting indigenous women's access to health care. For example, Amerindian women living in rural areas in the interior of Guyana live far away from any health facilities and transport is poor. Breast cancer is currently on the increase amongst them due to a lack of adequate cancer screening, caused in part by the remoteness of many Amerindian villages (Rodrigues, 2003:5).

Traditional cultural practices

There is a cultural conflict between scientific medicine and indigenous traditions, where illness is seen as a matter of the spirit, requiring holistic treatment. Indeed, indigenous peoples are still more likely to seek health assistance from traditional healers than from those trained in scientific medicine. In Tanzania, for example, there were between 30,000 and 40,000 traditional medical practitioners in 1982, compared with only 600 trained doctors (Indigenous Information Network, 2001). In India, where people from Scheduled Tribes make use of shamans and healers, "medical personnel are contacted as a last resort" (Ministry of Tribal Affairs, India, 2001:95).

While most traditional practices are harmless, some are dangerous. This is the case with the practice of female genital mutilation among the Pokot and other indigenous communities in Kenya.

4 Political Participation and Representation

Article 7 of CEDAW reads: "States Parties shall take all appropriate measures to eliminate discrimination against women in the political and public life of the country …" The Beijing +5 Outcome Document, 'Actions to be taken', urges governments to: "Address the barriers faced by women, particularly indigenous and other marginalised women, in accessing and participating in politics and decision-making …" (para. 66(b)) and to: "Apply and support positive measures to give all women, particularly indigenous women, equal access to capacity-building and training programmes to enhance their participation in decision-making in all fields and at all levels" (para. 95(j).

Traditionally, Commonwealth governments have not seen their accountability to indigenous peoples as of much importance. Few MPs in Commonwealth countries – with the exception of some Mäori MPs in New Zealand, some Adivasi MPs in India and the rather special case of Fiji Islands (where the native Fijians are in the majority) – are statutorily or in reality accountable to indigenous electorates. Indigenous electors are generally outvoted by larger groups of constituents, while indigenous MPs also are comfortably outvoted in assemblies and parliaments (except where State governments have been defined to help indigenous groups, as in Nunavut in Canada).

Political representation is one way of measuring the public profile of disadvantaged groups. While there are an increasing number of indigenous elected representatives on local govern-

While there are an increasing number of indigenous elected representatives on local government bodies, relatively few indigenous peoples have been elected to regional or national government bodies.

ment bodies, relatively few indigenous peoples have been elected to regional or national government bodies. In Australia, for example, there are no indigenous politicians in Australia's House of Representatives, although there is one indigenous man in the Senate. There is currently one indigenous woman Commissioner serving on the ATSIC Board.

Generally, as with indigenous peoples on the whole, indigenous women have unequal opportunities to political participation and representation. While they traditionally play a critical role in decision-making processes at the informal/community level, they rarely participate in politics at the formal/national level. Indigenous feminists argue that this is the result of a patriarchal system imposed on indigenous communities which is inherently discriminatory towards women and which prevents women from taking up political leadership roles despite their traditional role in informal politics. Traditional governance is characterised by an emphasis on participation of all community members (including women) in achieving consensus and consulting members for their knowledge and leadership on specific issues (Fox, 2002:6).

Even in Canada, where indigenous women enjoy far greater participation in the political processes than in other Commonwealth countries, they still find it difficult to participate in formal or national decision-making processes (ibid).

Funding agencies have traditionally ignored indigenous governance practices. They have failed to appreciate the scope and extent of consultation required in indigenous communities (ibid:7). Emphasising the importance of formal talks over community participation specifically excludes the participation of indigenous women, which is highly concentrated outside formal talks.

In addition, indigenous women have difficulty accessing decision-making processes, not only because they are indigenous and because of their gender, but because they belong to a numerical minority. Their numerical status and the prejudice of the majority non-indigenous community often prevails against indigenous peoples getting elected to public bodies.

Moreover, given the poor statistical data on indigenous peoples in many Commonwealth countries, some indigenous peoples of both sexes are not included on the electoral roll and therefore cannot exercise their right to vote.

Traditionally, tribal Pushtun women in FATA, Pakistan, have not been allowed to vote or have been discouraged from doing so. Tribal self-government has therefore been disadvantageous to Pushtun women. There has never been a tribal woman from FATA represented in the National Assembly or Senate in Pakistan.

Land security and management over traditional resources have to be at the heart of any national programmes designed to alleviate poverty amongst indigenous women.

Conclusion

This paper demonstrates that the Commonwealth needs to come into line with current international thinking on the rights of indigenous peoples. It also reveals that the Commonwealth is lagging far behind current efforts by the UN to address the specific issues facing indigenous women. As such, it encourages Heads of Government to make a commitment to the promotion and protection of the rights of indigenous peoples by including a statement of support in the 2005 Commonwealth Declaration.

Land security and management over traditional resources must be at the heart of any national programmes designed to alleviate poverty amongst indigenous women. However, any measures to end discrimination against indigenous women with respect to land rights, such as issuing them with individual titles, must be considered in the light of indigenous strategies to gain recognition of their collective land rights (see above). In other words, all national programmes directed at redressing the poverty facing indigenous women must recognise the importance of collective land for indigenous women.

If indigenous rights to education are to be realised, national governments must show more respect to the peoples whose children are to be educated. The educational process must be more of a partnership with communities and parents, and indigenous teachers must do more of the teaching.[29] Indigenous peoples are also calling for an increased role in the provision and development of health care. Community controlled health organisations offer the best chance of improving the health of indigenous men, women and children. They would offer culturally appropriate services that indigenous peoples would want to use. Moreover, indigenous peoples want their health care to be holistic in outlook, taking into account the intricate links between health and other issues they face. As with education, the first task in tackling health problems among indigenous peoples is to raise their visibility. This can only be done through the dedicated collection and collation of statistical data.[30]

At the heart of the indigenous rights movement is the demand for recognition of the right of indigenous peoples to self-determination, including the right to freely determine their political status. For the majority of indigenous peoples in the Commonwealth, self-determination is not about separatism, but about autonomy or self-government.[31] Indigenous self-determination is a pre-requisite for the exercise of their spiritual, social, cultural, economic and political rights, as well as their practical survival.[32]

Notes

1 The largest concentration of indigenous peoples in the Commonwealth is in India, where there are approximately 85 million Adivasis or Scheduled Tribes.
2 This project is funded by the European Commission and the UK Department for International Development. For more information, see the CPSU website: *www.cpsu.org.uk*
3 Beijing Declaration of Indigenous Women, Fourth World Conference on Women.
4 1993 was declared the International Year of the World's Indigenous People.
5 The World Bank is currently in the process of revising this policy.
6 For the full text of the Draft Declaration see: *http://www.unhchr.ch/indigenous/groups-02.htm*
7 There are many arguments over the wording of the Draft Declaration (to date only two of the 45 articles have been accepted). The Commonwealth States of Australia, Canada and the UK are at the forefront in opposing, along with the United States, the inclusion of the term 'self-determination' in the Draft Declaration. For more information on the Commonwealth and the Draft Declaration see Whall, forthcoming 2005.
8 Two of the current members of the 16-member forum are from a Commonwealth country.
9 For more information on the Commonwealth Association of Indigenous Peoples see the CPSU website at: *http://www.cpsu.org.uk/projects/CAIP.HTM*
10 Sri Lanka is presently considering accession to ILO 169.
11 For more information on Nunavut, see Dahl, Hicks and Jull, 2000.
12 In 2002, when the UN Committee monitoring the Convention on the Elimination of Racial Discrimination considered Canada's periodic report regarding domestic implementation, aboriginal issues were placed high on the agenda and members expressed much concern about what was referred to as "Canada's most glaring human rights problem". Amongst the concerns raised, special attention was paid to Ottawa's continuing effort to extinguish Aboriginal Title, which violates both Canadian Supreme Court of Canada decisions and international human rights law.
13 See 'Concluding Observations by the Committee on the Elimination of Racial Discrimination: Australia', 19/04/2000, CERD/C/304/Add.101, 19 April 2000.
14 See Note by the Secretary General, 11 July 2002, A/57/204.
15 The Beijing Declaration of Indigenous Women was signed by 118 indigenous groups from 27 countries worldwide. See also the Declaration of the International Indigenous Women's Forum, adopted in New York at Beijing +5 in 2000.

16 National Planning Commission, India.
17 Ministry of Mäori Development website, *Statistics New Zealand.*
18 In 1997, the Committee recommended to the Government of Australia that it "ensure women's equal access to individual ownership of native land". This recommendation was seen by many indigenous peoples as undermining rather than strengthening the human rights of indigenous women. See Kambel, 2004:3.
19 See Part VI, Land and Resources, of the Draft Declaration on the Rights of Indigenous Peoples.
20 General Recommendation XXIII (51) concerning Indigenous Peoples Adopted at the Committee's 1235th meeting, on 18 August 1997. UN Doc. CERD/C/51/Misc.13/Rev.4, at para. 4(d).
21 Concluding Observations by the Committee on the Elimination of Racial Discrimination: Australia. 24/03/2000. CERD/C/56/Misc.42/rev. 3, at para. 9.
22 Concluding Observations of the Committee on Economic, Social and Cultural Rights: Colombia. 30/11/2001. E/C.12/Add. 1/74, at para. 33.
23 Committee on the Elimination of Discrimination Against Women, General Recommendation No. 24, article 12 of the Convention on the Elimination of All Forms of Discrimination against Women – women and health (1999).
24 UN Press Release, HR/4597, 20 May 2002.
25 Aboriginal and Torres Strait Islander Health in the ACT, report no 10 of the Standing Committee on Health and Community Care, August 2001, p. 86.
26 For a copy of the Kuching Statement see: *http://www.cpsu.org.uk/projects/indigenous/indig_advoc.htm*
27 Information supplied by Ledum Mitee, President, Movement for the Survival of the Ogoni People (MOSOP), at a CPSU Consultation on the 'Socio-Economic Rights of Indigenous Peoples in the Commonwealth', London, March 2003.
28 For a fuller account of the current issues facing the Jumma people of Bangladesh, see Roy, 2002.
29 See Part IV, article 15, Education, of the Draft Declaration on the Rights of Indigenous Peoples.
30 See Part V, article 24, Health, of the Draft Declaration on the Rights of Indigenous Peoples.
31 Of the many indigenous groups in the Commonwealth that are claiming the right to self-determination, only the Nagas in North-east India are claiming the right to secession, from India. For more information on the Nagas, see: *http://www.cpsu.org.uk/projects/DELHI_P2.HTM*
32 See Part V, Participation and Development, and Part VII, Self-Government and Indigenous Laws, of the Draft Declaration on the Rights of Indigenous Peoples.

References

Bibi, Maryam (2002). 'How Can A Sustainable Female Education Programme be Introduced by a Women's NGO in Selected Federally Administered Tribal Areas of Pakistan?: A Feasibility Study', MA Social Policy Dissertation, University of York, September.

Bourne, Richard (2003). 'Invisible Lives – Undercounted, under-represented and underneath: the socio-economic plight of Indigenous peoples in the Commonwealth'. London: Commonwealth Policy Studies Unit, May.

Chakma, Kabita (2002). 'Security of Indigenous Women in the Chittagong Hill Tracts (CHT)', Paper presented at the 'Women and Leadership: Voices for Security and Development' conference, Ottawa, Canada, November.

Commonwealth Secretariat (2003). *Making Democracy Work for Pro-Poor Development. Report of the Commonwealth Expert Group on Development and Democracy*. London: Commonwealth Secretariat.

Dahl, Jens, Jack Hicks and Peter Jull (eds) (2000). 'Nunavut – Inuit Regain Control of their Lands and their Lives'. Copenhagen: IWGIA.

Fox, Stephanie Irlbacher (2002). 'Women's Participation in Self-Government Negotiations in the Northwest Territories, Canada', Paper presented at 'Taking Wing: Conference on Gender Equality and Women in the Arctic', Inari, Finland, August.

Government of Guyana (2000). 'National Development Strategy', Georgetown.

Hughes, Lotte (2003). *The No-Nonsense Guide to Indigenous Peoples*. London: Verso.

Indigenous Information Network (2001). *Nomadic News, 2000–2001*. Nairobi, Kenya.

Jackson, Dorothy (2003). 'Twa Women, Twa Rights in the Great Lakes Region of Africa'. London: Minority Rights Group International.

Jones, Nicky (2003). 'Poverty and Indigenous Rights in Australia'. Appendix B in Bourne, op cit.

Kambel, Ellen-Rose (2004). *A Guide to Indigenous Women's Rights under the International Convention on the Elimination of All Forms of Discrimination against Women*. Forest Peoples Programme, January.

Ministry of Mäori Development (1998). 'Trends in Mäori Employment, Income and Expenditure'. Wellington, New Zealand.

Ministry of Tribal Affairs, India (2001). 'Report of the Working Group for Empowering the Scheduled Tribes during the Tenth Five Year Plan (2000–2007)'. New Delhi, India.

Mulenkei, Lucy (2002). 'Indigenous Women's Rights in Africa', Paper presented at 'Indigenous Rights in the Commonwealth Project Africa Regional Expert Meeting', Cape Town, South Africa, October.

Naanen, Ben (2003). 'Progress of the Ogoni people in Nigeria towards the Attainment of the International Development Targets (IDTs) for Poverty, Education and Health', Appendix A in Bourne, op cit.

Nicholas, Colin (2000). 'The Orang Asli and the Contest for Resources'. Copenhagen: IWGIA.

Pridmore, Pat (1995). 'Learning and Schooling of Basarwa (Bushmen) children in Botswana', *Prospects*, XXV(4) (December).

Rodrigues, Carolyn (2003). 'Indigenous Rights in Guyana', Paper presented at the 'Indigenous Rights in the Commonwealth Caribbean and Americas Regional Expert Meeting', Guyana, June.

Roy, Raja Devasish (2002). 'Indigenous Rights in Bangladesh: Land Rights and Self-Government in the Chittagong Hill Tracts', Paper presented at 'Indigenous Rights in the Commonwealth Project South and South-East Asia Regional Expert Meeting', India, March.

Samson, Colin (2001). 'Teaching Lies: The Innu experience of schooling', *London Journal of Canadian Studies*, 16 (2000/2001).

Sen, Ilini (2002). 'An examination of sustainable food security systems in Chattisgargh, India: decentralised food security systems and women', Paper presented at 'Indigenous Rights in the Commonwealth Project South and South-East Asia Regional Expert Meeting', India, March.

Stegeborn, Wiveca (2002). 'Indigenous Rights in Sri Lanka: Assimilation of the Wanniyala-Aetto', Paper presented at 'Indigenous Rights in the Commonwealth Project South and South-East Asia Regional Expert Meeting', India, March.

Sujatha, K (2003) 'Education among Tribals', Paper presented at a CPSU Consultation on the 'Socio-Economic Rights of Indigenous Peoples in the Commonwealth', London, March.

Suzman, James (2001). 'Introduction to the Regional Assessment of the Status of the San in Southern Africa'. Windhoek, Namibia: Legal Assistance Centre.

Teul, Pulcheria (2003). 'Indigenous Socio-Economic and Cultural Rights in Belize, A Toledo Maya Women's Perspective', Paper presented at the 'Indigenous Rights in the Commonwealth Caribbean and Americas Regional Expert Meeting', Guyana, June.

Whall, Helena (2003a). 'Recognising and Protecting Indigenous Peoples' Rights in the Commonwealth', Memorandum to the Commonwealth Heads of Government attending the

Commonwealth Heads of Government Meeting (CHOGM), Abuja, Nigeria, 1–7 December.

—— (2003b), 'Indigenous Peoples in the Commonwealth: A Story of Exclusion'. In *The Parliamentarian, Commonwealth Parliamentary Association*, London, Issue 3/2003, pp. 249–56.

—— (2003c). 'The Challenge of Indigenous Peoples: The Unfinished Business of Decolonisation', *Round Table Journal of Commonwealth and Comparative Affairs*, London, October, pp. 635–59.

—— (forthcoming 2005). 'Indigenous Self-Determination in the Commonwealth of Nations'. In Hocking, Barbara A. (ed.). *Rethinking Indigenous Self-Determination*. Canberra, Australia: Aboriginal Studies Press.

World Bank (1991). *Operational Directive on Indigenous Peoples*. Washington DC: World Bank, September.

Appendix 1

Pan-Commonwealth Expert Group Meeting on Gender and Human Rights

Introduction

This Appendix contains a 'mini-report' of a pan-Commonwealth Expert Group Meeting on Gender and Human Rights, held at Marlborough House (Commonwealth Secretariat Headquarters in London), 17–19 February 2004.

The commissioned and background papers contained in the main body of this publication were the basis of discussion during the two-and-a-half day meeting. Although the Expert Group is not a decision-making body of the Commonwealth Secretariat, its members were asked to comment in a personal and professional capacities on the seven critical issues before them. The issues had been identified by Commonwealth Heads of National Women's Machineries at their meeting held in the wings of the United Nations Commission on the Status of Women in March 2003, as part of their brainstorming on the new Commonwealth Plan of Action for Gender Equality 2005–2015.

The format of the Expert Group meeting is reflected in the Agenda below, and a list of Experts who participated is also given. Discussants were asked to comment on the papers presented, and a general discussion followed – either in plenary or in small groups. There were seven critical areas to address and limited time allocated to each area, so discussion was focused on generating agreement on some of the critical issues relevant for Commonwealth action, with recommendations for the human rights section of the new Plan of Action for Gender Equality. All the key issues addressed were finally included in the Plan of Action, and this was adopted during the 7th Women's Affairs Ministers Meeting held in Fiji in May–June 2004. The final text of the Human Rights section of the Plan of Action for Gender Equality 2005–2015 can be found in Appendix II of this book.

We have included below the Discussants' comments, and have tried to capture the key recommendations made by Experts during the meeting. While the Commonwealth Plan of Action has not 'adopted' all of these recommendations, we include them as they may be useful for policy-makers and practitioners to draw upon in the course of their work.

Meeting Agenda

Day 1: Tuesday 17 February

08.30–09.30 Coffee and registration of participants

09.30–10.30 Welcome and opening remarks
Nancy Spence, *Director, Commonwealth Secretariat Social Transformation Programmes Division (STPD)*
Introductions of all participants

10.30–11.00 Overview on gender and human rights in the Commonwealth
The Plan of Action on Gender and Development to be agreed at the 7th Women's Ministerial Meeting in June.
'What have we achieved, where do we need to go?'
Rawwida Baksh, *Deputy Director, Head of Gender, STPD*

Expert Group Meeting: process, objectives and intended outcomes
Cindy Berman, *Gender and Human Rights Programme*, *STPD*

11.00–11.15 *Coffee break*

Session 1: CEDAW: Achievements and Challenges

11.15– 13.00 CEDAW: implementation of policies and legislation – progress, achievements, constraints and key priorities
Presentation: **Shanthi Dairiam**, *International Women's Rights Action Watch – Asia Pacific*
Discussant: **Betty Mould-Iddrisu**, *Director, Legal and Constitutional Affairs Division*, COMSEC

Plenary discussion

13.00–14.15 *Lunch in the Blenheim Saloon*

Session 2: Gender-based Violence

14.15 –15.15 Gender-based violence: overview of Commonwealth activities over the past decade; integrated approaches to gender-based violence; and recommendations for future action
Presentation: **Elsie Onubogu**, *Gender and Conflict Specialist*, COMSEC, on Tina Johnson's paper
Discussants: **Justice Athaliah Molokomme**, *High Court of Botswana*;
Professor Christine Chinkin, *London School of Economics (LSE)*, *UK*

15.15–16.00 Working groups

16.00–16.15 *Tea/coffee break*

16.15–17.30 Plenary report-back from Working Group Session 2

18.00–20.00 *Reception: Blenheim Saloon*
Participants and some Commonwealth Secretariat colleagues

Day 2: Wednesday 18 February

Session 3: Culture, the Law and Gender

09.00–10.30 Presentations:
1 Overview of key issues in culture, the law and gender
Catherine Muyeka Mumma, *Senior Counsel and Human Rights Commissioner, Kenya*
2 Conceptual/theoretical framework
Lisa Fishbayn, *legal consultant, academic, Harvard University*
Discussants: **Maiava Visekota Peteru**, *legal and human rights expert, Pacific region*; **Tracy Robinson**, *gender specialist, Caribbean region*

10.30–11.30 Working groups plenary report-backs

Coffee break included

Session 4: Trafficking and Migration

11.30– 13.00 Seeking rights: situating the trafficking in women – a human rights approach
Presentation: **Meena Shivdas**, *gender specialist and consultant, Asia region*
Discussants: **Lin Lean Lim**, *Director, Gender Promotion Programme, International Labour Organization*
Jarvis Matiya, *Chief Programme Officer, Human Rights Unit,* COMSEC

Plenary discussion

13.00 –14.15 *Lunch in the Blenheim Saloon*

Session 5: Indigenous Peoples' Rights

14.15–15.15 Indigenous peoples' rights in the Commonwealth – with a focus on indigenous women.
Presentation: **Dr Helena Whall**, *Commonwealth Policy Studies Unit (CPSU), UK*
Discussant: **Maryam Bibi**, *specialist and activist on Asian indigenous women*

15.15–15.30 *Tea/coffee break*

Session 6: Land and Property Rights

15.30–16.30 Key gender issues in land and property rights
Presentation: **Lucia Kiwala**, *UN-HABITAT*
Discussant: **Katalaina Sapolu**, *Legal and Constitutional Affairs Division*, COMSEC

16.30–17.30 Working groups to discuss Session 5 and 6

17.30–18.00 Plenary report-back from working groups

Day 3: Thursday 19 February

Session 7: Gender and Human Rights in the Life Cycle

09.00–10.30 Gender issues in the life cycle
Presentation: **Lin Lean Lim,** *Director, Gender Promotion Programme, International Labour Organization*
Discussant: **Fiona Clarke**, *Help Age International*

Plenary discussion

10.30–10.45 *Coffee break*

Session 8: Brainstorming and Recommendations

Identifying 'Niche' Areas for the New Commonwealth Plan of Action

10.45–11.45 Working groups: Discussion to put forward recommendations on focus areas in gender and human rights for the Commonwealth Plan of Action on Gender and Development 2005–2015.

11.45–12.45 Plenary report backs from working groups Session 8 and general discussion

12.45–13.00 Closing remarks, thanks and farewell to participants

13.00–14.00 *Final lunch in the Blenheim Saloon*

Notes from the Discussion and Recommendations

Session 1: CEDAW: Achievements and Challenges

Notes from the discussion

CEDAW provides for substantive equality. Although it has been signed by 49 Commonwealth countries, there is still no single country that lives up to the standards set out in the Convention and where implementation is promoted. There is a lack of political will: in some countries this is for cultural reasons; in others it because of limited resources or lack of political mobilisation.

Although all constitutions guarantee equality, they are subject to interpretation and the 'equality' provisions are used in a 'protectionist' way. Women have a right to equality, and governments have an obligation to promote legislation and policies that are more than gender neutral and to remove discriminatory provisions.

The conflict of legal systems within countries has impeded implementation of CEDAW. Implementation has also been hampered by delays. This is so despite the fact that CEDAW provides for the adoption of a policy for the elimination of discrimination without delay.

There are debates about the relevance of CEDAW to the daily lives of women, and questions are sometimes raised about whether all the articles in CEDAW are relevant to all women.

Access to justice is important and in this regard the Optional Protocol to CEDAW is an important step. However, not enough action has been taken to comply with the proviso of having exhausted domestic remedies and hence use the Protocol.

The problem of multiple discrimination against women was also raised. Women are discriminated against because they are poor or of a different ethnic group, as well as because they are women.

Recommendations

Commonwealth Secretariat

1 Promote ratification of CEDAW by those countries that have not become States parties (with the Commonwealth Parliamentary Association (CPA));

2 Target countries with a view to eliminating reservations (could be shared with NGOs);

3 Develop and share model legislation to incorporate CEDAW principles;

4 Use the process of constitutional/legislative reform as a mechanism to integrate CEDAW principles:
   a. include definition of discrimination, with explanatory recommendation for interpretation of discrimination to avoid misuse;
   b. develop model legislation for the incorporation of CEDAW (Legal and Constitutional Affairs Division (LCAD));

5 Assist States by providing tools/guidelines on reporting on CEDAW;

6 Assist States in linking CEDAW reporting to reporting on other human rights instruments and treaties (such as ILO/migrant workers, etc.), as well as on achievement of the Millennium Development Goals;

7 Provide assistance to civil society organisations in preparing shadow reports on international human rights instruments, including CEDAW/MDGs/ILO, etc. (with the Commonwealth Foundation);

8 Assist with the development of a toolkit for legal advocates to speed up the process for exhausting domestic remedies under CEDAW's Optional Protocol (with Commonwealth Lawyers Association (CLA)/Commonwealth Magistrates and Judges Association (CMJA));

9 Provide NGOs with information that will enable reporting back – see (6) above;

10 Provide a toolkit for States on different aspects of implementation of CEDAW principles.

Governments

11 Commit to human rights by ratifying and implementing UN human rights treaties, especially CEDAW, where this has not already been done;

12 Consider removing any reservations to CEDAW;

13 See (5).

14 Use the general recommendations of CEDAW to assist in implementation.

15 Promote CEDAW in all democratic institutions, especially amongst :
   a. parliamentarians
   b. public service
   c. justice system
   d. private sector
   e. legal advocates

16 Mobilise those at grassroots levels by informing them of their rights and how to take forward cases concerning discrimination (with NGOs);

17 Take special measures for affirmative action where required.

Non-governmental organisations

18 Undertake gender analysis of political processes, in particular those based on the Westminster process (CPA);

19 Women's NGOs to co-operate in a more cohesive way and with other human rights NGOs in reporting on international instruments – see (6);

20 Mobilise those at grassroots levels by informing them of their rights and how to take forward cases concerning discrimination (with governments);

21 Use reporting mechanisms more fully and also take into account regional instruments and the development of regional courts (with governments);

22 Look at new strategies and use the common law jurisprudence from other countries in advocacy work (CCA/CMJA).

Session 2: Gender-based Violence

Discussant comments

by **Christine Chinkin**

Gender-based violence is a cross-cutting theme that is relevant in different ways to all the other topics on the agenda of the meeting.

I have five brief points to make that arise from the excellent background paper. It is also important that the presenter has emphasised violence against women in armed conflict because of the continuum of violence that women experience in this situation, including post-conflict when domestic violence typically increases.

1 The definition of gender-based violence includes both violence that occurs exclusively to women and violence that affects women disproportionately. The latter includes disproportionate harm as well as the numbers of women affected by the particular form of violence. We should therefore bear in mind the gender-specific ways women are harmed by violence, including infection with HIV/AIDS and increased vulnerability to poverty (for example, through being unable to leave the home and work or becoming destitute on leaving an abusive relationship, and through prejudicial attitudes towards women being seen as the 'trouble maker' and thus being unable to return to their own families).

2 A number of the gender-based forms of violence listed in the paper relate to women's lack of access to property. Implicit also is the way women are perceived as property and are treated as commodities (trafficking) or as the possession of another person to be treated as that person wishes (for example, non-consensual sex in marriage). The linkage should also be made between violence, women as property and unequal access for women to economic and social rights, as enjoyment of economic and social rights militates against the treatment of women as property.

3 We should look not only at multiple discriminations but also at intersectional discrimination, that is, at the ways different forms of discrimination intersect and reinforce each other. Intersectionality covers the ways in which violence occurs and its forms (for

example, the targeting of minority or indigenous women for forced sterilisation) and the consequences of that violence (for example, an illegal immigrant woman who is subject to domestic violence is less likely to access the police or other agencies, including medical assistance, because of her vulnerability to deportation; a poorer woman in any society will be less likely to pursue legal remedies than one who has greater access to resources). The Committee on Racial Discrimination (CERD) produced an excellent report on the intersections between racial and gender discrimination before adopting its General Comment No. 25, and the same approach can be taken with respect to all other forms of discrimination such as ethnicity, age, disability, sexuality and class.

4 There have been a number of more recent developments with respect to international norms prohibiting violence against women and establishing redress for it. These include:

- The work of the International Criminal Tribunals for the Former Yugoslavia and Rwanda (ICTY/R) with respect to definitions of sex-based crimes, criminal procedures and protective measures;
- The inclusion of sex-based crimes of violence within the Statute of the International Criminal Court (ICC) and the potential work of the Court;
- The jurisprudence of the European Court of Human Rights, in particular the decision in MC *v. Bulgaria* (Case No. 39272/98), 4 December 2003;
- The Protocol to the African Charter on Human and Peoples' Rights on the Rights of Women in Africa, adopted July 2003, which mainstreams provisions on violence against women throughout.

5 In the current geo-political climate human rights are under challenge, for example, in the context of the war against terror. We have seen issues of violence against women manipulated by powerful Western governments for reasons not connected with guarantees of women's rights, for example in justifying the use of military force against the Taliban. The lack of genuine concern for reducing violence against women is shown by alliances with the Northern Alliance in Afghanistan and with other repressive groups/governments. The Commonwealth Secretariat should make a commitment to upholding the priority of reducing violence against women and of non-impunity of perpetrators (zero tolerance) as well as to the non-negotiability of crimes of violence against women in post-conflict peace processes and settlements.

Notes from the discussion

There is a need for a comprehensive definition of gender-based violence. This should refer to the fact that women are most affected, although men and boys are also victims. In addition, gender-based violence is most rampant in conflict and post-conflict situations. UN responses to violence relating to conflict situations are found in the ICTY, ICTR, ICC and Special Court for Sierra Leone.

Current policies around gender-based violence are inconsistent. CEDAW did not make specific reference to violence, although the CEDAW Committee's recommendation has incorporated this as a form of discrimination.

The Commonwealth Plan of Action promotes work with regional organisations, e.g. the Southern African Development Community (SADC), the development of national plans of action, and the development of a trainer's manual and training of leaders.

Possible national policy measures include:

1 Gender-sensitive laws;

2 Access to courts and justice;

3 Handling of domestic violence cases by law enforcement officers (police, magistrates);

4 Focus on negative cultural practices;

5 Police responses;

6 Men's initiatives;

7 Monitoring and evaluation efforts.

Some of the challenges faced in addressing gender-based violence include national frameworks, legal frameworks, traditional practices and religious beliefs.

Other players – such as UN agencies, regional inter-state institutions (Asia-Pacific, Africa, Caribbean, Europe, America) and NGOs – are already undertaking work in a number of important areas, including research, advocacy, policy development, education, protection, legal reform, service delivery, health, monitoring and evaluation and data collection.

Gaps that remain, however, include lack of co-ordination leading to no coherent picture of what is happening and the need for this to be evaluated. There is a need for localisation of policies, for effective national and regional interventions, for an assessment of good and bad practices and for the trickle up and trickle down of good practices and policies.

Recommendations

Commonwealth Secretariat

1 Continue to encourage an understanding of and commitment to the Integrated Approach to Eliminating Gender-based Violence by facilitating regional networking among various stakeholders (including the directors of committees set up to implement countries' national plans on violence against women and senior staff of national women's machineries), e.g. through managed e-mail lists;

2 Commission research on road mapping (who is doing what on this issue);

3 Document and share model laws, national plans of action, effective policies and good practices, e.g. through supporting regional good practice fairs or clinics on advocacy, services and legal frameworks;

4 Prepare a study on legal arguments and precedent and compilation as an advocacy tool;

5 Support training for personnel at all levels of the justice system, including judges and police officers, and periodic regional meetings for the exchange of experiences;

6 Encourage the incorporation by States of zero tolerance for gender-based violence, including no trade-off during post-conflict negotiations;

7 Develop educational materials, adaptable to national circumstances, to promote non-violent conflict resolution, respect for others and positive relationships. Governments could be encouraged to make these part of the official school curriculum and of teacher training programmes;

8 Work with governments and NGOs in sending and receiving countries to develop strategies to prevent, suppress and punish trafficking in women and girls. This would include ensuring that national legislation addressing the issue protects the human rights of those trafficked.

Governments

9 Implement the Commonwealth Secretariat's Integrated Approach to Eliminating Gender-based Violence, endorsed by Ministers Responsible for Women's and Gender Affairs, and incorporate a policy of zero tolerance – see (6);

10 If there is no national action plan on violence against women, develop such a plan as soon as possible and set up a national commission or committee that includes senior officials who can influence policy and budget allocation;

11 Ratify and implement the relevant human rights treaties where this has not already been done, consider removing any reservations to CEDAW and implement regional agreements;

12 Review and revise legislation to incorporate international standards and ensure gender sensitivity, identifying and amending discriminatory or oppressive laws, and enforce national laws against gender-based violence;

13 Allocate adequate financial support to address the issue, including the provision of women-friendly services such as shelters and other support for girls and women subjected to violence, in urban and rural areas, as well as medical, psychological and other counselling services and free or low-cost legal aid;

14 Ensure women's access to and safety at work through the development of appropriate policies and codes of conduct to address sexual harassment in the workplace, and

create an enabling environment for women's employment – including maternity and paternity leave, child care and transport – through affirmation action;

15 Recognise and support the work of NGOs and strengthen their capacity to provide services to women;

16 Ensure that gender-sensitive approaches and the promotion of non-violent conflict resolution – see (5) – are incorporated into school curricula and textbooks and are part of non-formal, continuing, adult and community education programmes;

17 Support public education campaigns and advocacy to eliminate traditional and cultural practices that constitute gender-based violence;

18 Create and fund training programmes to sensitise judicial, legal, medical, social, educational and police and immigrant personnel to the issue, and ensure that there is a gender balance in the composition of the bench, at all levels, and in all other court personnel.

Session 3: Culture, the Law and Gender

Discussant comments

by **Tracy Robinson**

The language of universalism and cultural relativism cannot capture the complexity of the issues or help us meaningfully imagine solutions. The Commonwealth Secretariat can contribute to changing that discourse to more productive terms. Whatever language we use must apply to the entire Commonwealth and not just developing countries and black and brown peoples. 'Culture' must be visible in all communities.

De jure *and* de facto

We have often talked about the dissonance between gains in legislation and the *de facto* position of women. But we should never lose sight of how legislation provides and has provided us with opportunities for cultural change.

In the Caribbean, for example, the Caribbean Community (CARICOM) designed model legislation dealing with domestic violence. Caribbean countries considered the model legislation, drafted and debated their own legislation and brokered slightly different arrangements for addressing domestic violence in each country. In Trinidad and Tobago, for instance, the legislation allows the perpetrator to give an 'undertaking' to not commit any further acts of violence as a way of avoiding the more onerous protection order. This does not exist elsewhere in the region. The process of law reform in the Caribbean has therefore produced domestic violence laws that represent negotiations about culture and growing consensus on the need for cultural change.

Additionally, we must create ways of assessing our progress and recognise slow, incremental gains that form part of a larger strategy with many elements. For example, the

Trinidad and Tobago Domestic Violence Act was first enacted in 1991 and substantial revisions were made in 1999. Although the Government has expressed scepticism about lower rates of domestic violence, it is clear that they are significantly lower.

The Commonwealth Secretariat can play a role in providing examples of best practice showing the range of strategies and, importantly, helping to create mechanisms for measuring or evaluating success. Research to make an assessment of what has been accomplished can offer a more realistic impression of this debate about culture and rights.

Women's agency

There is often a fascination with seeing women most where we hear them least. The debate about culture and women's rights will be strengthened if women's agency from inside/within a culture or community is recognised.

All systems that provide openings for the expression of 'cultural dissent' must be encouraged, so access to justice is key. More practically, the Commonwealth Secretariat can contribute by helping to build the capacity of the women's movement. And research is needed to show the genealogy of feminism in all countries.

Cultural conflict

While encouraging cultural dissent, we should be aware of the connection being made between gender conflict and women's security. By that I mean, the research (from the Caribbean at least) increasingly tells us that women engaged in resisting entrenched cultural practices that undermine gender equality may face a greater risk of intra-family violence. There is a tremendous challenge to enable women and keep them safe at the same time.

Notes from the discussion

Arguments in response to the cultural objection to women's human rights include: the fact that patriarchy is a feature of all societies, and that human rights and values are consistent with a wide range of cultural values.

There is a need to combine the best of jurisprudences of the various treaties (no matter their weaknesses) and the best in culture, and take advantage of the momentous transformations taking place to debate and transform culture.

Other issues that were raised include:

1 The role of law and judicial precedent in implementing women's human rights;

2 The limits imposed on the enjoyment of human rights by low socio-economic status;

3 The idea that culture is not necessarily an antithesis or hindrance to human rights, but that there is a need to understand and work with 'cultural structures';

4 There are at least two notions of culture, one static, organic and fragile and the other dynamic and shifting.

5 Certain factors complicate debates on women, culture and human rights: women as defenders of culture, the colonial legacy and globalisation;

6 Though legislative reform and judicial cases are not enough to realise women's human rights, they remain useful strategies and do result in changes over time or in the long term;

7 A multiplicity of strategies is needed to make the achievement of women's human rights a reality.

Recommendations

Commonwealth Secretariat

1 Support the collection and dissemination of case studies where legislation and court cases have brought about changes;

2 Develop ways of measuring the achievements that are being made.

Governments

3 Abolish cultural exceptions to laws protecting women's human rights and pass laws that eradicate traditional practices that violate women's human rights. Where there are conflicting law regimes, women must be given the option of opting out of private or customary law into general civil law;

4 Review and revise legislation to incorporate international human rights standards and ensure gender sensitivity, identifying and amending discriminatory or oppressive laws, including discriminatory provisions that take culture into account;

5 Supplement legislative change with educational programmes and use the law reform process to engage cultural communities in the process of reformulating traditional practices to conform to gender equality;

6 Identify cultural leaders and engage with them constructively on gender and human rights. Train local experts within the community, such as health practitioners and midwives, to engage community members in discussion about the cultural legitimacy of practices that negatively affect women;

7 Educate women and provide them with economic options to enable them to make their own choices about traditional practices and cultural norms;

8 Support efforts to build the capacity of the women's movement to advocate for better access to justice;

9 Facilitate community participation in the formulation and implementation of pro-rights policies that can enhance the enjoyment of economic, social and cultural rights.

Non-governmental organisations

10 NGOs, national human rights institutions together with civil society should develop tools to track gender and cultural issues in policy and public expenditure documents.

Session 4: Trafficking and Migration

Notes from the discussion

In considering what the Commonwealth can do on trafficking, it is important to bear in mind the following points:

1 Commonwealth Ministries of Women Affairs have urged governments to adopt and implement the 1996 Stockholm Declaration of the World Congress Against Sexual Exploitation of Children;

2 The Commonwealth Law Ministers Meeting in 1999 noted that the UN was preparing an international convention to combat transnational organised crime, with a protocol to prevent, suppress and punish trafficking in women and children. They encouraged the Secretariat to support this work and recommended the preparation of guidelines on measures to tackle the issues relating to trafficking of women and children in the Commonwealth;

3 One of the main problems is that trafficking has been regarded as an immigration/criminal issue as opposed to being a human rights issue. Current interventions remain largely gender blind and are often incompatible with a rights-based perspective. There is a need for a gender-responsive and rights-based approach to the problem, paying particular attention to the distinction between the individual and structural dimension of human rights of women and children;

4 Definitions of trafficking focus on the criminalisation of processes of movement rather than on remedies for women after they have been trafficked. It is preferable to use the Thai model of the "continuum of trafficking" – which includes coercion and trickery about conditions or hazards of work – as opposed to the definition in Sweden, which excludes those who come willingly but are deceived about expectations;

5 The issue of treatment of victims of trafficking in general, and children in particular, is a serious one. There is a need to change the perception that trafficking victims are criminals or offenders of the law. Strategies must be developed involving the community as well. This should be applicable both in countries of destination and of return;

6 Administrative procedures need to be more sensitive in handling victims in destination countries and in home countries, where women/girls sent back may be rejected by their family because they are seen as 'polluted'. Such repatriation to ostracism may result in vulnerability to re-trafficking to escape abuse in the home village;

7 The idea of women as 'property' is important as it is supported by women's lack of independent legal identity, e.g. independent rights of nationality that are not dependent upon their husbands;

8 The particular vulnerability of particular groups, such as indigenous peoples, should be given special consideration;

9 Trafficking also has class implications. For example, women's freedom from domestic work in developing countries is predicated on transferring that work to other women.

Recommendations

Commonwealth Secretariat

1 Undertake an assessment of who is doing what and to what extent in order to determine the added value that the Commonwealth could bring to existing initiatives. Many groups are active and there are already international standards in operation. It is suggested that the Secretariat should focus on prevention and treatment, and leave employment issues for the ILO;

2 Help to promote advocacy for the idea that trafficking should be addressed as a labour market and employment problem in both origin and destination countries;

3 Play a facilitating role in strengthening national capacity to ensure cohesiveness among countries' laws and policies, e.g. migrancy/AIDS policies;

4 Collect and share information about best practices.

Governments

5 Ensure that policies are guided by the UN Protocol to Prevent, Suppress and Punish Trafficking in Persons, Especially Women and Children 2000, the UN Recommended Principles and Guidelines on Human Rights and Human Trafficking 2002, CEDAW and other international instruments;

6 Ensure that there is legislation in place that covers trafficking not only for the purpose of sexual exploitation but also for forced labour, slavery or servitude;

7 Prosecute traffickers and ensure that those who have been trafficked have access to justice and are treated in a gender-sensitive manner;

8 Address the root causes of trafficking, including the feminisation of poverty and the gender discrimination that makes women and girls desperate, vulnerable and undervalued. Programmes need to have a broad anti-discrimination agenda;

9 Mainstream interventions at all levels of government in the development of policies and programmes and develop integrated and multisectoral programmes to address trafficking as a development issue at the national level.

10 Stress the importance of co-operation between ministries at all levels, since trafficking concerns not only the ministries of national security and law enforcement but also those of labour and other sectors and the national women's machinery.

11 Emphasise national level co-ordination to ensure cohesiveness among laws and policies within countries, e.g. migrancy/AIDS policies – see (3).

12 Ensure that labour legislation also covers domestic service and strengthen labour market institutions.

13 Follow the model of South Africa and Canada, which grant the same rights to aliens as nationals.

14 Co-operate to address the issue of trafficking at regional and international levels.

Session 5: Indigenous Peoples' Rights

Discussant Comments

by **Maryam Bibi**

The paper on Indigenous Peoples' Rights was very revealing and instructive for me as a tribal woman coming from Pakistan because I thought we were the only indigenous people and women facing discrimination, marginalisation and poverty. Now I realise that all indigenous women in the Commonwealth face similar issues, for example, poverty, poor health, low literacy rates and loss of language. Women suffer more as a result of continuing colonialism and as members of a poor class, though each situation can have unique problems.

I would like to endorse the definitions of indigenous peoples in the paper. I am very privileged to be here participating in this meeting today. However, I realise that I belong to a very small minority of indigenous women. The majority of indigenous women still live very traditional and hard lives in villages. Nevertheless, I share the same feelings, aspiration, belonging and kinship.

Indigenous peoples are perceived by others as on the one hand essential to sustainable development and the protectors of natural resources, while on the other hand their traditional practices are seen as conflicting with women's rights.

In the Federally Administered Tribal Areas (FATA) of Pakistan's North-West Frontier Province, development is mainly for political purposes and rarely for empowerment of ordinary indigenous peoples, especially women. Also funders of development projects, such as the World Bank, often involve indigenous peoples not only for empowerment purposes but for their self-interested reasons of cost-sharing.

Indigenous peoples are questioning the entire development process. For example, who is benefiting at the cost of whom?

Recommendations

Commonwealth Secretariat

1 Ensure that the rights of indigenous peoples, in particular indigenous women and girls, are addressed in the new ten-year Plan of Action on Gender and Development;

2 Encourage member States to allocate the necessary resources for social sector development for indigenous peoples;

3 Ensure that all Commonwealth Ministries Responsible for Women's Affairs recognise and protect the rights of indigenous women;

4 Ensure that all Commonwealth Ministries Responsible for Women's Affairs involve indigenous women in all stages of their decision-making processes;

5 Strengthen co-operation between Commonwealth Ministries Responsible for Women's Affairs and ministries or departments responsible for indigenous affairs, in order to co-ordinate greater understanding of issues facing indigenous women and responsibilities among member States;

6 Undertake appropriate data collection and research on indigenous women, with their full participation, in order to foster accessible, culturally and linguistically appropriate policies, programmes and services;

7 Create partnerships with indigenous women's organisations in Commonwealth countries and recognise the Commonwealth Association of Indigenous Peoples (CAIP) as a representative and special partner body;

8 Facilitate networking of indigenous women to develop support mechanisms and social capital;

9 Establish an Indigenous Women's Advocacy Unit to channel specific enquiry, advocacy or support;

10 Encourage States parties to CEDAW to report on the status of indigenous women in their reports to the Committee;

11 Assist indigenous NGOs to write and present 'shadow reports' to the Committee.

Governments

12 Consider establishing ministries or departments responsible for indigenous affairs in any States where there is a significant indigenous population;

13 Ensure that policy-making for indigenous peoples and women is sensitive to their unique situation, and is holistic and long term;

14 Recognise indigenous peoples' right of self-determination, including the right to freely determine their political status;

15 Take measures to end discrimination against indigenous women with respect to land rights (while recognising the importance of collective land for indigenous women);

16 Give indigenous people an increased role in the educational process, including as teachers, and in the provision and development of health care;

17 Collect and collate statistical data on the situation of indigenous peoples, especially women, and do more research on indigenous women particularly related to health issues, including HIV/AIDS.

Session 5: Indigenous Peoples' Rights

Notes from the discussion

Land rights are fundamental. There are different rights related to land and property: rights of ownership, of access and of use. Despite constitutional and/or legal guarantees prohibiting discrimination, this persists when it comes to interpretation and application.

It is not possible to talk about land without talking about issues of:

1 Culture;

2 Property rights;

3 Lack of credit, collateral and economic power;

4 Obstacles to women's rights to inherit land;

5 The registration of land (which is mostly ineffective in developing countries).

Land policies were inherited from the colonial period and agrarian reforms discriminated against women. We need to look at the different land tenure systems to understand the appropriate legal processes and mechanisms for land administration and land management. Much research is ongoing in the area of land and property, and there is a need to document positive experiences.

Women are not a homogeneous group. There are differences between single, married, divorced, rural, urban and indigenous/tribal women. Complicating the issue of land ownership is the fact that women are often seen as property themselves, and when people are property, they cannot own property. There are also problems of non-registered marriages and complications of occupational rights after a marriage breaks up.

Strong land policies will decrease poverty. If women have access to land and their use of land is increased, there will be greater economic empowerment, and this will also assist in achieving the Millennium Development Goals. At the same time, it is important to note the reality that urban populations will number more than 4 billion people by 2020 as rural populations are moving to cities in significant numbers.

The Legal and Constitutional Affairs Division (LCAD) of the Commonwealth Secretariat has been running workshops since the Kingston Declaration,[1] supporting Commonwealth countries to develop land policies and take forward recommendations of the Declaration.

Recommendations

Commonwealth Secretariat

1 Document existing examples and practices in land reform;

2 Identify NGOs working in the areas of land, property and housing rights for women and facilitate the establishment of Pan-Commonwealth or regional networks for advocacy and sharing of experiences;

3 Analyse, document and disseminate models of good practices, illustrating policies, legislation, successful strategies and processes for improving women's rights to land, property and housing.

4 Promote and set out processes for effective land registration systems, land acquisition processes and land valuation systems – looking at traditional systems and good practice to enhance security of tenure (also taking into account corporate takeovers of small landholdings).

Governments

5 Prioritise land, housing and property rights during the review of the Beijing Platform for Action and the preparation of the plans of action for women for the next decade. National women's machineries should lobby other government ministries and departments to ensure this is on the agenda (e.g. for Law Ministers);

6 Integrate land and property into poverty reduction strategy papers, national development plans, etc., which will lead to reformulation of land policy;

7 Develop and execute national policies that address gender discrimination and the feminisation of poverty, with a particular emphasis on women's rights to land and property;

8 National women's machineries should have legal officers/legal departments to train/sensitise officers on land management issues;

9 Improve registration in other areas such as marriage to assist in securing women's rights to land;

10 Review the legal and regulatory mechanisms governing land, land markets and land acquisition in order to facilitate poor women and men to access land and acquire property;

1 The Commonwealth Kingston Declaration on Land and Development was issued by Commonwealth Law Ministers meeting in St Vincent and the Grenadines in November 2002. This noted the strong link between the use, access to and ownership of land, and development and poverty reduction.

11 Collaborate with women's organisations and other NGOs to provide tools and information to help women and men understand their rights, policies and processes;

12 Take into account indigenous peoples' rights to land, particularly where land may not be registered formally but where security of tenure has been granted.

Non-governmental organisations

13 Conduct a national campaign to make existing inheritance laws gender equal and to ensure that there is gender equal distribution of all land, houses or other assets given by the government under resettlement schemes;

14 Enhance legal awareness about women's property rights, especially rights in inheritance laws, among women themselves as well as among NGO workers and the constituencies within which they work;

15 Ensure that the inheritance claims of women to family land are honoured and that their shares (as daughters or widows) are registered by the officials concerned.

Session 7: Gender and Human Rights in the Life Cycle

Recommendations

Commonwealth Secretariat

1 Collate information and promote understanding of the intergenerational nature of poverty, livelihoods and survival, and the need to support mutually supportive relationships between generations.

Governments

2 Undertake to adopt a life cycle approach to development, and gender and human rights, through the fulfilment of commitments made in the Convention on the Rights of the Child, the Convention on the Elimination of All Forms of Discrimination against Women, the UN principles for older people and the Madrid International Plan of Action on Ageing, and related regional plans of action and implementation strategies;

3 Fulfil commitments to the Millennium Declaration and Millennium Development Goals and other human rights and development instruments in an inclusive and intergenerational way that promotes a society for all ages and ensures the benefits of development are reaching the very poorest and most marginalised;

4 Ensure that policies and programmes designed to promote development and human rights are inclusive of all age groups ('from cradle to grave') and address the specific needs of people at different stages of the life course, including those of older people;

5 Disaggregate data and research by age and into all age groups, as well as by gender and other variables, for better information and understanding of the implications of policy

or programme interventions on people of all ages and at all stages of their life cycle;

6 Actively seek the involvement of both young and old people in consultations and the design, implementation and monitoring of policies and programmes.

General Recommendations by Experts on Gender and Human Rights in the Commonwealth

Commonwealth Secretariat

1 Carry out an assessment of who is doing what and to what extent in order to determine the added value that the Commonwealth could bring to existing initiatives;

2 Use its comparative advantage in advocacy to promote gender-sensitive policy-making;

3 Document and share national plans of action, effective policies and best practices;

4 Facilitate regional networking among various stakeholders and assist governments in strengthening regional human rights instruments;

5 Develop ways of measuring the achievements that are being made.

Governments

6 Prepare reports to the human rights treaty bodies as required in a timely manner;

7 Strengthen and implement regional agreements and instruments that address human rights and gender equality;

8 Ensure that laws are enforced, and support gender-awareness training for the police and judiciary;

9 Place legal officers/legal departments in national women's machineries to deal with legal issues;

10 Ensure that ministries co-operate at all levels when addressing issues that cut across portfolios, such as trafficking, gender-based violence and HIV/AIDS,

11 Ensure that, when mainstreaming diversity, gender does not take a back seat;

12 Collect and collate sex-disaggregated data that includes indicators that will reveal the situation of women and identify obstacles to gender equality;

13 Form partnerships with NGOs for needs identification, data sharing and identification of obstacles to gender equality;

14 Collaborate with women's organisations and other NGOs to provide tools and information to help women and men understand their rights, given the importance of legal literacy for the implementation of human rights instruments.

Participant List

Georgina Ashworth, *Director, CHANGE, UK*
Rawwida Baksh, *Deputy Director, STPD/Head, Gender Section, COMSEC*
Sylvia Beales, *Help Age International, UK*
Cindy Berman, *Gender and Human Rights Programme, COMSEC*
Maryam Bibi, *specialist and activist on Asian indigenous women*
Karen Brewer, *Commonwealth Magistrates and Judges Association*
Fiona Clarke, *Help Age International, UK*
Christine Chinkin, *Professor, legal specialist, London School of Economics (LSE), UK*
Rudo Chitiga, *Deputy Director, Commonwealth Foundation*
Christian Curran, *intern, Commonwealth Judges and Magistrates Association*
Shanthi Dairiam, *International Women's Rights Action Watch (IWRAW) – Asia Pacific*
Lisa Fishbayn, *Research Fellow, consultant, Harvard University*
Lucia Kiwala, *UN-HABITAT, Kenya*
Lin Lean Lim, *Director, Gender Promotion Programme, International Labour Organization*
Jarvis Matiya, *Chief Programme Officer, Human Rights Unit, COMSEC*
Justice Athaliah Molokomme, *High Court of Botswana*
Betty Mould-Idrissu, *Director, Legal and Constitutional Affairs Division, COMSEC*
Catherine Muyeka Mumma, *Senior Staff Counsel, Attorney General's Office and Human Rights Commissioner, Kenya*
Elsie Onubogu, *Gender and Conflict Specialist, COMSEC*
Maiava Vesekota Peteru, *legal and human rights expert, Pacific region, Samoa*
Tracy Robinson, *gender specialist, Caribbean region*
Katalaina Sapolu, *Legal and Constitutional Affairs Division, COMSEC*
Meena Shivdas, *gender specialist and consultant, Asia region*
Nancy Spence, *Director, Social Transformation Programmes Division, COMSEC*
Hanif Vally, *Deputy Director/Head of Human Rights, Human Rights Unit, COMSEC*
Helena Whall, *Commonwealth Policy Studies Unit (CPSU), UK*

Appendix 2

Extract from the Commonwealth Plan of Action on Gender Equality 2005–2015

3 Critical Areas for Human Rights Action

II Gender, human rights and law

3.15 The Commonwealth asserts its commitment to promoting a rights-based approach in all areas of its work. In issues related to gender equality and human rights, national constitutions and international human rights instruments such as the Universal Declaration of Human Rights and CEDAW [the Convention on the Elimination of All Forms of Violence against Women] are the primary instruments by which States parties have a duty to guarantee equality of rights between women and men. This framework is reinforced by provisions in national statutes, as well as regional treaties and instruments. In addition, other critical international or regional human rights instruments and monitoring bodies, which embed and extend these rights,[1] must also be recognised as key instruments for moving forward the gender-based rights agenda and integrating it into policies and programmes at all levels.

3.16 Although 49 Commonwealth countries have ratified CEDAW and 15 have ratified its Optional Protocol, there are still significant gaps in implementation. Many countries have ratified with reservations. Commonwealth countries should be encouraged to ratify CEDAW and other instruments such as the Convention on the Rights of the Child. The lack of a gender perspective in the administration of the law has stymied gains made in international and regional treaties and conventions. Even where sound legislation exists, application and interpretation of these laws are inadequate for many reasons: lack of political will, jurisdictional issues, lack of awareness in the public service and justice systems at all levels, lack of enforcement capacity, traditional or customary systems of law that discriminate against women, women's inadequate awareness or legal literacy concerning their rights and recourse to justice, limited human and financial resources for monitoring and enforcement at national, local and community levels, and inadequate evidence-based data collection. It is in this context that violations of human rights of women and girls, including elderly women and women with disabilities, occur and actions to redress these issues, such as human rights education, remain urgent priorities.

3.17 Women and girls, including women with disabilities and elderly women, experience different forms of discrimination and disadvantage at different stages in the life cycle. Even before birth, genetic selection may be used to reduce the proportion of girls being born; as children, they may be denied the right to an education. As girls mature, their sexuality and sexual identity may conflict with their society's legal, social or religious views about sex, marriage and child-bearing. In the labour market, women's work often has lower value, status and remuneration than men's; women and girls are more vulnerable to exploitation; and, together with men, women experience particular discrimination as they age. In order to ensure that progress and gains made at one stage in the life cycle are not negated by adverse experiences and discrimination later, adequate support needs to be given to enable transitions throughout the life cycle from one phase of life to another.

3.18 Customary and religious laws, practices and traditions often have greater significance and value for people in their daily lives than the established statutory and constitutional laws in a country. In addressing gender equality and human rights issues, it is critical to recognise the complex ways in which identity, values and behaviour are formed and regulated at household and community level, often being shaped by elders, traditional leaders or religious institutions.

3.19 It is therefore critical to promote active dialogue and engagement among members of judicial, religious, cultural, traditional and civil institutions and communities to address women's human rights in all cultures. It is critical that harmful practices that violate the rights of women and girls, such as female genital mutilation (FGM), early marriage and widow inheritance,[101] are eliminated as a matter of urgency. Where multiple legal systems and practices exist – including constitutional, religious and customary – full consideration should be given to the human rights of women, men, boys and girls and, where violations occur, effective recourse and consequences need to be established.

3.20 Gender-based violence remains one of the most intransigent forms of human rights violation because of its complex and varied causes, forms and contributing factors. The right to freedom from gender-based violence will only be effectively realised in the context of increased social, political and economic freedoms and rights for both women and men. There are clear links between gender-based violence and many other factors, such as poverty, HIV/AIDS, property and land rights, race/ethnicity, age and sexual orientation, and effective strategies to address gender-based violence need to recognise the full range of discrimination and prejudice in which it is perpetrated. Approaches to gender-based violence have often failed to recognise the special predicament of widows and older women who may be especially vulnerable due to their economic and social circumstances. There is evidence that widows of all ages are abused through traditional practices, which include discrimination in inheritance and property ownership. This situation is immeasurably compounded by conflict, which has not only increased the number of widows worldwide but renders them and their children more vulnerable to violations of their rights. Integrated approaches undertaken by all relevant agencies are required, underpinned by comprehensive laws and policies, monitoring and enforcement systems, and mechanisms to ensure accountability for implementation.

3.21 The rapid growth of trafficking in persons is causing increasing global concern. Many of those most exploited and subjected to slavery-like situations are women and girls. It is widely acknowledged that the root causes of trafficking include the feminisation of poverty, displacement as a result of natural and human made catastrophes, gendered cultural practices, gender discrimination and gender-based violence in families and communities. However, it is important to recognise clearly the distinctions between trafficking, smuggling and regular and irregular migration, and to ensure that solutions and strategies appropriate to each context are found. Anti-trafficking legislation must embrace a human rights approach and protect the rights of those most vulnerable to abuse.

3.22 In countries where indigenous peoples, particularly women, continue to be marginalised and disadvantaged in comparison to other groups in society, and face significantly greater poverty, social exclusion and discrimination, there has been a lack of recognition of their rights, despite acknowledgement of the history of colonialism and its role in the marginalisation of indigenous peoples in the CHOGM Lusaka Declaration of 1979.

3.23 Respect for land and property rights is fundamental to the realisation of human rights and gender equality. Despite constitutional and legal guarantees in many Commonwealth countries prohibiting discrimination against women with regard to ownership of, access to or inheritance of land and property, *de facto* discrimination persists.

3.24 Consequently, activities in this critical area will focus on:

i. Legislative and constitutional reform, judicial capacity building and strengthening of mechanisms for implementation, monitoring and accountability of gender equality commitments.

ii. Culture, violence against women, the law and human rights, including rights regarding access to and ownership of land and property.

iii. Gender-based violence, integrated with work on trafficking in persons (especially women and girls), conflict resolution, peace-building and post-conflict reconstruction.

iv. Indigenous peoples' rights, with a focus on indigenous women and girls.

v. Gender and human rights throughout the life cycle, addressing discrimination and opportunities at all stages of life and ensuring the maintenance of rights from one stage to another, linked with the achievement of the MDGs and poverty reduction strategies.

3.25 Governments are encouraged to take action to:

i. Recognise, ratify and implement international and regional human rights instruments that promote gender equality.

ii. Promote legal and, where appropriate, constitutional reform in accordance with the universal standards of human rights including CEDAW in support of gender equality and strengthen the knowledge and capacity of the justice system, parliament and local authorities on gender equality and rights issues through appropriate and ongoing gender training.

iii. Promote active dialogue and engagement between the justice system and religious, cultural, traditional and civil institutions and communities, to address women's human rights at all levels.

iv. Adopt an integrated, zero-tolerance approach to gender-based violence, including strengthening of the law, appropriate public education, provision of adequate institutional and financial support to address the needs of victims and witnesses, and rehabilitation of perpetrators.

v. Promote the implementation and enforcement of appropriate laws and policies against trafficking and the commercial sexual exploitation of women and children, including the UN Protocol to Prevent, Suppress and Punish Trafficking in Women and Children, and develop plans and strategies to give effect to this protocol at the national level.

vi. Foster and develop national, local and regional programmes of action with indigenous peoples, particularly women, in accordance with international human rights standards and Commonwealth values on development, democracy and good governance, where required.

vii. Promote the maintenance of gender-related rights throughout the life cycle, through the fulfilment of commitments made in the Convention on the Rights of the Child and CEDAW, as well as other agreements such as the Madrid International Plan of Action on Ageing and related regional plans of action and implementation strategies.

viii. Ensure that women's rights to land, housing, property and inheritance are promoted and protected, having recourse to relevant international and national instruments on human rights and poverty reduction.

ix. Codify positive customary laws that protect women as a process of reviewing the existing laws to ensure that all laws are in conformity with both international and domestic human rights obligations.

3.26 The Secretariat will support member countries by:

i. Working with governments and in collaboration with CSOs [civil society organisations] to develop appropriate laws and policies for the promotion and protection of women's human rights.

ii. Documenting and disseminating case studies of good practice that address customary laws and practices that promote the rights of women and girls; examples of dialogue and synergy between customary systems and constitutional and statutory institutions;

and good practices in land reform processes that take into account gender equality.

iii. Providing training on the elimination of gender-based violence, using integrated approaches, and promoting the sharing of good practice at all levels.

iv. Supporting governments in the development of national plans and strategies to implement the UN Protocol to Prevent, Suppress and Punish Trafficking in Women and Children.

v. Promoting the rights of indigenous peoples, especially women, in political, social, economic and cultural spheres.

Notes

1 For example, the International Covenant on Economic, Social and Cultural Rights; the Additional Protocol to the African Charter on Human and Peoples' Rights on the Rights of Women in Africa; the Convention on the Rights of the Child; and the four key gender-related ILO Conventions (C100 on equal remuneration, C111 on freedom from discrimination at work, C156 on workers with family responsibilities and C183 on maternity protection).

2 Widow inheritance refers to the passing of a widow from one male relative to another in some societies.